Pivotal

Interpretations

of American History

Vol. II   ★   Edited by CARL N. DEGLER

HARPER TORCHBOOKS, The Academy Library

HARPER & ROW, Publishers, New York

PIVOTAL INTERPRETATIONS OF AMERICAN HISTORY: VOLUME II

Notes and compilation copyright © 1966 by Carl N. Degler.

Printed in the United States of America.

First edition: HARPER TORCHBOOKS, 1966
Harper & Row, Publishers, Incorporated
New York, N.Y. 10016.

Library of Congress Catalog Card Number: 66-10532.

Contents

Volume II

11

IF THE principal provisions of the federal land acts are reviewed in their order of enactment, they appear to describe a steady trend toward facilitating the acquisition of land by actual settlers. The trend begins early in the nineteenth century. In the land act of 1820 the federal government offered to sell public land to settlers at a minimum price of $1.25 per acre, in plots as small as 80 acres. Although the act abolished sales on credit, the new low minimum price and low acreage size meant that a substantial farm could be purchased for as little as one hundred dollars. Then in 1841 Congress, by passing the Pre-emption Act, went a step further in providing easy access to the public domain. The new law permitted settlers to stake claims to the land they settled upon up to a maximum of 160 acres and at a minimum price of $1.25. The act was a triumph for the western contention that the public lands should be opened up to settlement as rapidly and at as low cost to actual settlers as possible. Furthermore, it not only legalized the frontier practice of "squatting" on land before it was surveyed but also permitted the squatter to secure his land later at the minimum price without having to compete for it at a land auction as required under previous laws. For these reasons, as Gates observes, the act is usually taken to mark the decisive shift in federal land policy from one of using the public lands as a source of government revenue to one of settling the West quickly. With the Graduation Act of 1854, Congress pushed still further the principle of settling the West rapidly. This act, in a series of steps, reduced the price of land that remained unsold after being on the market for ten years or more. For example, land that was unsold after thirty years was offered at a mere 12.5 cents per acre.

1

The logic of these three laws leads clearly to the conclusion that land should be granted free to settlers. In fact, for half a generation small groups of land reformers and western politicians had been urging just that approach to land disposal. But the idea was not enacted into law until the passage of the Homestead Act in 1862. This act provided that public lands would be granted in amounts up to 160 acres, to any citizen over twenty-one who was head of a family and lived on the land for five continuous years. Only a small registration fee was demanded.

The homestead law was followed by other measures designed, like it, to encourage settlement of the West. The Timber Culture Act of 1873 offered land up to 160 acres to anyone who, settling on the treeless Great Plains, would plant trees on the land. The Desert Land Act of 1877 permitted individuals to buy up to 640 acres of land at 25 cents per acre in the arid areas of the West in return for irrigating the land for a period of three years. The Timber and Stone Act of 1878, confined in its application to the Pacific coast states and Nevada, authorized, at a price of $2.50 per acre, up to a limit of 160 acres, the sale of lands on which timber and stone were to be found but which were unfit for agriculture.

Confronted with the content of this formidable series of laws spread over a half century, historians understandably drew the conclusion that the trend of land legislation was steadily and clearly in the direction of opening the West to settlers and minimizing large holdings and monopoly. As Gates's article shows, however, the actual workings of the laws and other legislation pertaining to land disposal reveal a quite different picture. The actual effect of Congressional policy differed from the obvious interpretation in at least two important respects. Very little good land was opened to settlement by the homestead law, despite its supposed intention to be a boon to the pioneer and the small farmer. In fact, the records of the Land Office now make evident that more entries under the Homestead Act were made in the twentieth century than in the nineteenth. Furthermore, as Gates's article makes abundantly clear, speculation in land continued at a vigorous pace long after the passage of the homestead law. (In passing, and in order to put some of the large holdings that are mentioned in the article into a meaningful context, it might be recalled that there are 640 acres in a square mile.)

One of the striking aspects of Gates's article is not only its large amount of detail, marshaled to substantiate a position, but its obvious bias. There is no doubt that Gates approves the idea behind the Homestead Act. Several times he calls it "idealistic"; conversely, he dislikes and distrusts those who pushed through legislation contrary to what he calls the homestead principle. Thus in writing about the Congressional grants of land to railroads he refers to the "cynical indifference to the idealistic expressions constantly voiced concerning the principles." At another place, after showing that Congress did not always follow the principle of the Homestead Act, he denominates that body as "insincere." Yet despite this obvious bias his conclusions are unaffected by it. One can certainly disagree with the aspersions Gates casts upon Congress and the railroad and timber interests of the time. But because of the amount and character of his evidence it is not possible to ignore his conclusions. Here is a good example of where the bias of the investigator—assuming that his facts are accurately presented— does not vitiate his evidence or his conclusions. Another instance, though from an opposite bias, is the article by Robert S. Henry which follows this one. Though Gates's indictment of Congress for inconsistency has at times obscured the point, he has shown that the passage of the Homestead Act was neither a sharp break with earlier land policy nor the culmination of a single line of policy. Rather it was simply one of several policies that Congress adopted to deal with the many problems of the West. Sometimes, as in the Pre-emption and Homestead Acts, Congress sought to open the West to small settlers. At other times, however, Congress employed its land disposal power to help in the construction of railroads or to deal with the Indian question, or at still other times to open up land unsuited to agriculture, as in the Desert Land and Timber Culture Acts. And at least once, in its restriction on sales of land in the post-Civil War South, Congress sought to encourage the purchase of land by newly freed Negro slaves.

On the other hand, Gates's hostility to land speculators and his commitment to the homestead principle do lead him into unsubstantiated minor conclusions. He has not, for example, proved his contention that "speculation and land engrossment were not retarded" by the Homestead Act. His conclusion is based on a number of examples of land speculation and engrossment after 1862. But without a measure of the amount of speculation before and after 1862, his conclusion is no more than an impression at best. Also, with his obvious distaste for the land speculator Gates leaves the impression from his many examples that the acquisition of large amounts of land always resulted in huge profits for speculators. Obviously this was not always the case, or else there would have been no speculation involved; investment in land would have been a sure thing. As Robert S. Henry points out in article No. 12, studies of the average sale price of railroad lands show very modest returns, on the order of $2.81 and $3.38 an acre. For a more recent and balanced investigation of the land speculator that notes that he was not always a winner nor always to be despised, see Allan G. and Margaret B. Bogue's " 'Profits' and the Frontier Land Speculator," *Journal of Economic History*, XVII (March 1957), 1–24. Nevertheless Gates's point that speculation continued after the passage of the Homestead Act is certainly established.

More important, his conclusion that the Homestead Act was not consistent with earlier and subsequent land disposal practices has become the standard interpretation. In the very same issue of the *American Historical Review* that carried Gates's article, Fred A. Shannon's "The Homestead Act and the Labor Surplus" appeared. Although Shannon's purpose was quite different from Gates's, his conclusion that few settlers took advantage of the Homestead Act in the years between 1862 and 1900 strongly supports Gates's conclusion. Furthermore, Shannon's evidence on land speculation reinforces Gates's point. More recent writers have also shown their acceptance of the Gates interpretation of the Homestead Act. Henry Nash Smith, in *Virgin Land: The American West as Symbol and Myth* (Cambridge, 1950), echoes Gates's own words when he writes: "The Homestead Act failed because it was incongruous with the Industrial Revolution."

Since the terms "scrip" and "warrant" appear frequently in the article, it might be worthwhile to identify them. In general, both scrip and land warrants are certificates that entitle the holder to take up a specified piece of public land. Often they were issued as payment for services to the government. Inasmuch as such certificates were usually transferable, others could purchase them from the original owners.

Mr. Gates is professor of history at Cornell University. His publications have centered on studies of land policy and the history of agriculture. His most recent book is *The Farmer's Age: Agriculture, 1815–1860* (New York, 1960), which is Volume III in the "Economic History of the United States" series.

The Homestead Law in an Incongruous Land System [1]

BY PAUL WALLACE GATES

THE Homestead Act of 1862 is one of the most important laws which have been enacted in the history of this country, but its significance has been distorted and grossly misinterpreted. An important misconception concerning the Homestead Act is that its adoption marked a more or less complete break with the past, in that the lands which previously had been considered as a source of revenue were now to be given free to settlers. As part of this interpretation it is held that direct land sales virtually ceased except for transactions under the Pre-emption Law, the commutation clause of the Homestead Act, the Timber and Stone Act, and the Desert Land Act. Each of the first three of these acts permitted the purchase by individuals of 160 acres and the Desert Land Act permitted the purchase of an additional 640 acres, making a total which could be acquired under them of 1120 acres. Aside from this maximum which was open to purchasers, the accepted view is that speculators [2] in lands were barred from direct transactions at the land offices and that, to secure large tracts, they were forced to operate through dummy entrymen or buy from states and railroads.

To state this view differently, it is held that after 1862 the chief way in which settlers and speculators alike acquired land from the government was through the Pre-emption and Homestead laws and their subsequent modifications. Indeed, some writers have maintained

SOURCE: Reprinted by permission of the American Historical Association from the *American Historical Review*, XLI (July 1936). Copyright, 1936, by The Macmillan Company.

[1] The material for this article was gathered in part while the writer was Fellow of the Social Science Research Council in 1933 and 1934. Grateful acknowledgments are due to the Council and especially to Donald Young of its staff for many kindnesses. The article was completed while the writer was engaged in a study of Recent Land Policies of the United States for the Land Policy Section of the Agricultural Adjustment Administration, later the Resettlement Administration.

[2] The word "speculator," as used in this article, refers to large-scale land operators, and does not include many farmers who speculated in a small way.

that the region beyond the Mississippi was largely settled by homesteaders taking up free land under the Act of 1862. Congressman
Harvey B. Ferguson stated in 1914, "It was great statesmanship
that created the homestead laws under which such a State as Iowa
developed." [3] Another writer made an even broader statement as
follows: "Under the homestead law were taken up the rich agricultural alluvial lands of the central Mississippi basin. . . ." [4] Even
Professor Hibbard, the authority on American land policies, has
misunderstood the developments in land matters after 1862. He states
that land sales made after 1862 were "only in connection with
preemption and miscellaneous parcels of land, the preemptions
covering by far the larger part of the operations." He also states
that a congressional resolution, expressing opposition to the further
sale of agricultural lands, which passed the House in 1868 but
failed of adoption in the Senate, was virtually "tantamount to a
law." [5] As these views have been widely accepted it is essential
to examine briefly their source and then to test their accuracy.

The principle of free homesteads for settlers had long been the
goal for which the West had struggled, and as each succeeding land
law, more liberal than its predecessor, was passed, that goal came
constantly nearer until, in 1862, it was attained. So generous seemed
this policy in contrast with the earlier one of regarding the lands
as a source of revenue, and so significant did it appear prospectively,
that it became the subject of eulogy at the outset. Furthermore, the
measure had been sponsored by the Republican party and when
this party was later accused of representing the interests of large
capitalistic combines and of neglecting the farmers, its leaders
pointed to the Homestead Act as a refutation of the accusation.[6]
Consequently there was built up around the law a halo of political
and economic significance which has greatly magnified the importance to be attributed to it and which has misled practically every

[3] "Grazing Homesteads and the Regulation of Grazing on the Public Lands,"
Hearing before the Committee on the Public Lands, House of Representatives, 63 Cong., 2 sess., pt. 1, p. 358.

[4] Leifur Magnusson, *Disposition of the Public Lands of the United States
with Particular Reference to Wage-Earning-Labor* (Washington, 1919), p. 29.
See also Arthur C. Cole, *The Irrepressible Conflict, 1850–1865* (New York,
1934), pp. 119, 357; John Ise, *The United States Forest Policy* (New Haven,
1920), p. 56.

[5] Benjamin Horace Hibbard, *History of the Public Land Policies* (New
York, 1924), pp. 111, 112.

[6] The shallowness of this contention was pointed out by George W. Julian
in 1884 (*Political Recollections, 1840 to 1872*, Chicago, 1884, p. 218). Speaking of the continuation of cash sales, railroad grants, and disposal of the
Indian lands as fatal to the homestead principle, he said that they furnished
"a remarkable commentary upon the boasted friendship of the Republican
party for the landless poor."

historian and economist who has dealt with land policies. The Homestead Law has been considered the capstone of an increasingly liberal land policy, and to it has been ascribed the rapid settlement of the West and the large percentage of farmer owners in the United States. It has also been regarded as providing an outlet for the discontented and surplus labor of the East with the result that, as compared with European countries, high wage rates have prevailed in that section. The influence of free land has been blithely discussed by writers who have never taken the time to examine the facts with which they dealt so lightly.[7]

The source of most of these ideas concerning the Homestead Law is, of course, the *Congressional Globe,* later the *Record,* upon which so many writers completely depend. A careful reading of the congressional debates should, however, lead one to question the general conception above outlined. Professor Hibbard bases his generalizations upon even more untrustworthy evidence. He quotes from the *Report* of the Commissioner of the General Land Office for 1863 wherein it is stated that it is not the design of Congress "to look to the public lands as a source of direct revenue," [8] and, from the exceedingly small amount of sales reported in the first year that the Homestead Law was in operation, draws the inference that cash sales were thenceforth of no importance. Professor Hibbard may also have been depending upon a statement made by that great compiler of land statistics. Thomas Donaldson, in his book, *The Public Domain,* originally published in 1880, in which it is stated that lands available for cash entry are few and isolated, except for those in the five Southern states of Alabama, Louisiana, Florida, Arkansas, and Mississippi. The statement was correct in general in 1880, in so far as it applied to the lands ordinarily described as "public domain," [9] but there were many million acres of rich agricultural lands which at that time were rapidly being brought into the market for cash sale by the Federal government.[10] It would not apply at all to the period prior to 1880 when large areas of the best agricultural lands in the country were subject to sale.

[7] In contrast, Herbert Heaton ventures the view that the importance of free land in drawing immigrants to America has been overestimated while the influence of high wages has been underestimated. "Migration and Cheap Land—the End of Two Chapters," *The Sociological Review,* XXVI (July, 1934), 237.

[8] *Report,* 1863, p. 7. See also *Report,* Secretary of the Interior, 1862, p. 4.

[9] 1884 edition, pp. 25, 415. It is worth noting that a total of 4,851,296 acres was entered in Michigan, Wisconsin, and Minnesota in the eighties with cash, scrip, and warrants. This is exclusive of pre-emption, homestead, and other limited entries.

[10] These lands, which were being ceded by the Indians, are neglected by both Donaldson and Hibbard.

It is the purpose of this paper to show that the Homestead Law
did not completely change our land system, that its adoption merely
superimposed upon the old land system a principle out of harmony
with it, and that until 1890 the old and the new constantly clashed.
In presenting this view it will appear that the Homestead Law did
not end the auction system or cash sales, as is generally assumed,
that speculation and land monopolization continued after its adoption as widely perhaps as before, and within as well as without the
law, that actual homesteading was generally confined to the less
desirable lands distant from railroad lines, and that farm tenancy
developed in frontier communities in many instances as a result of
the monopolization of the land. The efforts to abolish cash sales
will also be outlined briefly.

The moderate land reformers of the mid-nineteenth century
believed that the enactment of a homestead measure would retard
if not end speculation in public lands.[11] They argued that once free
homesteads were available to settlers speculators would no longer
have a market for their lands and all inducements to purchase in
advance of settlement would be ended. Parenthetically, similar arguments have been advanced by certain historians to prove that there
was little or no profit in land speculation.[12] The land reformers
reckoned too lightly, however, with the astuteness of the speculators
who in the past had either succeeded in emasculating laws inimical
to their interests or had actually flouted such laws in the very faces
of the officials appointed to administer them.

From the outset the cards were stacked against the efficient and
successful operation of the Homestead Law. Other acts in existence
in 1862 greatly limited its application and new laws further restrict-

[11] The more advanced reformers demanded that all sales should be discontinued, grants to railroads and other special interests ended, and all the
public lands reserved for actual settlers under the provisions of the homestead measure. The differences between what may be called the moderate and
the radical land reformers is apparent in the congressional debates. See also
George M. Stephenson, *The Political History of the Public Lands from 1840
to 1862* (Boston, 1917), p. 166 and elsewhere; Roy M. Robbins, "Horace
Greeley: Land Reform and Unemployment, 1837–1862," *Agricultural History*,
VII (Jan., 1933), 26, *passim*; St. George L. Sioussat, "Andrew Johnson and
the Early Phases of the Homestead Bill," *Mississippi Valley Historical Review*, V (Dec., 1918), 253, *passim*; Hibbard, p. 347, *passim*; John Bell San-
born, "Some Political Aspects of Homestead Legislation," *Am. Hist. Rev.*, VI
(Oct., 1900), 19, *passim*.

[12] Speaking of the period from 1836 to 1876 Professor Joseph Schafer
writes: "It was, in this period, a rare thing for an outside speculator in wild
lands to make any profit on his speculation." *Wisconsin Magazine of History*,
XIII (June, 1930), 428. See also his *The Wisconsin Lead Region*, *Wisconsin
Domesday Book*, "General Studies," III (Madison, 1932), p. 153; *Wisconsin
Domesday Book, Town Studies* (1924), I, 10.

ing it were subsequently enacted. The administration of the law, both in Washington and in the field, was frequently in the hands of persons unsympathetic to its principle,[13] and Western interests, though lauding the act, were ever ready to pervert it. The existence of the Pre-emption Law and its later variations, the Desert Land Act, the Timber Culture Act, the Timber and Stone Act, the land grants to railroads and states, the cash sale system, the Indian land policy, the acts granting land warrants to ex-soldiers or their heirs, and the Agricultural College Act of 1862, which granted millions of acres of land scrip to Eastern states, tended to make it practically as easy for speculators to engross huge areas of land after 1862 as before.

The retention of the Pre-emption Law and the commutation clause of the Homestead Law made it possible for timber dealers,[14] cattle graziers, mining interests, and speculators to continue to acquire lands through the use of dummy entrymen, false swearing, and, often, the connivance of local land officers. That this was done on a large scale is evident by the frequent and sometimes pathetic admissions of the apparently helpless land commissioners. The Desert Land Act, the Timber Culture Act, and the Timber and Stone Act provided even greater opportunities for dummy entrymen to enter lands

---

[13] Wm. A. J. Sparks, commissioner of the General Land Office, in his *Report* for 1885 (pp. 3–4), writes as follows concerning the administration of the land laws:

I found that the magnificent estate of the nation in its public lands had been to a wide extent wasted under defective and improvident laws and through a laxity of public administration astonishing in a business sense if not culpable in recklessness of official responsibility.

The widespread belief of the people of this country that the land department has been very largely conducted to the advantage of speculation and monopoly, private and corporate, rather than in the public interest, I have found supported by developments in every branch of the service. It seems that the prevailing idea running through this office and those subordinate to it was that the government had no distinctive rights to be considered and no special interests to protect; hence, as between the government and spoilers of the public domain, the government usually had the worst of it. I am satisfied that thousands of claims without foundation in law or equity, involving millions of acres of public land, have been annually passed to patent upon the single proposition that nobody but the government had any *adverse* interest.

The vast machinery of the land department appears to have been devoted to the chief result of conveying the title of the United States to public lands upon fraudulent entries under strained constructions of imperfect public land laws and upon illegal claims under public and private grants.

[14] Ise, *passim*, has drawn together and summarized the published information concerning the vast frauds committed by the lumber interests in their efforts to acquire great areas of timber lands. See also Jenks Cameron, *The Development of Governmental Forest Control in the United States* (Baltimore, 1928), *passim*.

and assign them to hidden land engrossers.[15] The palpable frauds committed and the large areas transferred under these acts and their interference with the homestead principle lead one to suspect that their enactment and retention were the results of political pressure by interested groups.

It was not entirely necessary, however, for speculators to resort to these illegal and fraudulent methods of acquiring land since Congress proceeded to aid their schemes by enacting a series of laws which went far toward vitiating the principle of land for the landless. By continuing after 1862 the policy of granting lands to railroads to encourage their construction, Congress from the outset struck a severe blow at the principle of free homesteads. In the eight years after the passage of the Homestead Law five times as much land was granted to railroads as had been given in the twelve preceding years; 127,628,000 acres were granted between 1862 and 1871 to aid in the extension of the railroad net and 2,000,-000 acres were granted for wagon roads and canals. Such imperial generosity was at the expense of future homesteaders who must purchase the land.[16] As it was necessary to withdraw all lands from entry in the regions through which such roads were projected to prevent speculators from anticipating the railroads in making selections of land, and as the routes were rarely definitely established when the grants were made, more than double this amount of land was withdrawn from entry and remained unavailable to settlement for a long period of years.[17]

The railroads were, of course, built through undeveloped regions and, other things being equal, routes were selected which would ensure to the companies the largest amount of what was then considered to be the best agricultural land. When the alternate govern-

[15] The commissioners of the General Land Office from 1875 onward recommended annually the repeal of the Pre-emption Law; in 1883 the commissioner recommended the repeal of the commutation clause of the Homestead Law and the Timber Culture Act (*Report*, 1883, pp. 6–7); in 1884 the commissioner suggested the repeal of these laws and the Desert Land Act and the Timber and Stone Act. *Ibid.*, 1883, pp. 6–8. These documents are cited hereafter as G.L.O. *Report*.

[16] Computed from Donaldson, pp. 258–273. The best criticism by a contemporary of the railroad land grant policy, is found in Henry George, *Our Land and Land Policy, National and State* (San Francisco, 1871). See also George W. Julian, "Railway Influence in the Land Office," *North American Review*, CXXXVI (Mar., 1883), 237–256, and his "Our Land-Grant Railways in Congress," *International Review*, XIV (Feb.-Mar., 1883), 198–212.

[17] G.L.O. *Report*, 1885, pp. 26, *passim*. As late as 1883, twelve years after the last land grant was made to railroads, it was estimated that more than 100,000,000 acres were withdrawn from settlement pending selection of the railroad sections: Julian, *N. Am. Rev.*, CXXXVI, 252.

ment sections were finally restored to market settlers were frequently outbid for them by speculators.[18] Moreover, the provision in the Homestead Law which confined the homesteader to eighty acres within the limits of a railroad grant[19] was sufficient to send many homeseekers farther afield. On the railroad sections, of course, no free homesteading was permitted and thus the prospective settler found it necessary to go far from transportation facilities in order to take advantage of the government's bounty. In numerous instances the land policies of the railroads encouraged speculative and large-scale purchases with the result that millions of acres were turned into bonanza farms, such as those found in Dakota Territory,[20] or were rented or leased to incoming settlers who had expected to find free land available to them.

These grants to railroads after 1862 were a limitation on the homestead principle and indicate cynical indifference to the idealistic expressions constantly voiced concerning the principle. That some doubt existed among members of Congress as to the propriety of continuing to make grants for railroads is revealed by a resolution adopted by the House in 1870[21] which stated:

> That in the judgement of this House the policy of granting subsidies in public lands to railroad and other corporations ought to be discontinued; and that every consideration of public policy and equal justice to the whole people requires that the public lands of the United States should be held for the exclusive purpose of securing homesteads to actual settlers under the homestead and preemption laws, subject to reasonable appropriations of such lands for the purposes of education.

Although adopted without any debate the resolution was just a bluff, for within the next twelve months Congress made one of the largest and most indefensible of the railroad grants which, together with a number of smaller ones, totaled nearly 20,000,000 acres.[22] The anti-railroad feeling which swept over the West in the early

---

[18] For large speculative purchases within the limits of the Illinois Central Railroad grant, see Paul Wallace Gates, *The Illinois Central Railroad and its Colonization Work* (Cambridge, 1934), pp. 107, 123 ff.

[19] This provision was practically repealed by the acts of Mar. 3, 1879 (20 *U.S. Stat.*, 472), July 1, 1879 (21 *U.S. Stat.*, 46), and June 15, 1880 (*ibid.*, p. 238).

[20] James B. Hedges, "The Colonization Work of the Northern Pacific Railroad," *Mississippi Valley Hist. Rev.*, XIII (Dec., 1926), 327; Harold E. Briggs, "Early Bonanza Farming in the Red River Valley of the North," *Agricultural History*, VI (Jan., 1932), 26, *passim*; Alva H. Benton, "Large Land Holdings in North Dakota," *Journal of Land and Public Utility Economics*, I (Oct., 1925), 405–413.

[21] *Cong. Globe*, 41 Cong., 2 sess., p. 2095.

[22] Donaldson, p. 272.

seventies finally brought these grants to an end. After 1871 no more grants were made [23] although various interests were at the time seeking additional grants which, if made, would have required practically all the valuable lands remaining to the government.

The continuation of the policy of granting to the states Federal lands within their borders was likewise contrary to the homestead principle. With the exception of the swamp land grants, the purpose of these donations was to provide the states with a valuable commodity, the sale of which would produce revenue or endowment for educational and other state institutions. Over 72,000,000 acres were granted to states which came into the Union after 1862 while other states had their grants increased subsequent to the enactment of the Homestead Law.[24] It is safe to say that over 140,000,000 acres of land were in the hands of the states for disposition after 1862.[25] The philosophy behind the grants, and frequently the conditions embedded in the donations, required their sale at the highest market price. The states were prevented, therefore, from giving homesteads to settlers and the prices asked for their lands, with the exception of the swamp lands which were generally sold at low prices or granted to railroads, made them the prey of speculators. It is true that limitations were sometimes placed on the amount of land which individuals could purchase, but dummy entrymen were usually employed to circumvent such restrictions.[26] The states, like the railroads, naturally endeavored to secure the best possible lands in order to ensure large returns therefrom. The following table,[27] showing the land sales of and the prices received by representative states, reveals clearly that persons seeking cheap or free lands found little encouragement from state officials.

The maintenance of the cash sale system after the Homestead Law went into operation did even greater violence to the principle

[23] Lewis H. Haney, *A Congressional History of Railways in the United States* (Madison, 1910), II, 20–22; Stephenson, p. 122, n.

[24] Computed from G.L.O. *Report*, 1932, pp. 45–50.

[25] A total of 230,088,219 acres have been patented to the states of which 38,206,487 acres were given for railroads, 3,359,188 acres for wagon roads, and 6,842,921 acres for canals. Most of these special grants were quickly transferred to construction companies or disposed of by the states. The total also includes 7,672,800 acres in land scrip which was granted to the states in which there were no remaining public lands for the endowment of agricultural colleges. The scrip could not be located by the states and had to be sold promptly. Of the remaining lands granted, or which were subsequently granted to the states, it seems safe to say that at least 140,000,000 acres were still unsold to 1862.

[26] U.S. Department of Commerce and Labor, Bureau of Corporations, *The Lumber Industry* (1913), pt. 1, p. 252.

[27] Computed from reports of the land offices of the respective states.

State	Net amount of land sold to date	Average price per acre
Idaho [28]	838,140	$16.90
Kansas	3,064,547	3.22
Minnesota	2,306,600	6.53
Montana	1,587,488	15.50
North Dakota	1,686,436	16.73
South Dakota	873,960	35.22
Utah	3,448,876	2.44

of free lands. It is not generally appreciated that there were available in 1862 for cash sale 83,919,649 acres of land.[29] Contrary to the views of Hibbard and others, this figure was later increased to well over 100,000,000 acres by the opening up of new lands to the auction and cash sale system.[30] Throughout the sixties and seventies and, indeed, until 1888 the government continued to offer land at auction in Oregon, Washington, California, Kansas, Nebraska, Colorado, New Mexico, and in practically all of the states in the Lakes region and in the Mississippi Valley where it still had land. It is true that after 1870 most of the land so offered was timbered but by then a goodly portion of the arable lands had been surveyed and opened to sale. The richest and most fertile sections of Kansas, Nebraska, Missouri, California, Washington, and Oregon were thus open to the cash purchaser after the enactment of the Homestead Law and, as will be seen later, great landed estates were acquired through outright purchase in these states.

Little attention has been devoted by historians to the Indian lands and yet there is a story involved in their disposition totally at variance with the conventional account of the era of free land. At the time the Homestead Law was passed the government was following the policy of concentrating the Indians on reservations where they would be in less conflict with white settlers. The rights of the Indians in lands claimed by them were recognized and, when they were persuaded to leave a hunting area over which they claimed ownership to dwell in a reservation, they were generally compensated for their lands either by the Federal government or by a purchaser acting with the consent of the government. Some of the lands were

[28] To 1918.
[29] G.L.O. *Report*, 1862, p. 8.
[30] Volumes of "Proclamations for Public Land Sales," General Land Office; G.L.O. *Reports*, 1862 and following. It is true that 46,000,000 acres in the South were withdrawn from cash entry under the Act of June 21, 1866, but these lands were restored to sale in 1876 and during the interval the amount of land disposed of was small, amounting to only 2,000,000 acres by 1871. Computed from G.L.O. *Report*, 1871, p. 343.

ceded outright to the government for a consideration; others were ceded in trust, the lands to be sold for the benefit of the Indians; the disposition of still others to railroads was authorized in a number of treaties. As these Indian lands were frequently the very choicest and contained some improvements they were much desired by speculators. No uniform policy concerning their final disposition was worked out—both legislative and administrative regulations as to their disposal varying widely—and consequently speculators were able to get their grasp on them more easily than if the lands had been subject to a clearly defined policy. The only consistent rule concerning them was that they must be sold for a consideration, which, of course, denied to the homesteader the right to enter them free. The obligation of the government to compensate the Indian for his land did not necessitate a policy of sale to settlers but the revenue complex with reference to the public lands was still prevalent in spite of the Homestead Law, and the Indian lands were reserved for cash sale.

The amount of land in Indian reservations or claimed by the Indians in 1862 was probably 175,000,000 acres.[31] The land was scattered throughout the Western states, but large amounts were concentrated in the states of Kansas and Nebraska and the Dakota and Indian territories into which settlers were eagerly pressing in the sixties, seventies, and eighties, or where they looked longingly for lands. At the outset, these lands were sold in large blocks to groups of capitalists and railroads, as is seen below, without being offered in small lots. Slightly later they were appraised, generally at high valuations, offered at auction and sold to the highest bidders. Still later, some of the Indian lands were sold in small tracts to settlers, a slight concession to the home-seekers.[32]

The Indian Allotment Act of 1887, as modified by the Burke Act of 1906 [33] and subsequent measures, was undoubtedly in part the result of Western pressure to have the lands of the Indians made available to white settlement. These acts provided for the allotment of Indian lands and eventually for their sale. The Dawes Act contin-

[31] Indian reservations and claims were not sharply defined in 1862, much of the area not having been surveyed. In 1875 the Commission of Indian Affairs (*Report*, 1875, p. 142) gave the acreage in Indian reservations as 165,729,714 acres. The amount of Indian lands sold directly to individuals and corporations and that sold through the General Land Office during the years 1862–1875 would bring this figure to 175,000,000 acres for 1862.

[32] There is little available information on the Indian lands and their disposition, the most important published source being the *Annual Reports* of the Commissioners of Indian Affairs during the years after the Civil War.

[33] 24 *U. S. Stat.*, 388; 34 *U. S. Stat.*, 182.

ued the policy whereby the government purchased the surplus lands from the Indians and subsequently resold them, but it provided that lands so acquired in the future should be reserved for actual settlers in tracts of 160 acres. This provision did not apply to ceded lands transferred before 1887 nor did it open the ceded lands to free homesteading. Congress has been consistent at least in requiring payment for Indian land. Between 100,000,000 and 125,000,000 acres of Indian land have been sold since 1862, practically one half as much as the total acreage which has been entered under the Homestead Law.[34]

With over 125,000,000 acres of railroad lands,[35] 140,000,000 acres of state lands, 100,000,000 acres of Indian lands, and 100,000,000 acres of Federal lands for sale in large or small blocks, and with the opportunities for evasion of the Homestead and Pre-emption laws and their variations outlined above, it is obvious that there were few obstacles in the way of speculation and land monopolization after 1862. As before, it was still possible for foresighted speculators to precede settlers into the frontier, purchase the best lands, and hold them for the anticipated increase in value which the succeeding wave of settlers would give to them. It has heretofore been maintained that the existence of free land after 1862 greatly diminished the speculators' chances of profit and consequently limited their activities. This view will not bear careful scrutiny. Except for the squatters' claims, the speculators were generally able to secure the most desirable lands, that is, those easily brought under cultivation, fertile and close to timber, water, markets, and lines of

[34] Recent addresses by John Collier, commissioner of Indian Affairs, and Senator William H. King have called attention to the alienation of Indian lands since the Allotment Act of 1887, but they have not been concerned with the previous crowding of the Indians on the reservations and the forced cession or sale of their surplus lands which antedated that act. See the speech of Senator King on "Condition of Indians in the United States," *Senate Document,* 72 Cong., 2 sess., no. 214. It is difficult to estimate the total amount of Indian land which was sold prior to 1887 and after 1862 but it would certainly bring the total Indian land sales since 1862 to over 100,-000,000 acres.

[35] The railroads have received 132,425,574 acres of land directly from the Federal government or from grants originally given to the states for railroad construction. *Report,* Secretary of the Interior, 1934, p. 73. This amount would be greatly augmented by grants made by the State of Texas from its public lands and by other states from the swamp lands received from the Federal government, and also by the lands purchased by railroads from the Indians. As used here only the 132,425,574 acres are considered. Only a small part of this vast area was sold prior to 1862. Not all of it was available for sale even by 1871 but this total represents all the land which the railroads received from congressional land grants.

communication. The subsequent settler had the choice of buying at the speculators' prices, from the land grant railroads which held their alternate tracts at equally high prices, from the states whose land policies were less generous than those of the Federal government, or of going farther afield to exercise his homestead privilege where facilities for social and economic intercourse were limited. The fact that their lands were more advantageously situated was effectively advertised by the land companies. Thus the American Emigrant Company in advertising its Iowa lands in the sixties, summed up under the caption "Better than a Free Homestead" all the disadvantages of free land:

> Under the homestead law the settler must, in order to get a good location, go far out into the wild and unsettled districts, and for many years be deprived of school privileges, churches, mills, bridges, and in fact of all the advantages of society.[36]

Settlers arriving in Kansas—to consider a typical state—between 1868 and 1872 were greeted with advertisements announcing that the choicest lands in the state had been selected by the State Agricultural College which was now offering 90,000 acres for sale on long term credits. The Central Branch of the Union Pacific Railroad offered 1,200,000 acres for prices ranging from $1.00 to $15.00 per acre; the Kansas Pacific Railroad offered 5,000,000 acres for $1.00 to $6.00 per acre; the Kansas and Neosho Valley Railroad offered 1,500,000 acres for sale at $2.00 to $8.00 per acre; the Capital Land Agency of Topeka offered 1,000,000 acres of Kansas land for sale; [37] Van Doren and Havens offered 200,000 acres for $3.00 to $10.00 per acre; T. H. Walker offered 10,000 (or 100,000) acres [38] for $5.00 to $10.00 per acre; Hendry and Noyes offered 50,000 acres; and even the United States government was advertising for bids for approximately 6000 acres of Sac and Fox Indian

---

[36] Pamphlet: *Two Thousand Families Wanted For Iowa*, n. d., n. p.

[37] Letterhead of letter of W. C. Fitzsimmons, a member of the firm, July 15, 1871, to E. S. Parker, commissioner of Indian Affairs, file of material on Indian land sales, Indian Office.

[38] In June, 1870, Walker was advertising 10,000 acres of Kansas land for sale (Leavenworth *Bulletin*, June 13, 1870), while in February, 1871, he was advertising 100,000 acres for sale (*ibid.*, Feb. 7, 1871). Thaddeus H. Walker of Topeka, Kansas, formerly of Washington County, New York, had entered in 1855 to 1859 in the Kickapoo, Kansas, Land District 16,000 acres, 46,000 acres in the Lecompton, Kansas, Land District, 14,000 acres in the Junction City, Kansas, Land District, and 4600 acres in the Decorah, Iowa, Land District. The lands were entered mostly with military land warrants. See the abstract and entry books of the above-mentioned land districts in the General Land Office.

lands.[39] That virgin lands in Kansas were selling for substantial prices in this period is shown by the following tables:

Table showing Sales of State Lands [40]

		Acres	Average price per acre
Common School lands	(1865–1882)	450,764	$4.00
Agricultural College lands	(1868–1882)	48,465	4.78
University lands	(1878–1882)	6,224	2.88
Normal School lands	(1876–1882)	4,966	4.72

Table showing Land Sales of Atchison, Topeka, and Santa Fe Railroad [41]
Total Sales from March 1, 1871, to Dec. 31, 1879

Year	Acres	Principal	Average price per acre
1871	71,801.51	$ 425,013.75	$5.91
1872	45,328.81	269,627.66	5.94
1873	133,507.30	748,977.25	5.61
1874	200,459.96	900,973.30	4.49
1875	75,415.33	416,409.85	5.52
1876	122,201.17	665,455.17	5.44½
1877	85,047.78	423,477.49	4.98
1878	267,122.47	1,206,527.64	4.52
1879	104,744.41	494,353.73	4.72
Total	1,105,628.74	$5,550,815.84	$5.02

Such sales—and many others might be cited—are evidence that free homesteads on the most desirable land were not available in this state to incoming settlers.

A strong impulse to speculation was provided by the existence of large amounts of land warrants, chiefly those of the Act of March 3, 1855,[42] which were to be had in the market at prices of a dollar an

[39] The advertisements appeared in the *Kansas Farmer*, the Leavenworth *Bulletin*, the Lawrence *Republican Daily Journal*, the *Cultivator and Country Gentleman*, and the *American Agriculturist*.

[40] *Biennial Report*, Auditor of State, Kansas, 1882, pp. 359–360.

[41] Compiled from *Annual Reports* of the Atchison, Topeka, and Santa Fe Railroad, 1873–1880.

[42] 10 *U. S. Stat.*, 701–702. It should be pointed out that prior to the adoption of the prospective pre-emption principle public lands were not subject to disposal until they had been surveyed and offered at public auction. Lands then remaining unsold were subject to private entry for cash, scrip, or warrants. After prospective pre-emption was adopted settlers could make claims upon surveyed but unoffered lands, thus preceding the speculators. When the homestead idea was being debated its advocates argued that its effects would be largely mitigated unless all lands were withdrawn from speculative entry upon its passage. Such a radical proposal was too much for many homestead advocates and it failed of serious consideration. Nevertheless, it was expected by many people that no additional lands would be offered at auction after 1862 and therefore the area open to private entry would become progressively smaller as time passed. Unfortunately, additional land was put up at auction

acre or less.[43] They could be used to locate solid blocks of land wherever the surveyed area of the public domain was open to cash entry. In addition, it is startling to find a provision in the Agricultural College Act of July 2, 1862, whereby 7,672,800 acres in land scrip,[44] which likewise could be used to locate surveyed lands open to cash entry, were thrown on the market. Within a comparatively short time this scrip depreciated greatly in value. Some states sold their scrip for an average price of less than fifty cents an acre and such prices tempted many individuals to purchase and locate large areas in the Western states.[45] Probably no other scrip or warrant act was used so extensively by speculators to build up large holdings as was this Agricultural College Act. Other special acts were passed after 1862 creating smaller amounts of Indian land scrip and other compensatory scrip, part of which possessed the special privilege of being subject to location on any part of the public domain, whether or not it was surveyed or had been offered for sale.[46]

The existence of large areas of rich lands open to speculative entries and the availability of warrants and scrip at depreciated prices made possible large-scale engrossment after the Homestead Law was passed. Some of the richest and most fertile sections of Iowa, Kansas, Nebraska, Missouri, California, Washington, and Oregon were thus open to cash or warrant entry and after the adoption of the Homestead Law they were quickly engrossed by speculators.

Some of the land entries [47] made after 1862 are interesting to note.

---

in the sixties, seventies, and eighties, thus increasing the areas open to speculative and large-scale entries. At the same time land was being opened to homestead and pre-emption entry which was not offered at auction and therefore not subject to private entry for cash, scrip, or warrants.

[43] G.L.O. *Report*, 1862, p. 9. In 1862 there were 7,123,380 acres of military warrants outstanding.

[44] 12 *U. S. Stat.*, 503–505; "Report of the Public Lands Commission," 1905. *Sen. Doc.*, 58 Cong., 3 sess., no. 189, p. 361.

[45] Of course the Southern states did not receive their scrip until after the Civil War but it took some time for the Land Office to handle the details involved in issuing it and consequently most of it was located between 1864 and 1868. The price which each state received for the sale of its scrip is given in *History of the Agricultural College Land Grant of July 2, 1862, together with a Statement of the Conditions of the Fund derived therefrom as it now exists in each State of the Union* (Ithaca, 1890), pp. xvi, xvii.

[46] G.L.O. *Report*, 1875, p. 69; *Public Land Statutes of the United States*, Daniel M. Green, compiler (Washington, 1931), pp. 637–639.

[47] These land entries were compiled from hundreds of volumes of abstracts in the General Land Office, Department of the Interior, Washington, the listing of which would be almost impossible and equally futile. Following are the chief types of entry books: Abstracts of Lands Entered (for cash), Military Warrant Abstracts, Agricultural College Scrip Abstracts, Indian and other miscellaneous scrip abstracts, and Registers of Receipts.

Senator John Sherman, who, like most politicians of his day, was not averse to speculating in lands, located with Agricultural College scrip 2560 acres in Missouri in 1868; Robert Mears with the same kind of scrip located 29,280 acres in the Boonville district of Missouri; Amos Lawrence, prominent among the promoters of the Emigrant Aid Company at an earlier date, located 58,360 acres in Kansas in 1866 with Agricultural College scrip; Charles and Henry Stebbins and Henry M. Porter entered 53,760 acres in Kansas and Nebraska in 1866, 1867, and 1868 with the same kind of scrip; John C. Work and Rufus Hatch of New York, John J. Blair of New Jersey, and James C. Cusey of Sioux City, Iowa, entered in western Iowa in 1869 and 1870, 12,200, 28,671, 20,970, and 9280 acres respectively; John P. Crothers, of Berks County, Pennsylvania, later of Clark County, Ohio, entered with scrip and cash, 44,140 acres in Nebraska; William Scully, one of the greatest landed proprietors in the United States whose relations with his tenants have been the subject of much hostile comment and legislation,[48] purchased for cash in a single land district in Nebraska in 1870, 41,421 acres; Ira Davenport of Steuben County, New York, whose land operations extended throughout most of the Northwestern states entered with cash and land warrants 16,949 acres in the Dakota City district of Nebraska. Perhaps the largest purchasers of land in Nebraska were a group of Providence, Rhode Island, speculators, consisting of Robert H. Ives, John Carter Brown, Charlotte R. and Moses B. J. Goddard. Ives alone had previously purchased 82,431 acres in Illinois, 50,000 acres in Iowa, and smaller amounts in Minnesota and Missouri, while Brown had acquired over 30,000 acres in Iowa and Illinois. These four individuals entered with cash over 96,000 acres in the Dakota City district. Between 1862 and 1873, twenty-seven other persons entered a combined area of 250,000 acres in Nebraska. Numerous other illustrations could be cited to indicate that speculation in agricultural lands in the Great Plains area did not cease with the passage of the Homestead Law.

Not only were the best agricultural lands being snapped up by speculators but the richest timber lands remaining in the possession of the United States were being rapidly entered by large dealers during the post-Civil War period. There were three areas in which vast amounts of timber land were still owned by the Federal government, the Lake states, the Gulf states with Arkansas, and the Pacific Coast states. In each of these three regions millions of acres of pine, spruce, hemlock, and fir were available for cash entry and in the

---

[48] See C. F. Taylor, ed., *The Land Question from Various Points of View* (Philadelphia, 1898), pp. 44, *passim*.

Pacific area lands covered with the rich redwood and other trees peculiar to that region had been or were just being brought into the market. In the timber lands of these three sections some of the largest purchases by speculators or lumber men took place. Many thousands of acres in Wisconsin and Michigan were located by Isaac Stephenson, Philetus Sawyer, and Russell A. Alger, influential lumber dealers, who were subsequently to become members of the Senate of the United States. Ezra Cornell located 385,780 acres in the Eau Claire, Wisconsin, land district, 76,180 acres in the Bayfield district, 29,200 in the Stevens Point district, 12,480 acres in Minnesota, and 4000 acres in Kansas, all with Agricultural College scrip of New York. A group of New York magnates, Thomas F. Mason, George B. Satterlee, and William E. Dodge, entered 232,799 acres in the Marquette, Michigan, district, 10,850 acres elsewhere in that state, and 10,359 acres in Wassau, Wisconsin. Francis Palms purchased in Wisconsin and Michigan 286,208 acres, and with Frederick E. Driggs entered in the eighties about 200,000 acres more in the Marquette district. Three Ithaca, New York, lumber dealers, Henry W. Sage,[49] John McGraw, and Jeremiah W. Dwight, like Ezra Cornell, benefactors of Cornell University, entered 277,000 acres in Michigan, Wisconsin, and Minnesota, and 75,000 acres in Mississippi, Alabama, and Arkansas. Other large timberland entrymen in the Northwest were Calvin F. Howe of New York who acquired 105,000 acres in Minnesota, Thomas B. Walker [50] who alone and with others acquired 166,000 acres in the St. Cloud, Minnesota, district, George M. Wakefield who accumulated 110,000 acres in the Marquette district, and Jesse Spaulding and H. H. Porter of Chicago who purchased 113,000 acres in the same district. Fifty-six other persons purchased a total of 1,514,000 acres in Michigan, mostly in the Marquette district.

The same concentration of ownership of timber lands developed in the South after 1877. Some of the large purchases in this section were Daniel F. Sullivan's purchase of 147,000 acres in the Montgomery, Alabama, district in 1880–1882; Jabez B. Watkins's purchase of 145,000 acres in the New Orleans district; Delos A. Blodgett's purchase of 136,000 acres in the Jackson, Mississippi, district in 1885 to 1888; Lutcher and Moore's purchase of 108,000 acres in Louisiana in the eighties; and Franklin Head's and Nathan

---

[49] The land empire of Henry W. Sage alone is said by a local historian to have included over 500,000 acres. John H. Selkreg, ed., *Landmarks of Tompkins County, New York* (Syracuse, 1894), pt. 2, p. 4.

[50] Walker acquired 700,000 acres of valuable sugar pine and western pine timber land in California, chiefly through the use of dummy entrymen. Bureau of Corporations, *The Lumber Industry*, pt. 2, p. 91.

B. Bradley's puchases of 110,000 and 111,200 acres respectively in the New Orleans district. Sixty-eight other persons entered 2,110,000 acres in the Southern districts. Altogether, over five and one half million acres of land were sold in the five Southern states between 1880 and 1888, exclusive of pre-emption sales. Practically all of this area went to large land and lumber dealers. These lands comprised some of the very choicest timbered areas in the South and within less than a generation were selling at prices which brought enormous profits to the owners. It is worthy of note that many of the large timber dealers in Wisconsin, Michigan, and Minnesota made great acquisitions in the South.

The engrossment of timber and agricultural lands on the Pacific Coast proceeded at an even more rapid rate than in other sections of the country. Here in the years immediately following the Civil War a relatively small group of speculators sought to monopolize the best timber and agricultural lands. A group of Eastern speculators consisting of W. W. Corcoran of Washingotn, ex-Senator Bright of Indiana, and Elisha and Lawrason Riggs, whose land acquisitions in the Middle West had been very profitable, purchased over 7000 acres in Washington and Oregon in the early seventies; another group of San Francisco speculators purchased 59,000 acres in the Olympia, Washington, district; J. W. Sprague of Minnesota purchased 24,000 acres in the same district, and five other persons acquired 42,000 acres. More spectacular were the huge entries in California.

Land monopolization in California dates back to the Spanish and Mexican periods when large grants were made to favored individuals. After investigation by an American commission, 588 of these claims amounting to 8,850,143 acres, or an average of 15,051 acres each, were confirmed.[51] Following 1848 there came a rapid influx of settlers which, together with the large profits realized from the grazing industry in the interior valleys, created a land boom and led to extensive purchases. With great areas of land in the San Joaquin and Sacramento valleys open to cash purchase the opportunity for speculative profits was unparalleled elsewhere; nor was the opportunity neglected. From 1862 to 1880 land sales and warrant and scrip entries in California were on an enormous scale, surpassing all other states for the period and in some years comprising well over half of the sales for the entire country. In the single year, ending June 30, 1869, 1,726,794 acres were sold in this state by the Federal government, and for the entire period from 1862 to 1880 well over 7,000,-

[51] "Report of the Public Lands Commission," 1905, *op. cit.*, p. 140.

000 [52] acres were entered with cash, warrants, or scrip. It should also be remembered that the State of California which received 8,426,-380 [53] acres from the Federal government was disposing of its most valuable holdings at this time.

Greatest of all the speculators operating in California was William S. Chapman whose political influence stretched from Sacramento to St. Paul, Minnesota, and Washington, D.C. Of him it was said, with apparent justice, that land officers, judges, local legislators, officials in the Department of the Interior, and even higher dignitaries were ready and anxious to do him favors, frequently of no mean significance. Between 1868 and 1871 Chapman entered at the Federal land offices approximately 650,000 acres of land in California and Nevada with cash, scrip, and warrants. At the same time he entered additional land through dummy entrymen, purchased many thousands of acres of "swamp" lands from the State of California, and otherwise added to his possessions till they totaled over 1,000,000 acres. Fraud, bribery, false swearing, forgery, and other crimes were charged against him but he passed them off with little trouble.[54] The most remarkable feature about his vast acquisitions is that when plotted on a land-use map today they appear to be among the choicest of the lands. Chapman was not able to retain this vast empire for long. He became deeply involved in a grand canal project and eventually lost his lands, many of them going to a more constructive but equally spectacular land plunger, Henry Miller.[55]

Miller, unlike Chapman, bought lands for his cattle business which was his main interest. As the activities of his firm—Miller and Lux, of which he was the chief promoter—expanded, he pushed its land acquisitions until they mounted to over a million acres. One hundred and eighty-one thousand acres of this amount were acquired directly from the Federal government, with cash, Agricultural College scrip, and military warrants; large amounts were purchased from Chapman and other big land speculators and from the State of California. Miller's lands were slowly irrigated, parts were disposed of to small farmers, and upon them today exists a veritable agricultural empire.[56]

[52] G.L.O. *Reports*, 1862–1880.

[53] G.L.O. *Report*, 1932, p. 46.

[54] There is a mass of testimony offered to prove these charges in *Reports of the Joint Committees on Swamp and Overflowed Lands, and Land Monopoly*, presented at the Twentieth Session of the Legislature of California (Sacramento, 1874).

[55] Edward F. Treadwell, *The Cattle King* (New York, 1931), p. 73.

[56] The story of Henry Miller is interestingly told in Treadwell, *op. cit.* A more detailed and objective study of the land and cattle business of Miller and Lux would shed much light on the history of the Far West.

Other large purchasers of land in California were Isaac Friedlander, E. H. Miller, and John W. Mitchell, who acquired 214,000, 105,000, and 78,000 acres respectively. The total amount purchased from the Federal government by Chapman, Miller and Lux, Friedlander, E. H. Miller, and Mitchell was one and a quarter million acres. Forty-three other large purchasers acquired 905,000 acres of land in the sixties in California. Buying in advance of settlement, these men were virtually thwarting the Homestead Law in California where, because of the enormous monopolization above outlined, homesteaders later were able to find little good land.

Further details concerning the widespread speculative activity in public lands—both agricultural and timbered—after the passage of the Homestead Act are unnecessary; it is clear that speculation and land engrossment were not retarded by the act. Homeseekers in the West, being unwilling to go far afield from means of transportation or to settle upon the inferior lands remaining open to homestead, and lacking capital with which to purchase farms and to provide equipment for them, were frequently forced to become tenants on the lands of speculators. Thus farm tenancy developed in the frontier stage at least a generation before it would have appeared had the homestead system worked properly. In the states of Kansas and Nebraska, in which large-scale land monopolization has been revealed, sixteen and eighteen per cent respectively of the farms were operated by tenants in 1880, the first year for which figures are available, and in 1890 twenty-eight and twenty-four per cent respectively were operated by tenants.[57] This continued monopolization of the best lands and the resulting growth of farm tenancy led reformers and others who feared the establishment of a landed aristocracy similar to that existing in many European countries to advocate the ending of the cash sales system entirely. Their demands were expressed in petitions to Congress, agitation in the press, and union of effort with other antimonopoly groups which were coming into prominence in the last third of the nineteenth century. Their agitation and the growing seriousness of the monopoly movement led to a series of halting steps toward the abandonment of cash sales, which frequently were offset by movements in the opposite direction.

The first step in the direction of abolishing the cash sale system

[57] *Eleventh Census,* 1890, "Statistics of Agriculture," p. 4. There is some detail on the relation of land policy and farm tenancy in an article by the present writer on "Recent Land Policies of the Federal Government" which is to appear in part VII of the Supplementary Report of the Land Planning Committee to the National Resources Board, entitled "Certain Aspects of Land Problems and Governmental Land Policies."

was taken in June, 1866, when Congress provided that all public lands in the five Southern states of Alabama, Arkansas, Florida, Louisiana, and Mississippi should be reserved from sale and subject only to entry under the Homestead Law.[58] The avowed purpose of this apparent discrimination against land speculation in the South while it was permitted to flourish elsewhere, was to prevent speculators from monopolizing the land when it was restored to market—all land transactions had of course ceased in these states during the Civil War—and to encourage the growth of small holdings among the freedmen. By the South, the act was regarded, perhaps rightly, as a punitive measure. Certain it is that much of the 46,398,544 acres [59] thus reserved from cash entry was unsuited to small-scale farming and the freedmen showed no great desire to take advantage of the homestead privilege thus safeguarded. Nevertheless, the act was the first attack on the cash sale system.

Two backward steps were tried the same year, however. In the same month that the law was passed restricting Southern public lands to homestead entry an apparently innocuous measure slipped through Congress without much debate or opposition, giving to the New York and Montana Iron Mining and Manufacturing Company the right to purchase at $1.25 per acre twenty sections—12,800 acres—of unsurveyed and unopened lands in the territory of Montana, three sections of which might contain iron ore or coal and the remaining sections would presumably be timber lands. This measure was put through by Benjamin Wade of Ohio and Thaddeus Stevens of Pennsylvania of whom it cannot be said that the interests of the homesteaders were nearest to their hearts.[60] It gave a gross extension of privilege to a group of speculators or land monopolists. Never had such a *carte blanche* grant been made before, though frequently petitioned for, and it aroused the indignation of President Johnson who, in a ringing veto message, declared that the privileges conferred by the act "are in direct conflict with every principle heretofore observed in respect to the disposal of the public lands." [61] If the measure had been signed, the principle of granting lands free or for the minimum price to mining companies and other industrial organizations might have been established and the remaining portion of the public domain might have been divided among such capitalistic groups, just as millions of acres were being parceled out among

[58] Act of June 21, 1866, 14 *U. S. Stat.*, 66–67.
[59] *Cong. Globe*, 39 Cong., 1 sess., pp. 715ff.; p. 2736.
[60] *Ibid.*, pp. 2193, 2218, 2219, 2303, 2965, 2966.
[61] Message of June 15, 1866, *Senate Journal*, 39 Cong., 1 sess., p. 532.

the railroads. In placing himself squarely against the law, President Johnson aided in preserving the lands from speculators.

President Johnson's opposition to the granting of such special privileges to private business groups did not end the matter, however, for a similar measure passed the Senate in 1870. This second measure would have authorized the Sierra Iron Company of California to purchase 640 acres of land containing iron ore in the vicinity of Gold Lake, California, and 3200 acres of timber lands for $2.50 per acre. As originally proposed by Senator Cole of California it would have permitted the purchase of 10,000 acres of timber lands at $1.25 per acre but was amended as above. The measure was rushed through the Senate at a night session when there was a very small attendance, but was later reconsidered, amended to provide further safeguards, and sent to the House where the opponents of land monopoly succeeded in preventing its adoption.[62] Eternal vigilance on the part of true friends of the homesteaders was essential to prevent such laws being slipped through without adequate consideration.

The second backward step was a series of Indian treaties and administrative measures by which substantial areas of land in the Great Plains were sold to railroad companies and other speculative groups. When railroads were projected through Kansas and Nebraska, it was found that they must run through Indian reservations. Congressional land grants did not apply to such lands and the railroad officials therefore sought to purchase the lands which they could not receive as a gift. Instead of asking for alternate sections, however, as in the grants, they sought to purchase solid areas which would enable them to secure the entire benefits resulting from the construction of the railroads. As the Granger period had not yet arrived, railroads were still popular throughout most sections of the country. Furthermore, they possessed great influence at the seat of power and it was not difficult for them to prevail upon the proper officials to make treaties for the cession or sale of Indian lands. The Senate at this time was far more friendly to the railroads than to the homeseekers, as shown by its generous land grants and financial subsidies to the former and its refusal to place restrictions upon speculative purchases of land. Apparently it saw little difference between making donations of alternate sections of the public domain to the railroads and selling solid blocks of Indian lands to them for a low price. It therefore ratified such treaties with little hesitation.

In the years immediately following the enactment of the Homestead

[62] *Ibid.,* 41 Cong., 2 sess., pp. 3659–3670, 4543–4546.

Law, a number of such treaties and subsequent sales contracts were ratified, providing for the sale of several million acres in Kansas to railroad companies.[63] That which aroused the greatest local opposition was the sale of some 800,000 acres of Cherokee Indian lands in southeastern Kansas. A treaty was negotiated with the Cherokees which permitted the sale of 800,000 acres to a single individual or corporation for $1.00 per acre, and which completely disregarded the white settlers already on the lands. Before ratification, the treaty was amended to permit the sale of tracts of 160 acres to the squatters.[64] In the meantime, the Secretary of the Interior had sold this great tract to the American Emigrant Company. This company was organized to operate under the nefarious contract labor law of 1864 but quickly saw that larger profits were to be realized in land speculation and it began to deal in lands. Its record of land deals is obscure but is accompanied by sufficient evidence to indicate that the transactions were not always legitimate.[65] The purchase of 800,-000 acres of Cherokee lands at $1.00 per acre on long credit was the result of secret negotiations; the lands were not offered at public sale, and the settlers were given no opportunity to purchase the tracts upon which they were squatting. The sale was, then, an outrageous violation of the principle of land for the landless and was immediately attacked as a gross fraud upon the public. Subsequent investigations revealed much that could not be satisfactorily explained and the Attorney General held that it was not in conformity with the treaty with the Cherokees.

Meantime, the Cherokee tract, through widely circulated rumors as to its fertility and desirability for settlement, was attracting the attention of many interested people. Following 1866 settlers flocked to the area in large numbers so that by 1867 there were reported to be 10,000 or 12,000 people there [66] and the number was shortly increased to 20,000. The settlers expected from the government the same lenient attitude toward their intrusions upon land not open to

[63] These treaties are included in *United States Statutes-at-Large*, vols. XII, XIII, XIV. They are analyzed and the areas conveyed by them are pictured on maps in Charles C. Royce, *Indian Land Sessions in the United States* (Eighteenth Annual Report of the Bureau of American Ethnology to the Secretary of the Smithsonian Institution, 1896–1897), pt. 2.

[64] 14 *U. S. Stat.*, 799–809.

[65] The sale of 18,000 acres of "swamp lands" in Wright County, Iowa, to the American Emigrant Company for $1500 and the subsequent recovery of a portion of the land is described by W. J. Covil in the Webster City *Freeman-Tribune*, July 13, 1904, republished in *Annals of Iowa*, 3d ser., VII (1905), 360.

[66] Governor S. J. Crawford, Topeka, Kansas, Aug. 19, 1867, to Secretary Browning, file of material on Indian land sales, Indian Office.

settlement as was being rendered to other people in similar circumstances elsewhere. Unfortunately for them the value of the tract was appreciated by a number of railroad groups which desired to secure ownership of the entire area as a means of financing the construction of their lines. Concrete proposals for the purchase of the tract were made by three railroads—the Tebo and Neosho Railroad Company of Missouri,[67] the Atlantic and Pacific Railroad, and the Kansas City, Fort Scott, and Gulf Railroad. Prominent Missouri and Kansas politicians, John C. Fremont and James F. Joy—"The Railroad King"—were interested in these lines and each sought to secure the much coveted lands for his company. Although not the highest bidder, the sale was finally awarded to James F. Joy who purchased the land for the Kansas City, Fort Scott, and Gulf Railroad. After the sale was made and the rival proposals turned down, the lenient officials of the Department of the Interior permitted Joy to surrender his contract and to substitute the original but less exacting contract with the American Emigrant Company which was now assigned to him. This necessitated a supplementary treaty with the Cherokees to validate a contract previously held to be illegal. The contract was modified, however, to permit settlers who resided upon the land in 1866 to purchase their tracts at the appraised value.[68] Joy was required to pay but $1.00 an acre and generous credit was allowed him, while the settlers were asked to pay an average of $1.92 per acre in cash.[69]

The second sale was an equally great violation of the principle of free homesteads, and, it should be noted, was ratified by the Senate the same year that the House resolution frowning upon the further sale of agricultural land was passed. Secretary Browning who, as Harlan's successor, had negotiated the sale, came in for as bitter accusations as had his predecessor and, it must be admitted, with some justification. The sale was made to his brother-in-law, Joy; his partner was at the time employed by Joy to negotiate the transaction; Browning himself had earlier represented Joy, and the following year was again retained by him in a series of important

[67] P. A. Ladue, St. Louis, Missouri, Jan. 19, 1867, to L. C. Bogy, commissioner of Indian Affairs, *ibid.*

[68] The sale of the Cherokee lands is discussed in a letter of Charles Mix, acting commissioner of Indian Affairs, Apr. 21, 1869, to J. D. Cox, secretary of the Interior, Cherokee File, Indian Office. Secretary Harlan's interpretation of the sale may be read in *Cong. Globe*, 40 Cong., 3 sess., pp. 409ff., and 41 Cong., 1 sess., pp. 21–23; also in Johnson Brigham, *James Harlan* (Iowa City, 1913), pp. 235ff. See also Eugene F. Ware, "The Neutral Lands," Kansas State Historical Society, *Transactions*, VI (1900), 147–169.

[69] *Report*, Commissioner of Indian Affairs, 1869, p. 502.

cases.[70] Furthermore, as was pointed out in a joint resolution adopted by the House on July 13, 1868,[71] the sale failed to consider the rights of a large number of people who had settled upon the tract between 1866 and 1868 and who were subsequently forced to purchase their lands from the railroad. Petitions from settlers upon the Cherokee tract demanding the abrogation of the sale poured in upon the Interior Department; [72] the governor of Kansas denounced the sale as "a cheat and a fraud in every particular, and should have been encircled with hell's blackest marks," a "gigantic swindle"; [73] and in 1868 both the Republican and Democratic state conventions condemned the policy of disposing of Indian lands to "speculators and foreign corporations." [74] The campaign to have the second sale annulled was unsuccessful but, combined with the opposition to similar sales of Indian lands, it was eventually to end the policy.

Equally inconsiderate of the rights of settlers were the sales of the lands of the Delaware, Pottawatomie, Kickapoo, and Sac and Fox of the Mississippi Indians in Kansas. Treaties authorizing the sale of the surplus Delaware and Pottawatomie lands to the Leavenworth, Pawnee, and Western Railroad for $1.25 per acre were proclaimed on August 22, 1860, and April 19, 1862, respectively.[75] This railroad was unable to carry through the purchase of the Pottawatomie lands but did succeed in negotiating a sufficiently liberal contract for the Delaware lands whereby it acquired title to 223,966 acres of rich farming lands in Leavenworth, Atchison, and Jefferson counties for $286,742 paid in its own bonds, instead of cash as originally required.[76] In 1866, the Delaware Indians having decided to abandon their diminished reserve in Kansas, which had been allotted in severalty, accepted a second treaty which provided for the sale of the

[70] Theodore Calvin Pease and James G. Randall, eds., *Diary of Orville Hickman Browning* (Illinois State Historical Library, *Collections*, vols. XX, XXII, 1925–1933), I, 645–646; II, 219, 239, 257, 276, *passim*.

[71] *Cong. Globe*, 40 Cong., 2 sess., pp. 4000–4001.

[72] These petitions are filed in the Indian Office, Cherokee File.

[73] Samuel J. Crawford, *Kansas in the Sixties* (Chicago, 1911), p. 310. Crawford, as governor, took an active part in the campaign to end the sale of large tracts of Indian lands to railroads and other speculative groups. Aside from his interest in the settlers who were being deprived of the right of buying their holdings directly from the government he opposed the Indian land policy on the ground that it deprived the state of the 16th and 32d sections which it would otherwise get for its public schools.

[74] D. W. Wilder, *Annals of Kansas* (Topeka, 1886), pp. 481, *passim*. In this book are found a number of items indicating the emotions which were aroused in the settlers of the Cherokee tract by the arbitrary sale of the lands.

[75] 12 *U. S. Stat.*, 1129, 1193. This railroad later became the Union Pacific Railway Company, Eastern Division, and still later the Kansas Pacific Railroad.

[76] *Ibid.*, p. 1177.

92,598 acres contained in the reserve to the Missouri River Railroad for $2.50 per acre, exclusive of improvements, which were to be appraised and sold at a fair valuation.[77]

The Pottawatomie lands were subsequently sold, in 1868, to the Atchison, Topeka, and Santa Fe Railroad. This sale called for the payment of $1.00 per acre, not $1.25 as the earlier treaty provided, and five years' time was given during which no payments were required except advance interest of six per cent annually upon the purchase sum. The government thus not only denied to settlers the right to acquire the land directly but gave the railroad company the use of 340,180 acres of rich agricultural lands for annual payments of $20,410 for five years. At the end of this time a payment of 340,180 was required, which could be paid in greenbacks.[78] The policy of making land sales to settlers on credit had been abandoned in 1820 and Congress had resisted all efforts to restore the credit system but credit was extended to railroads in the sixties. The Atchison, Topeka, and Santa Fe Railroad proceeded to sell the lands at prices well over double their cost, and charged seven per cent interest on delayed payments. By 1873 it had received in cash and notes $646,784 and valued the remaining lands at $507,366,[79] no small profit for the times. A substantial part of the amount due the government in 1873 was paid from cash sales. The mortgage bonds based on these lands, obtained for only $20,410 down, enabled the railroad to begin construction without the promoters having to supply any capital of their own worth mentioning.

A treaty similar to that w'th the Pottawatomie Indians was concluded with the Kickapoo Indians under the terms of which 123,832 acres were sold in 1865 to the Atchison and Pike's Peak Railroad for $1.25 per acre, on generous credit.[80] This treaty was negotiated with a railroad whose president, Samuel C. Pomeroy, was not only senator from Kansas and thus in a position to support its adoption, but was also very close to the administration of the Indian Office and the Department of the Interior. Pomeroy represented the attitude of his state in demanding the speedy removal of the Indians and the dis-

[77] 14 *U. S. Stat.*, 793–794; O. H. Browning, secretary of the Interior, Oct. 21, 1867, to C. E. Mix, commissioner of Indian Affairs, Delaware Files, Indian Office.
[78] 15 *U. S. Stat.*, 535–536; *Report*, Commissioner of Indian Affairs, 1869, p. 504.
[79] *Report*, Atchison, Topeka, and Santa Fe Railroad, 1873, p. 10. It is true that in later reports the meager data given indicate the estimate of return contained in the *Report* for 1873 as somewhat optimistic.
[80] 13 *U. S. Stat.*, 623ff.; *Cong. Globe*, 40 Cong., 2 sess., p. 1715; Royce, *passim*.

posal of their lands but he went against popular opinion in supporting the sale of the Cherokee, Delaware, Pottawatomie, Kickapoo, and
Osage lands to railroads.

The sale of the Sac and Fox Indian lands differs somewhat from
those previously mentioned. These lands, comprising 272,200 acres,
were advertised for sale to the highest bidders but, unlike the public
land auctions, the bids were to be submitted by letter. This of course
had the effect of preventing settlers upon the lands from combining
into a claims association and preventing outsiders from bidding as
was done at the public auctions. As a result most of the land was
acquired at low prices by speculators, among whom the largest
buyers were John McManus,[81] William B. McKean, Fuller and
McDonald, Robert S. Stevens, and the Hon. Hugh McCulloch who
acquired respectively 142,915, 29,677, 39,058, 51,689, and 7014
acres.[82]

The treaty providing for the largest sale of Indian lands was negotiated in 1868 between the Osage Indians of Kansas and representatives of the Department of the Interior, according to which 8,000,000
acres of land were to be sold to the Leavenworth, Lawrence, and
Galveston Railroad for $1,600,000.[83] This was at the rate of twenty
cents an acre for lands to which settlers were eagerly looking for
homes. Characterized by Governor Crawford as "one of the most
infamous outrages ever before committed in this country," it was
indeed a most disgraceful and unjustified action. If adopted it would
have deprived the State of Kansas of 500,000 acres of school lands,
robbed the Indians of a fair price for their lands, and would have
killed a number of rival railroads, including the Atchison, Topeka,
and Santa Fe. Worst of all, the treaty ignored the rights of settlers
already on the lands. Furthermore, it was stated that a substantially
higher bid had been turned down in order to accept that of the
Leavenworth, Lawrence, and Galveston Railroad. The hand of James
F. Joy was again seen, for the latter road had already come under
his control as part of the great transportation system he was con-
structing. The Osage treaty brought to a climax the utter disregard
shown by the officials of the Department of the Interior for the
rights of settlers and aroused a storm of criticism, both in Kansas
and in Washington.[84]

[81] John McManus, of Reading, Pennsylvania, was a director of the Kansas
Pacific Railway Company which had the largest land grant in Kansas. *Report*,
Kansas Pacific Railway Co., 1870.

[82] *Report*, Commissioner of Indian Affairs, 1865, p. 549ff. See also speech
of Representative Julian in *Cong. Globe*, 40 Cong., 2 sess., p. 1715.

[83] *Report*, Commissioner of Indian Affairs, 1868, p. 5.

[84] Crawford, pp. 299ff.

Representative George W. Julian, than whom no one had the interests of the homesteader more at heart, saw the iniquity in these Indian treaties and subsequent land sales to railroads and others. He introduced a resolution into the House of Representatives to the effect that these sales were a usurpation of power by the Senate which was endangering the entire land system and urged upon the Senate the advisability of ratifying no more such treaties. He pointed out that by using the treaty making power in this way it was possible for the Senate to transfer all the public lands to the Indians and then by other treaties to arrange for their sale to railroads or other speculative groups, thus completely frustrating the Homestead Law and subverting the land system. Julian succeeded in winning the support of the House for his view and the resolution was adopted.[85] The enactment of this resolution and the storm of criticism which rained upon the Senate apparently had some effect, for the treaty with the Osage Indians, although urgently supported by the Commissioner of Indian Affairs, was not ratified and Congress later provided for the sale of the Osage lands to actual settlers.

One may plainly see from events in Congress during 1867 and 1868 how insincere that body was in rendering lip service to the homestead principle. In this year Representative Julian introduced two measures into the House, the action on which throws a flood of light on the question. The first was a resolution that:

> In order to carry into full and complete effect the spirit and policy of the preemption and homestead laws of the United States, the further sale of the agricultural public lands ought to be prohibited by law and that all proposed grants of land to aid in construction of railroads, or for other special objects, should be carefully scrutinized and rigidly subordinated to the paramount purpose of securing homes for the landless poor, the actual settlement and tillage of the public domain, and the consequent increase of the national wealth.[86]

The second was a bill to prevent any further sale of the public lands except as provided for in the Pre-emption and Homestead laws.[87] In support of these measures Julian made a number of strong speeches in which he described the evils resulting from speculation in lands, showed that, except for the Southern states, free homesteading was restricted to the least attractive lands, and denounced the land monopoly which was rapidly being created by the lavish grants to the railroads. Julian was followed by two congressmen from Michigan districts in which lumbering was the chief industry. They favored

[85] *Cong. Globe*, 40 Cong., 2 sess., pp. 2753, 2814, 3278–3279.
[86] *Ibid.*, p. 97.
[87] *Ibid.*, p. 371.

large grants to railroads and no restrictions on land sales, and argued that Julian's bill, if passed, would ruin the lumber industry, increase speculation and fraudulent entries, and thus frustrate its own purpose.[88] Although unanimously reported by the Committee on Public Lands, nothing further was heard from the bill to end cash sales. The resolution, on the other hand, which had no binding effect but which favored exactly the same policy toward cash sales as the bill, passed the House without any important opposition.[89] Congress was far from ready in 1868 to end cash sales, and the passage of the resolution was certainly not "tantamount to a law." [90]

Between the enactment of this resolution in 1868 and 1876, the forces interested in opening up the public domain to large-scale purchases were fighting the advocates of the homestead principle on two grounds; they struggled to repeal the Act of 1866 which placed restrictions on cash sales in the South, and they tried to prevent further limitations on land engrossment in the West.

The discriminatory character of the restrictions upon cash sales in the South and its obviously punitive features rankled with the Southern congressmen who sought to repeal the act of 1866. They were vigorously supported by representatives from other sections who were either interested in the lumber industry themselves or whose constituents looked with longing eyes upon the rich pine lands of the South. In the early seventies the movement for repeal gained headway. Its leaders harped on the discriminatory features of the Act of 1866, its retarding effects upon immigration and the lumber industry, and argued that it led to the public lands being stripped of their only valuable commodity—timber. In 1875 the commissioner of the General Land Office came to the support of the repealists. Indeed, the land commissioners in their reports of 1875, 1876, and 1877 favored opening up all public lands to cash sale.[91] Strong opposition was voiced against the repeal measure by the Northern radicals for political purposes and by land reformers who foresaw the effects of such a backward step, but the combination of Southern resentment and Northern economic interests was too strong, and the measure became a law on July 4, 1876, without the approval of President Grant.[92] Southern lands were again made subject to cash

[88] *Ibid.*, pp. 1712–1715, 2380–2387.
[89] *Ibid.*, p. 1861.
[90] See p. 653 of this article.
[91] *Cong. Globe*, 41 Cong., 3 sess., pp. 539–540; *Cong. Record*, 43 Cong., 1 sess., pp. 4633, *passim*; 44 Cong., 1 sess., pp. 815ff., 1090, 3655. G.L.O. *Report*, 1875, pp. 8–9, 17–19; 1876, p. 7; 1877, p. 34.
[92] *Cong. Record*, 44 Cong., 1 sess., p. 4469; 19 *U. S. Stat.*, 73–74. The debates on the repeal measure are discussed in Ise, pp. 49–53.

entry, the unfortunate results of which have already been seen in the large-scale monopolization by lumber interests, mostly from the Northern states.

Although defeated in the South, the land reformers, under the leadership of Senator Harlan of Iowa and Representative Julian of Indiana, continued the fight to limit or end cash sales to large purchasers. In the House three measures were passed in 1870, one to end cash sales in California, another to end cash sales in Dakota Territory, and the third to prevent cash sales in Nebraska, Nevada, California, Arkansas, and Utah.[93] Similar measures were introduced in the Senate but were uniformly unsuccessful, because here the interests of lumber men, mining groups, and large speculators were well represented. In 1872 a congressman from California proposed an amendment to the Constitution which would have prohibited the further disposal of the public lands except to actual settlers but it made no progress.[94]

From the date of the repeal of the restrictions on cash entry in the South until 1889 there was not a session of Congress in which the question of reserving all the public lands for homestead entry was not fiercely debated. Continued efforts were made to end the cash sale system. Following 1880, the Pre-emption, Timber and Stone, Timber Culture, and Desert Land acts came in for much criticism since it was apparent that, like the commutation clause of the Homestead Law, they lent themselves to abuse and fraud. In the eighties the movement was given a great impetus by the discovery of enormous frauds in which foreign corporations and titled noblemen were engaged for the purpose of building up vast estates. The fact that most of this alien ownership was English[95] was used effectively by the Anglophobes and, added to the antimonopoly movement which was rapidly gaining in strength, it made easy the conversion of many politicians to the cause of land reform.

President Cleveland's land commissioner, William A. J. Sparks, dramatically brought the issue to the front by revealing with overwhelming evidence that "the public domain was being made the prey of unscrupulous speculation and the worst forms of land monopoly through systematic frauds carried on and consummated under the public land laws."[96] In cold, biting language, he accused the ad-

[93] *Cong. Globe*, 41 Cong., 2 sess., pp. 738–739, 5129.
[94] *Cong. Globe*, 42 Cong., 3 sess., p. 84.
[95] In 1884 the Senate called for an investigation of the foreign land holdings and the resulting report contains some interesting information on the practices and holdings of a number of well-financed British land and cattle companies. See *Sen. Doc.*, 48 Cong., 1 sess., no. 181.
[96] G.L.O. *Report*, 1885, p. 48.

ministration of the General Land Office of being either extra-
ordinarily inept in its management or directly involved in the great
frauds which he unearthed. So general were the illegal or fraudulent
entries that within a month after his accession to office he suspended
all final entries under the Timber and Stone Act and the Desert Land
Act, and in Colorado, Dakota, Idaho, Utah, Washington, New
Mexico, Montana, Wyoming, Nevada, and parts of Minnesota, Kansas, and Nebraska suspended all entries except those made with
cash and scrip. The evidence of fraud continued to come in, and,
as the demand for complete suspension of all non-homestead entries
stimulated speculators and monopolists to feverish activity, Sparks
in desperation, in 1886, ordered the land officers to accept no further
applications for entries under the Pre-emption, Timber Culture, and
Desert Land acts.[97] This precipitate action stirred up a veritable
hornets' nest of opposition and the order was rescinded, but its
effect remained.

The onslaught of the antimonopolists had the effect of stimulating
the speculators, cattlemen, lumber and mining companies to prompt
action before the public domain should be closed to them. Land sales
and entries under the Pre-emption, Timber Culture, Timber and
Stone, and Desert Land acts and the cash sale system shot up to a
high point in 1888, exceeding those of any year since 1856 and being
surpassed only four times in our entire history.

This enormous speculation, added to the widespread frauds which
were being uncovered, produced a demand for reform which swelled
to a tremendous volume. Hundreds of petitions with innumerable
signatures flooded Congress urging changes in land policy and administration. They made it plain that public opinion had been
aroused and could no longer be ignored.

Measure after measure providing for repeal of the objectionable
laws passed the House in the eighties only to be defeated in the
Senate. Finally, under the stimulus of Sparks's dramatic gesture, repeal measures passed both houses in 1886 and again in 1887, but
were defeated through failure to harmonize conflicting views. These
were to be the last defeats, however, because Congress was rapidly
being forced into a position where it had to take action. In May
and July, 1888, two measures were passed by which land sales in
the five Southern states were temporarily suspended, and the Act of
1876 was reversed. This was followed, on March 2, 1889, by an act
ending all cash sales of public lands except in Missouri where the
remaining lands were mostly mineral in character or scattered frag-

[97] *Report*, 1886, p. 43, 135.

ments of little value for agriculture. In 1890 a rider was attached to an appropriation act by which it was stipulated that henceforth no person should acquire title to more than 320 acres in the aggregate under all of the land laws.[98] Finally, in 1891 a combination of antimonopoly land reformers and conservationists placed upon the statute books a law which was as far reaching, as important, perhaps, as the Homestead Act of 1862. This law [99] repealed the Pre-emption and Timber Culture acts and placed additional safeguards in the Desert Land Act and the commutation clause of the Homestead Act. Except for Indian lands and small isolated tracts the speculators could no longer purchase whole counties for the minimum price and land engrossment by fraudulent means was at least made more difficult. Unfortunately these land reforms were not enacted until the best of the area suitable for farming without irrigation had passed into private ownership.

The most important section of the Act of 1891 was that which authorized the creation of forest reservations on the public lands. Here was the first fundamental break with the underlying philosophy of our land system—the desire to dispose of the lands and hasten their settlement. The conservationists had now convinced the country that a part of our natural resources must be retained in public ownership and preserved for the future. Unfortunately, conservation, when first adopted, was embedded in an outworn laissez-faire land system of a previous age just as the free homestead plan had been superimposed upon a land system designed to produce revenue. In both cases the old and the new clashed with disastrous effects.

[98] 25 *U. S. Stat.*, 622, 626; 854–855; 26 *U. S. Stat.*, 371, 391.
[99] 26 *U. S. Stat.*, 1095–1103.

12

THERE is no need to describe the general interpretation of federal land grants to railroads that prevailed prior to the publication of Henry's article. He has fully described it in his first few pages, and as his use of the word "legend" in his title suggests, he has shown it to be substantially in error.

Aside from the article's correction of an erroneous and established view, it merits study for at least two additional reasons. To be able to show, as he does, that textbooks, those bibles of American history for the student, can be erroneous is certainly a salutary lesson. Unfortunately the dryness of a text is sometimes equated with a guarantee of its accuracy. There is no more dramatic way for a student to learn that all authors are fallible than to see the textbook proved to be in substantial error. The second justification for this article is that it nicely demonstrates how an investigation of a rather narrow subject can have broad implications, extending beyond the immediate subject.

Once Mr. Henry has shown that the usual picture of the amounts of land granted to the railroads has been exaggerated, he goes on to draw other conclusions about the role of land grants in the economic history of the United States. Like Paul Wallace Gates in the previous article, Henry has an ax to grind. At the time he wrote this article, he was an official of the Association of American Railroads. Indeed, some of the criticism of this article that professional historians leveled against it made much of this connection. But as other historians pointed out, a man's motives for undertaking a piece of research are never at issue in the search for the facts of the past. All that one should ask is that the reporting of the facts be accurate and that the interpretations fit, more or less easily, all the known facts, not just those used by the author. It is true, of course, that Henry in this article was interested in showing that the granting of land to the railroads was not just a giveaway nor simply a sordid deal in which the United States government was "taken" by unscrupulous and greedy railroad interests in league with equally avaricious politicians. Simply because he was interested in defending railroad companies, historians gained new information and new insights into the past.

Thus he argued that the government not only received much in return from the grants but, more important, that American society gained important transportation links that most Americans at the time believed indispensable to the economy and society. This point of view has now been widely accepted. (An exception is Paul W. Gates, "The Railroad Land Grant Legend," *Journal of Economic History*, XIV [Spring 1954], 143–146.) Thomas Cochran, for example, in "Land Grants and Railroad Entrepreneurship," in *The Tasks of Economic History* (supplement of the *Journal of Economic History*, X [1950], 53–67), follows the view of Henry. From his investigation of the correspondence of the officials of the transcontinental railroads Cochran concludes that the grants were necessary if any railroads were to be built. Recent general works, like Carter Goodrich's *Government Promotion of American Canals and Railroads, 1800–1890* (New York, 1960) and John F. Stover's *American Railroads* (Chicago, 1961), have followed the broader conclusions of Henry on the role of government aid to railroad construction. From a slightly different angle, Robert Fogel, in his *The Union Pacific Railroad, A Case in Premature Enterprise* (Baltimore, 1960), also concludes that only through government land grants was such an enterprise as the Union Pacific possible, given the high financial risk involved in building a railroad through unsettled territory where profitable return was extremely problematical.

On the other hand, Henry's desire to minimize the role of the land grants in the creation of the American railroad network is evident in a less convincing conclusion. He apparently would like to see private enterprise receive more credit for the job. Thus he speaks of land grants being made to only 8 per cent of the mileage of all railroads in the country. This comparison, though, seems a little disingenuous. It assumes a claim for the importance of land grants no one has made; it sets up a straw man. By comparing the length of tracks aided by land grants with the total trackage of the nation, Henry arrives at a very small percentage. But land grants to railroads ceased after 1871, while railroad construction continued well into the twentieth century. A comparison with total mileage by, say, 1890 would have given a much fairer picture, one would think, of the part government aid played in the spread of the railroad net in the nineteenth century. It would also have been a considerably larger figure than 8 per cent. Or one could ask what part land grants played in the all-important and dramatic transcontinental roads. Here, too, the significance of the government aid appears large. Three of the four transcontinental lines were recipients of land grants from the federal government. Finally, in making his case for a downward revision of the part played by the government in railroad construction, Mr. Henry ignored the grants made by the states. Yet, as his critics were quick to point out, the states provided to the railroads almost 49 million acres, in addition to the federal grants.

Although from what has already been said it is clear that Henry's interpretation of the land grants has given a new turn to the study of the subject, at the time his article appeared it aroused great opposition. So vehement was the criticism that the editors of the journal in which it appeared took the very unusual action of reprinting some of the criticisms: *Mississippi Valley Historical Review*, XXXII (March 1946), 557–576. Communications from eight historians were printed, of which two were extremely critical, calling the article an example of "special pleading." Three accepted his corrections of the texts but doubted his conclusion that the government made a good bargain. The others defended the publication of the article and found it an important corrective to earlier views. One of the critics raised a point that perhaps needs to be elaborated upon. That was the conclusion of Henry that the use of land grants was a desirable use of public resources because it did get the railroads constructed. Shouldn't some other criteria of desirability be used, the critic asked, besides simply that it "worked"? But as Henry himself observes in his article, given the spirit of the times, what other device could have been used? Isn't it from hindsight, from the wiser vantage point of a closed frontier and a settled nation, that such arguments arise? Henry answered his critics in the same journal (XXXIII [June 1946], 115–120).

Robert S. Henry is the author of several works on railroads, including *Trains* (1934), *On the Railroad* (1936), and *Portraits of the Iron Horse* (1937), as well as books on the Civil War and the Reconstruction period. In 1957 he served as president of the Southern Historical Association.

The Railroad Land Grant Legend in American History Texts*

BY ROBERT S. HENRY

IN 1850, the United States government had a public domain of approximately 1,400,000,000 acres, vacant, unoccupied, and, for lack of transportation, largely unusable and unsalable.[1] Between that year and the end of 1871, the government undertook to use a portion of this land to encourage and assist the building of railroads in vacant or sparsely settled sections, in the same way in which previously it had aided the building of wagon roads and canals. The resulting series of transactions came to be known as the Federal railroad land grants, a subject frequently mentioned in high school and college texts which are the first, last, and only works on the history of their country read by many, if not most, Americans. This paper is the result of an examination of the treatment of the Federal land grant transactions in thirty-seven representative texts.

Since the treatment of a subject of this sort in such works must be brief, and even, in a sense, incidental, accuracy both as to the essential facts themselves and as to their place and proportion in the whole setting becomes all the more important. This inquiry is directed, therefore, to these facts and the manner of their treatment. It is limited to the Federal land grants because those are the grants which, for the most part, are discussed in the works examined, and are the grants about which the most complete information has been compiled, published, and made available.

SOURCE: Reprinted by permission from the *Mississippi Valley Historical Review*, XXXII (September 1945). Copyright, 1945, by the Mississippi Valley Historical Association.

* Mr. Henry wishes to acknowledge the assistance given him in preparing this article by Carlton J. Corliss and L. I. McDougle.

[1] On June 30, 1852, the public domain remaining unsold or not used for public purposes amounted to 1,387,534,000 acres. From the opening of the land office in 1812 up to that time, the government had sold only 102,113,861 acres. Grants to wagon roads and canals had amounted to 10,007,677 acres. J. D. B. DeBow, Superintendent of the U. S. Census, *Statistical View of the United States . . . Being a Compendium of the Seventh Census* (Washington, 1854), 191.

A balanced story of the Federal land grant transactions requires reasonably correct answers to these questions, at the very least:

How much land was granted to railroads, and what proportion was this of the whole public domain?

What proportion of the railroad mileage of the country received land grants from the government?

What was this land worth?

What were the terms and conditions of the grants? Were they gifts, or did the government get as well as give?

HOW MUCH LAND?

The first of these questions, purely a matter of recorded fact, deals with the amount of land granted to railroads by the United States government. In the standard general work on the subject, Donaldson's *Public Domain*, published by the government in 1884, the total amount of land that would be necessary to fulfill all the acts granting lands to railroads was estimated at 155,504,994 acres.[2] The amount of land actually patented to railroads, however, fell substantially short of this acreage, for a variety of reasons—noncompletion of the lines or other failure to comply with the conditions of the grants, or lack of sufficient acreage within the designated limits to fulfill the terms of the grants. The acreage to which the railroads actually received title appears in the annual reports of the Commissioner of the General Land Office, the latest such report showing a total of 131,-350,534 acres.[3]

Of the thirty-seven American history textbooks examined, twenty-four make specific reference to the area granted to railroads by the

[2] Thomas Donaldson, *The Public Domain* (Washington, 1884), 753.

[3] U. S. General Land Office, *Annual Report of the Commissioner*, June 30, 1943, table 76. Corresponding figures, with slight variations from year to year, appear in this entire series of reports. The report cited is for the latest year available. In addition to Federal land grants, it is estimated that railroads received from the states grants totaling 48,883,372 acres. U. S. Federal Coordinator of Transportation, *Public Aids to Transportation*, 1938, Vol. II, 32, and Table 13, p. 115, based on Federal or state records to June 30, 1933. The state land grants are not dealt with in this discussion. For a detailed and careful study of the state grants of Texas, which were by far the most significant, see S. G. Reed, *A History of the Texas Railroads* (Houston, 1941), Chap. XXIV. Right-of-way grants, by which the Federal government granted to pioneer railroads running through the public domain strips of land from 80 to 400 feet wide (the most common grants being 200 feet wide) for right-of-way purposes, are mentioned in some of the works examined but are not dealt with in this study. While in the aggregate they amounted to a considerable acreage, the grants were of so little value without railroads, and they were relatively such a minor part of the whole picture, that no separate discussion of them seems necessary. Donaldson, 286–7, 769–71, 940–43, 1262–3. *Public Aids to Transportation*, II, 48–51.

Federal government. Of these twenty-four, one gives clear and approximately correct figures as to the whole area granted, while one other comes within 10 per cent of the correct figure.[4] Two others which do not state the area as a whole, give correct partial figures.[5] In seven works, a substantially correct statement at one place is contradicted elsewhere, either by another larger figure or by a graphic presentation which greatly exaggerates the area granted.[6] Eight others show the area granted, either graphically or in text, or both, as anywhere from nearly one-fifth more than it was, up to about four times the correct area.[7] Five give partial figures only, which either are incorrect or are so presented as to give a misleading impression.[8] Others make neither arithmetical nor graphic presenta-

[4] Ralph Volney Harlow, *The Growth of the United States* (2 vols., New York, 1943), II, 15, gives 132,500,000 acres. George M. Stephenson, *American History to 1865* (New York, 1940), 407, compares the grants with states having a total area of 144,224,000 acres.

[5] Carl Russell Fish and Howard E. Wilson, *History of the United States* (New York, 1936), 545; John D. Hicks, *The Federal Union: A History of the United States to 1865* (Boston, 1937), 552.

[6] Charles H. Coleman and Edgar B. Wesley, *America's Road to Now* (Boston, 1942), 401, 502; Harold U. Faulkner, Tyler Kepner, and Hall Bartlett, *The American Way of Life* (New York, 1941), 296–7; Harold U. Faulkner and Tyler Kepner, *America, Its History and People* (New York, 1942), 388, 455; Willis Mason West and Ruth West, *The American People* (Boston, 1937), Map Underline facing p. 474, 554–5; Melville Freeman and Eston V. Tubbs, *The Story of Our Republic* (Philadelphia, 1943), Part II, 47, 68; Charles A. and Mary R. Beard, *The Making of American Civilization* (New York, 1942), 552; Edward C. Kirkland, *A History of American Economic Life* (New York, 1941), 379.

[7] Asa Earl Martin, *History of the United States* (2 vols., Boston, 1938), II, 122; Charles A. Beard and William C. Bagley, *The History of the American People* (New York, 1943), 501; Rolla M. Tryon, Charles R. Lingley, and Frances Morehouse, *The American Nation Yesterday and Today* (Boston, 1942), 439; Louis M. Hacker and Benjamin B. Kendrick, *The United States Since 1865* (New York, 1943), 160; William A. Hamm, *The American People* (Boston, 1939), 517–18; David Saville Muzzey, *The United States of America* (2 vols., Boston, 1937), II, 27; Samuel Eliot Morison and Henry Steele Commager, *The Growth of the American Republic* (2 vols., New York, 1937), II, 112 and map facing p. 112; George Earl Freeland and James Truslow Adams, *America's Progress in Civilization* (New York, 1942), map facing p. 324.

[8] John T. Greenan and Albert B. Meredith, *Everyday Problems of American Democracy* (Boston, 1943), 451; Arthur Meier Schlesinger, *Political and Social Growth of the American People, 1865–1940* (New York, 1943), 47; Gertrude Van Duyn Southworth and John Van Duyn Southworth, *American History, from the Discovery of America to the Present Day* (Syracuse, 1940), 226. In the three works above, the areas granted to the original Pacific railroads are shown as 100 million acres, as against actual grants to these routes of less than three-fourths that amount. Dwight Lowell Dumond, *A History of the United States* (New York, 1942), 535, states the grants to the first Pacific railroad as 33 million acres, as against an actual grant of slightly more than 18 million acres. Jacob Lewis Stockton, *A Topical Survey of American History*

tion of the area granted, but rely entirely on adjectives. In most of the books, in fact, such adjectives as "huge," "vast," "enormous," "staggering," and "breath-taking" are parts of the treatment of the subject of area.

LAND GRANT MAPS, RIGHT AND WRONG

The most potent source of this exaggerated impression of the size of land grants, and the prevailing confusion of thought and inaccuracies of statement in their measurement, seems to be uncritical acceptance of land grant maps which are incorrectly understood and described by the text writers.

To understand the official land grant maps, it is necessary to bear in mind the "checkerboard pattern" in which land was granted to the railroads. First, there were original, or primary, limits within which the grantees were to receive alternate sections, non-mineral in character, or a total of one-half the area within a strip of land of a given width lying on both sides of the track, provided these sections had not previously been granted or otherwise disposed of, or reserved from grant for other public purposes, such as school grants, forest, and other reservations. In lieu of the land which had been previously disposed of or was reserved, the grantee was to be allowed to select a like amount of land from a contiguous zone— the so-called indemnity limits.[9] (It is necessary to bear in mind, also, the fact that the official maps include not only grants to railroads, but also grants for wagon roads, canals, and river improvements.) The four principal patterns followed, with variations, in the several different land grants were:

1. Grants of alternate sections of land in primary strips embracing the area within *six* miles on either side of the proposed railroad, with indemnity limits outside thereof extending fifteen or twenty miles from the railroad.

2. Grants of alternate sections of land in primary strips embracing the area within *ten* miles on either side of the proposed railroad, some without indemnity limits, others with indemnity limits outside thereof extending twenty or thirty miles from the railroad.

3. Grants of alternate sections of land in primary strips embracing the area within *twenty* miles on either side of the proposed railroad, some without

(New York, 1944), 148, takes as an example the grants to the railroad which received almost one-third of all the lands granted by the government to railroads, raises the amount of this grant from its actual figure of 36 million to 47 million acres, and then declares that "other roads were granted proportionate amounts."

[9] Donaldson, 261–2, 274–9, 756–63.

indemnity limits, others with indemnity limits outside thereof extending twenty-five, thirty, or fifty miles from the railroad.

4. Grants of alternate sections of land in primary strips embracing the area within *forty* miles on either side of the proposed railroad, with indemnity limits outside thereof extending fifty, and in some cases sixty, miles from the railroad. This pattern applied to territories only.

Under Pattern 1, for instance, the railroad received the equivalent of six sections of land (three on either side of the railroad) within the primary strips if available; otherwise within the indemnity limits. In no case did the railroad receive more than six sections per mile of road. Thus, where the primary and indemnity limits embraced an area forty miles in width, the railroad actually received a maximum of only slightly less than one-seventh of that area, or the equivalent of a solid strip six miles in width.

Under Pattern 3, the railroad was granted the equivalent of twenty sections of land (ten on either side of the railroad) within the primary strips if available; otherwise within the indemnity limits. Where the indemnity limits extended fifty miles from the railroad, the maximum area that the railroad could receive was one-fifth of the total area embraced by the primary and indemnity strips.

The earliest of the general land grant maps, apparently, was published by the government in 1878, in connection with a report on arid lands. Revised and brought up to date, it was again published by the government in 1883, and is included in Donaldson's well-known and widely available *Public Domain*. Again brought up to date, the map was republished in 1913 by the United States Department of Commerce and Labor in its report on *The Lumber Industry*.[10]

Each of these maps showed the limits of both the primary and indemnity zones, while the latest of the maps, that of 1913, showed also, by a special hatching, the grants which had been forfeited for noncompletion of the roads within the terms of the acts making the grant and under which, therefore, no railroad had received lands. The whole was covered, on this map, by the correctly descriptive caption: "Map of the United States showing the limits within which

[10] The original government map and its two revisions and republications are as follows: (1) accompanying an historical article by Willis Drummond on "Land Grants in Aid of Internal Improvements," published in connection with the report of Major J. W. Powell on the "Lands of the Arid Region of the United States," *House Executive Document* No. 73, 45 Cong., 2 Sess., 1878; (2) Donaldson, facing p. 949; and (3) U. S. Department of Commerce and Labor, Bureau of Corporations, *The Lumber Industry: Part I — Standing Timber* (Washington, 1913), 222 and facing.

land grants were made by the Federal Government to aid in the construction of railroads and wagon roads." The map also carried a legend explaining that "the maximum amount of land obtainable was one-half that within the primary limits, the lands granted being in the alternate survey sections. The maximum was often not obtained."

The last sentence refers to the fact that in many of the grants, especially in the older and more settled land grant states, it was not possible to locate the maximum acreage allowed even within the indemnity limits. The situation is thus outlined on page 222 of the 1913 report referred to:

> In this connection the caution is repeated against assuming that the entire area within the limits shown on the map was granted to the railroads. The first set of heavy lines on each side of a road indicates the "primary limits" of the grant . . . within which limits it was to receive each alternate section (or part thereof) not already disposed of or reserved. The possible maximum of a grant, therefore, was half of the land within the primary limits. The second set of heavy lines, seen farther out on each side of the road in many grants, indicates the "indemnity limits" referred to above within which the railroad could select vacant alternate sections (or parts thereof) to make up for lands within the primary limits that had been previously disposed of or reserved. Often so much land had been disposed of or reserved both in the primary and the indemnity limits that a road received considerably less than its possible maximum. In Iowa so much land had already been disposed of at private sale, under warrants and to settlers, that although the State appears practically covered by grants, only a little more than one-eighth its area was received by the railroads. But in regions where there was less of prior purchase and settlement the railroads secured a higher proportion; in some cases the whole of the possible maximum.[11]

The several government publications of the map became the basis of two privately published maps, that of Professors Hart and Bolton in their series of American history maps published in 1919,[12] and that in Paullin's *Atlas of the Historical Geography of the United States*,[13] published in 1932, both of which are careful to give like

[11] One publication (not included in the present study) which printed the usual land grant map did so with the caption: "The black bands on the map show the land that the government granted to the railroads. Notice that almost the entire State of Iowa was given to them"—an interesting example of the error against which particular warning is given in the explanation quoted. *Building America: Railroads* (New York, 1940), V, No. 6, p. 174.

[12] Albert Bushnell Hart, assisted by David Maydole Matteson and Herbert Eugene Bolton, *A Teacher's Manual Accompanying the Hart-Bolton American History Maps* (Chicago, 1919), 87–8, and Map A-18: "Western Statehood and Land Grants to Railroads."

[13] Charles O. Paullin, *Atlas of the Historical Geography of the United States* (Washington, 1932), 39–40, and plate 56-D.

information, either on the map itself or in accompanying explan-
atory material.

Even with the most scrupulous explanation, however, it is difficult not to get an exaggerated impression of size from maps which
show a shaded area twice as great as the actual grants, as in the
case of the Hart map, and approximately four times as great, as
in the case of the government publications and the Paullin map.
Without such understanding and explanation, the maps become
downright wrong. And, unfortunately for popular understanding of
the facts of history, it is in this misleading form and with incorrect
captions that almost all land grant maps have been circulated.

The first such use of the map, apparently, was in the presidential
year of 1884, when the Democratic party issued a campaign poster
featuring what purported to be a map of lands granted to railroads,
but was actually a map of the extreme limits of the widest zones
within which some lands might have been granted not only to railroads but also to wagon roads and river improvements, under the
caption: "How the Public Domain Has Been Squandered—Map
showing the 139,403,026 acres of the people's land . . . worth at
$2 an acre $278,806.052 given by Republican Congresses to Railroad Corporations. . . ." [14]

Apparently those who compiled the poster overlooked the fact
that the shaded area on the featured map represented about four
times the number of acres stated in the accompanying text. The
figures given in the text, however, are completely overshadowed
by the pictorial impression of the map itself—an interesting example
of the validity of the Chinese proverb as to the comparative force
and effectiveness of words and pictures.

This effective pictorial exaggeration is perpetuated in the maps
subsequently appearing in history texts. Nine of the works examined
in this study present maps which include wagon road and river
improvement grants as well as those for railroads, and which show
the full area of the indemnity limits of both completed and non-
completed grants, without explanation or distinction as between
primary and indemnity zones, and with captions which, in all but
two cases, unqualifiedly describe the shaded strips as showing lands
granted to railroads.[15]

[14] Democratic Party Platform, 1884, *How the Public Domain Has Been
Squandered*, broadside, with land grant map.
[15] The seven works which show the whole of the shaded portions of the map
as representing lands granted to railroads are Faulkner and Kepner, 455;
Faulkner, Kepner, and Bartlett, 296; Morison and Commager, II, facing p. 112;
Hamm, 518; Muzzey, II, 27; Freeman and Tubbs, Part II, 68; Freeland and

One work, indeed, enlarges upon its erroneous caption by declaring that "the nation gave the railroad builders a kingdom in land. No such lavish generosity was ever dreamed of before. The map on page 68 tells better than words what vast areas were presented to the railroad companies." [16]

The two books which qualify the statement that the shaded areas of the map show lands granted to railroads point out that they were to receive only alternate sections, or one-half the area shown, but show on their maps not the primary limits but the much more extensive indemnity limits.

Accompanying this article are two maps (page 48) identified by number. Map No. 1 is typical of the sort published in many of the textbooks examined. In contrast, Map No. 2 is drawn so as to show the approximate location of the grants which were actually completed. The widths of lines are proportioned to show the equivalent of the areas actually certified and patented to the railroads. In many instances, the acreage certified and patented was considerably less than the acreage granted, due to forfeitures, previous transfers, federal reservations, and other causes. The startling contrast between the two maps indicates the extent of the vivid misinformation about railroad land grants which has become all but staple in history texts.

Besides the works which reproduce the erroneous land grant map (No. 1) itself, others seem to have used it uncritically as the source of information for textual comparisons of area which, of course, reflect the map's own exaggerations and inaccuracies. Thus, according to one work, "more than half of the northern tier of states lying against Canada from Lake Michigan to the Pacific" and "about half of New Mexico, Arizona and California," were included in Federal land grants.[17] That would be approximately 272,000,000 acres in only eight states, and yet the same work gives the total area of all the Federal railroad grants in twenty-six states as only 155,000,000 acres—which itself is one-sixth more than the railroads actually received.

The table in the Appendix to this paper shows, by states, the discrepancy between the approximate acreage of land grants as they appear on Map No. 1 and the actual acreage received by the railroads as reported by the General Land Office.

Of course, the total Federal grants, whether the figure be the

---

Adams, facing p. 324. The two works which state that the railroads received only half the area shown are Coleman and Wesley, 401; West and West, map underline facing p. 474.

[16] Freeman and Tubbs, part II, 47.

[17] Beard and Beard, 552.

155,000,000 acres which it was originally contemplated might be turned over to the railroads, or the 131,351,000 acres which were finally patented to them, when looked at by themselves, are indeed a great quantity of land. That objection was made in the debate on the bill for the first of the railroad grants, back in 1850. "We are met by the objection," said Senator William R. King, afterwards vice president of the United States, "that this is an immense grant— that it is a great quantity of land. Well, sir, it is a great quantity; but it will be there for five hundred years; and unless some mode of the kind proposed be adopted, it will never command ten cents." The Senator was looking at the land involved not as an absolute quantity but as a portion of a domain which, as he said, "can never be of any value . . . unless some direct communication by railroad, or some other way, is made." [18]

That was the way the land grant transaction was looked upon by the men who urged its adoption in the beginning—the Whigs, Henry Clay and William H. Seward among them, and the Democrats, Stephen A. Douglas, Thomas H. Benton, and Lewis Cass. It was the way in which it was regarded by Abraham Lincoln, in whose administration and with whose approval the policy found its widest use and application. Part of a domain, immense in itself, was to be used to give value to the vastly more immense whole.

This point of comparison, so essential to any proper understanding of the transaction, is almost wholly lost sight of in the works examined. Only three of the twenty-four which discuss the area of the Federal land grants, in fact, in any way relate the areas granted to the size of the public domain as a whole, and but one of the three gives the proportion correctly. Of the others, one says that the land grants were "one-seventh" of the public domain, and another 14 per cent.[19] The actual figure was less than one-tenth.

A fourth work lumps the area of railroad land grants with grants for wagon roads, canals, and river improvements, to arrive at a total of 337,740,000 acres, "equal," the author says, "to one-sixth of the total area of the United States and three times that of France." [20]

[18] *The Congressional Globe*, 31 Cong., 1 Sess., April 29, 1850, pp. 845–6.

[19] Coleman and Wesley, 502, gives correct figures for the areas of the land grants to railroads and the public domain. The other works referred to are Muzzey, II, 27, and West and West, map underline facing p. 474.

[20] Beard and Bagley, 501. In a number of the books examined, areas are compared not with the areas of such states as those in which the lands were located, but with foreign countries, as in this case, or with thickly settled eastern states, a favorite selection for that purpose being the six New England states, New York, and Pennsylvania combined. While such comparisons might be arithmetically accurate, they do not present so true a picture as would comparisons with western acreage, such as used in two works: Coleman and Wesley, 401; Schlesinger, 47.

This map, originally drawn to show the extreme outer limits of areas within which some land *might be granted* to railroads, is frequently reproduced in American History texts with captions describing it as showing lands *actually granted*—thereby exaggerating by approximately four times the area received by railroads.

MAP NO. 1

U. S. LAND GRANTS TO RAILROADS

The Federal Government granted lands to railroads in alternate sections, retaining the sections between. It is impossible to present this "checkerboard" pattern on so small a map, but the shaded areas show the approximate locations of the land grants, and are in proportion to the amounts actually received by railroads.

MAP NO. 2

The acreage given checks with no official report on the subject, but the Federal grants to railroads—on which the whole attention of the passage is focused—are much less than half the area mentioned.

HOW MUCH RAILROAD WAS BUILT WITH THE AID OF LAND GRANTS?

The second, and equally simple, question deals with the extent of railroad mileage, the construction of which was aided by the government's land grants. Such grants were made in aid of a total of 18,738 miles of railroad line [21]—less than 8 per cent of the total mileage of railroads built in the United States. The fact that more than 92 per cent of all the railroad mileage in the United States was built without the aid of an acre of Federal land grants is nowhere brought out in the texts examined—an omission which tends to throw the land grant transaction out of all proportion as a factor in the development of the national network of railroads.

The same tendency to exaggerate the government's financial part in railroad building appears in the treatment of the bond aid extended to six of the companies chartered to build the pioneer "Pacific" railroads. The government made a loan of its bonds to these railroads, in the total amount of $64,623,512. The roads were to pay 6 per cent interest on the bonds and to pay them off. During the long period of development and light traffic they were not always able to meet these charges, but in the final settlement in 1898 and 1899 the government collected $63,023,512 of principal plus $104,722,978 in interest—a total repayment of $167,746,490 on an initial loan of $64,623,512. [22] Professor Hugo R. Meyer of Harvard was well justified in saying that "for the government the whole outcome has been financially not less than brilliant" [23]—but none of this appears in the treatment of the transaction in the texts. Thirty-four of the thirty-seven texts examined mention the bond aid to these Pacific roads. In one-third of the works, it is not made

[21] U. S. General Land Office, *Notice of Releases of Land Grant Claims by Railroad Carriers*, May 17, 1941. Similar figures appear in earlier statements and reports of the General Land Office and other governmental departments and agencies concerned. In Lewis Henry Haney, *A Congressional History of Railways in the United States* (2 vols., Madison, Wisc., 1910), II, 14, the total mileage is given as 17,724 miles. The total route mileage of railroads on December 31, 1943 in the United States was 227,999 miles. Interstate Commerce Commission, *Statistics of Railways in the United States* (Annual).

[22] *Public Aids to Transportation*, II, 59, and table 19, p. 138.

[23] Hugo R. Meyer, "The Settlements with the Pacific Railways," *Quarterly Journal of Economics*, XIII (July, 1899), 443–4.

clear whether the financial assistance referred to was a loan or a gift. Three describe the aid definitely as gifts—which they were not.[24] Twenty-one refer to the transactions as loans, but only four [25] mention the fact that the loans were repaid, while three [26] make the positively erroneous statement that the loans were never repaid.[27]

WHAT WERE THE LAND GRANTS WORTH?

One measure of the value of the lands granted—though no one would contend that it is the correct one—would be the cost to the government of acquiring them, which, according to Donaldson, was an average of 23.3 cents an acre.[28] On that basis, the 131,351,-000 acres which the railroads received could be said to be worth less than $31,000,000.

Another possible measure is the standard "minimum" price at which the government offered the public domain for sale in the land grant period. This price was $1.25 an acre, though the government was never able to realize even this figure as an average selling price. But if the new railroad companies had bought from the government the 131,350,534 acres actually received, and had paid the full established price, the lands would have cost them $164,188,167.

[24] Howard C. Hill, *The Life and Work of the Citizen* (Boston, 1942), 392; Jeremiah S. Young and Edwin M. Barton, *Growing in Citizenship* (New York, 1941), 521; Sister of St. Joseph, *American History* (St. Augustine, Fla., 1932), Book II, 116.

[25] Repayment is mentioned in Hacker and Kendrick, 161; George M. Stephenson, *American History Since 1865* (New York, 1939), 84; Kirkland, 380; Morison and Commager, II, 113.

[26] West and West, 464; Bruce Winton Knight, *Economic Principles in Practice* (New York, 1942), 262; W. E. Woodward, *A New American History* (Garden City, N. Y., 1938), 618.

[27] The same sort of disregard of repayment may be observed in the treatment of the government loans made to the railroads at the close of World War I, in connection with the difficult transition from government to private operation at that time. These loans, which totaled $1,080,575,000, are mentioned in three of the books examined. All of this huge sum except $28,698,000 has been repaid, with a total of $220,891,000 in interest (*Annual Report of the Secretary of the Treasury . . . for fiscal year ended June 30, 1944*, p. 173), but the fact is mentioned in none of the texts. The more recent depression loans made by the Reconstruction Finance Corporation and other federal agencies receive the same type of treatment. Twenty books mention the fact that these loans were made. More than three-fourths of the loans made have been repaid or sold to the public, with a profit to the government in interest. Mention of repayment of any sort is made in only two of the books: Kirkland, 743; Hicks, II, 671.

[28] Donaldson, 21 and 524. This figure for cost of acquisition covers not only purchase price and payments to Indian tribes, but also costs of surveying and disposition.

Still another measure of the value of the lands during the period of the grants is to be found in the Graduation Act, under which the price of lands long on the market and unsold was graduated downward, starting with a price of $1 an acre after ten years, and ending with a price of 12½ cents an acre for lands unsold after thirty years. Total sales in the years 1854–1862, during which the Act was in effect, even under such price arrangements as these, were only 25,696,420 acres.[29]

A more correct measure of value is the one applied in all ordinary transfers between buyer and seller—the worth of the land granted and received at the time of sale. During the period in which the land grants were being made to the railroads, the average sale price of government lands in the land grant states was less than $1 an acre.[30] Applying that price to the lands granted to the railroads gives a value as of the time of the grants, of less than $130,000,000.

It is sometimes contended that the measure of value in this case should be the amount finally realized by the railroads on their lands, after the roads had been built and after years of colonizing, advertising, sales effort, and development costs had been put upon them.[31] There is no more basis for setting up such a measure of value than there would be for putting it at the 23 cents an acre which it cost the government to acquire the lands in the first place, but because the point is raised in some of the works examined, it may be noted that the average realizations of the railroads from their Federal land grants, plus the estimated value of the lands remaining unsold, was put at $3.38 an acre according to one government

---

[29] Donaldson, 205–206, 291; *Public Aids to Transportation*, II, 35.

[30] The latest and most complete calculation of proceeds of Federal land sales during the period 1850–1871, when the land grants were made, shows an average sale price of 97.2 cents per acre. This calculation, however, is not restricted to the sale of lands in the land grant states, but covers also lands sold during this period in the older and more settled states. Eliminating these sales, the average per acre from sales of Federal public lands in railroad land grant states during this period was 94 cents per acre. From report of Federal Coordinator of Transportation, *Public Aids to Transportation*, II, 36.

[31] The extent of the effort and expense to which railroads went in marketing and settling their granted lands is indicated in the studies of Paul W. Gates, *The Illinois Central Railroad and Its Colonization Work* (Cambridge, 1934); James B. Hedges, "The Colonization Work of the Northern Pacific Railroad," Mississippi Valley Historical Review, XIII (December, 1926), 311–42, and "Promotion of Immigration to the Pacific Northwest by the Railroads," *ibid.*, XV (September, 1928), 183–203; Richard C. Overton, *Burlington West: A Colonization History of the Burlington Railroad* (Cambridge, 1941). The somewhat similar situation in Canada is treated in James B. Hedges, *Building the Canadian West: The Land and Colonization Work of the Canadian Pacific Railway* (New York, 1939).

study,[32] while in another report, including both state and Federal grants, the average is $2.81 an acre.[33]

Few of the works examined deal in detail with the question of value. An impression of richness is built up with such adjectives as "lavish," "munificent," and "princely," but figures are scarce. One suggests a value of two dollars an acre, which is the same figure used in the Democratic campaign document of 1884.[34] Others undertake to measure value by what the railroads realized from the lands when sold. One work states this as an "average price of $4.76 an acre." [35] Another quotes a "careful investigator" to the effect that it "has been under rather than over ten dollars an acre," out of which there had to come the costs of selling, from all of which the author concludes that "the actual financial assistance to the railroads from the land grants has probably been overestimated." [36]

The real contribution of the Federal land grants to the spread of the rails in the West and the newer South was not the cash realized upon them, but the fact that they furnished a basis of credit which got the job started and made it possible to get it done. The land grant acreage could be certified, patented, and sold only as the railroad itself was completed, in sections, and then could be sold mostly on long time credit. The selling price had to be low to get it sold at all, and the expense of sale was necessarily high. The net realizations from the sales, particularly during the period of construction, were but a tiny fraction of the cost of building the railroads. Thus, the Auditor of Railroad Accounts of the Department of the Interior reported that up to 1880 the several companies going to make up the five pioneer "Pacific" routes had sold only $36,383,-795 worth of land. "The lands have been sold in small tracts, some for cash, but most of them on time," the Auditor wrote in describing the sales of one of the several companies concerned. The cost

---

[32] U. S. Board of Investigation and Research, *Report and Comments on H. R. 4184 . . . to the Committee on Interstate and Foreign Commerce of the House of Representatives*, March 9, 1944, p. 28, shows net proceeds of sales of both Federal and state land grant lands to December 31, 1941 of $434,806,671, plus an estimated value of the unsold grant lands of $60,684,032. Of this total of $495,490,703 the sum of $55,090,652 is attributed to state land grants and $440,400,051 to Federal land grants.

[33] The report of the Federal Coordinator of Transportation, *Public Aids to Transportation*, II, 52, estimated the "aid received from all such grants," that is, state as well as Federal, at $516,144,749. This includes both proceeds of sales under Federal and state land and right-of-way grants, and also the estimated net value of lands still held by the railroads on December 31, 1927.

[34] Hacker and Kendrick, 161.

[35] Harlow, II, 15.

[36] Kirkland, 381.

up to that time of building the several Pacific routes is shown in the same report as having been $465,584,029. This, the Auditor thought and so reported, was excessive, or at least much more than similar roads could have been built for when the report was made. Even the lesser figure of $168,045,000, which he estimated as enough to reproduce the roads, however, was considerably more than four times the realizations from land sales up to that date. Looking to the future, the Auditor estimated that the value of the railroad lands unsold in 1880 was $78,889,940, making a total estimated value for all lands sold and to be sold of $115,273,735, as against a total estimated cost of the several "Pacific" railroads, to completion, of $634,165,613. The Auditor thought that similar railroads could be built for $286,819,300, but even this figure is more than double the estimated total realizations from the lands granted to the "Pacific's." [37]

The estimated worth of all lands which these and all other land grant railroads had received, or were to receive, from the Federal government was estimated by the Interior Department's Auditor as of November 1, 1880, at $391,804,610.[38] By way of comparison, the total investment in railroads in the United States in that year was $4,653,609,000.[39]

THE NATURE OF THE LAND GRANT TRANSACTION

The questions dealt with so far—that is, the amount of land granted and its relationship to the whole, the extent of the railroads thus aided and their relationship to the whole, and the value of the aid so extended—are, after all, matters of detail. While these details are more important than the treatment accorded them in so many of the works examined would indicate, they are not of the essence of the land grant transaction. The main question is, what was the nature of that transaction? Were the Federal land grants gifts? Or were they trades by which the government got, as well as gave, direct consideration?

No reference is made here to the immense indirect benefits arising from the early building of the railroads so aided, but only to the

[37] Department of Interior, Office of Auditor of Railroad Accounts, *Report on the Quantity and Value of Public Lands Granted by Congress to Aid in the Construction of the Pacific Railroad* (Washington, Jan. 26, 1881) ; Donaldson, 912–33 (figures on 932).

[38] *Ibid.*, 753.

[39] Interstate Commerce Commission, Bureau of Statistics, *Railway Statistics Before 1890*, Statement No. 32151 (Washington, Dec., 1932), 4.

direct monetary return which the government of the United States received for the lands which it granted.[40]

Almost without exception, the works examined treat the transactions as "gifts," or "donations," or, as some put it, "free" or "outright" gifts, without in any way referring to the fact that the railroads which received these "gifts" or "donations" were required to haul mail and government freight and passengers at less than their regular charges.[41]

While the conditions of the several grants vary, in the overwhelming majority of cases the Acts of Congress making grants to railroads adopted the phraseology of the earlier canal and wagon road grants in requiring that the railroad to be built should "be and remain a public highway for the use of the government of the United States, free from toll or other charge upon the transportation of any property or troops of the United States." The effect of this clause, as finally determined by the Supreme Court, was that the government was entitled to the use of the roadbed without toll, by analogy to the free right of passage for its vehicles or boats over grant-aided wagon roads and canals, but that this did not extend so far as to require the railroad company to provide and operate without charge the engines, cars, and other equipment needed for transportation over the railroads.[42]

Under a formula subsequently worked out by the United States Court of Claims, the deduction from ordinary charges on account of this provision of the land grant acts was established at 50 per cent.[43] Still later, by a series of Acts of Congress, the same percentage of deduction from commercial rates was made applicable to the limited number of land grant roads whose grants did not contain

[40] These indirect returns to the government are suggestively outlined in U. S. General Land Office, *Transportation: Information Concerning Land Grants for Roads, Canals, River Improvement and Railroads*, Information Bulletin, 1939 Series, No. 5 (Washington, 1940), 1–2. While no figures are available, and the point is developed in none of the reports and studies examined, it is obvious that transfer of lands from Federal to private ownership had a substantial effect upon the taxable resources of the states, territories, and local governments. Only in recent years, with the increasing tendency in the other direction, with property passing from private to government ownership, has the importance of this fact begun to be appreciated.

[41] This is true of twenty-six of the texts examined. Only two, Stephenson, *American History to 1865*, 407, and Robert I. Adriance, *Using the Wealth of the World* (Boston, 1943), 268, make reference to deductions from railroad rates because of land grants.

[42] Lake Superior and Mississippi Railroad *vs*. United States, 93 *U. S. Reports*, 442, October term, 1876. Decided Jan. 15, 1877.

[43] Atchison, Topeka & Santa Fe Railway *vs*. United States, 15 *Court of Claims*, 126, December term, 1879.

the "toll-free" provision in this form,[44] while even railroads which received no land grant whatever from the government have long since entered into "equalization agreements" by which they also undertake to handle government traffic at the same rates applying by law on the land grant lines.[45] Compensation for handling mail on land grant lines was fixed by Act of Congress in 1876 at 80 per cent of the rates applying on other railroads.[46]

In the Transportation Act of 1940, the Congress eliminated these provisions in so far as they applied to mail pay and to rates on the government's civilian passenger and freight traffic. Deductions of 50 per cent were continued, however, on the charges for transportation of military and naval personnel and property moving for military and naval and not for civil uses.[47]

The resulting situation is thus described by a Committee of the House of Representatives in the most recent statement on the subject:

> Certain of our railroads, because of lands granted by the Government many years ago to aid in the construction of lines of road now owned by them, are under statutory obligation to transport certain specified classes of Government traffic over such land-grant lines at 50 percent of their established tariff charges for such transportation. While that statutory requirement applies to only 14,411 miles of railroad, the reduced charges for which it provides have been extended to many times that mileage as the result of so-called equalization agreements entered into with the Government by other railroads to enable them to handle Government traffic.[48]

Thus it is that although less than 10 per cent of railroad mileage received grants of land, either Federal or state, the whole railroad system of the nation has paid for them a direct monetary return far exceeding the value of the lands granted.

"It is probable," said the Congressional Committee report already referred to, "that the railroads have contributed over $900,000,000 in payment of the lands which were transferred to them under the Land Grant Acts. This is double the amount received for the lands sold by the railroads plus the estimated value of such lands still under railroad ownership. Former Commissioner Eastman estimated

[44] The first of these Acts of Congress was adopted July 16, 1892. 27 *Statutes at Large*, 174, 180.
[45] Since 1914 this agreement has been between the government and the railroads collectively.
[46] 19 *Statutes at Large*, 78–82.
[47] Transportation Act of 1940, Part II, Section 321 (a), 54 *Statutes at Large*, Vol. I, 954.
[48] Committee on Interstate and Foreign Commerce, *House of Representatives*, *Report No. 393*, 79 Cong., 1 Sess., March 26, 1945, pp. 1–2.

that the total value of the lands at the time they were granted . . . was not more than $126,000,000." [49]

The total of deductions was not so large when the texts examined were written, of course, but even the fact that deductions are made is completely ignored in all but two of the books examined.

THE MAJOR FACT

The net result of the treatment of the land grant transaction as a whole is to present to the student a picture of a wastrel Uncle Sam scattering his substance with reckless extravagance, instead of the much more nearly correct picture of a canny landowner using part of his holdings to increase immeasurably the value of the rest, not as a gift but on terms which constituted a bargain shrewder than he realized. As far back as 1859, indeed, Charles Russell Lowell wrote that with the continued movement of troops and military supplies into the West "it may be found that even with the most liberal construction of the grant, the government has not been so 'munificent' as sharp." The same observer noted, about the same time, "that he who buildeth a railroad west of the Mississippi must also find a population and build up business." [50]

The "best and highest interests of the people of the United States in regard to this domain," said William H. Seward in the Senate debate on the passage of the first land grant bill, "is not to derive from it the highest amount of current revenue" from the sales of lands," "[b]ut it is to bring them into cultivation and settlement in the shortest space of time and under the most favorable auspices." [51]

To that end, the land grant device was adopted. Its adoption was sought not only by the people of the West and the newer parts of the South, but also by the people of the manufacturing East.[52] In its administration there were errors and abuses, both on the part of government authorities and on the part of railroads, as revealed, for example, in connection with the movement for forfeiture of land grants which reached its height in the 1880's. But the essential thing is that through the use of land grants, the result sought was accomplished. It may not have been the wisest way to achieve these results,

[49] The several authorities for the details of this statement as to the amount of the direct return to the government from the land grant acts are given in detail in *ibid.*, 4.

[50] Overton, 156, 159.

[51] *Cong. Globe*, 31 Cong., 1 Sess., April 29, 1850, p. 851.

[52] This may be substantiated by sectional analysis of the vote in Congress on the land grant acts. See, for example, the 1856 vote on four grants in Iowa. Overton, 73–86.

though no one even yet has suggested a better way by which a nation long on land and short on cash and credit could have enlisted the driving forces, which, in the short space of less than a generation, laced the West with rails. It may not have been the wisest way, but it worked. The job was done.

While the existing monographs on the actual working out of specific grants confirm this fact,[53] few of the texts examined take note of it. Two books note the need of some such device for getting railroads built ahead of settlement.[54] Four refer to the value added to the lands retained by the government.[55] Another, although treating the grants as the bestowal of "great gifts of land," recognized that "the transcontinental railroads opened the way for settlers." [56] Two others, while questioning the wisdom of the "gifts" to the railroads, nevertheless recognized the part which the grants played in the earlier development of the country.[57] Although joining in the almost universal description of the land grants as gifts, one book declared that the railroads "earned" what they got, and that it was a "wise use of the public domain." [58]

But for the most part, this essential element in the transaction—its very heart, indeed—is ignored or glossed over in the history texts which form the foundation of the American citizen's idea of the history of his own nation and the forces which have shaped and built it. From most of these texts, no one could learn that here was a transaction by which lands constituting less than one-tenth of the nation's public domain were granted to railroads constituting less than 8 per cent of the United States mileage, not as gifts but under terms and conditions by which the government received a direct monetary return far greater than the value of the lands granted.

This direct monetary return, however, is by far the smallest part of the gain to the government and the people of the United States from the working out of the land grant transaction. When the policy was first adopted, nearly two and one-half centuries after the beginnings of permanent settlement on the Atlantic seaboard, the frontier

[53] See works cited in footnote 31, above.

[54] Coleman and Wesley, 401; Dumond, 535.

[55] Kirkland, 378, 380; Stephenson, *American History to 1865*, 407; Fish and Wilson, 355; Richard J. Purcell, *The American Nation* (Boston, 1937), 529.

[56] Roy F. and Jeannette P. Nichols, *A Short History of American Democracy* (New York, 1943), 270, 272.

[57] Eugene C. Barker, William E. Dodd, and Henry Steele Commager, *Our Nation's Development* (Evanston, Ill., 1937), 387; Kirkland, 381.

[58] Purcell, 532.

of the United States was but a little way beyond the Mississippi River—still not half way across the continent. And then, within less than a generation, the frontier almost literally leaped across the Great Plains, the mountains, and the vast areas which the old maps showed as the "Great American Desert." Such a difference in the rate of settlement was not due to any one thing, of course, but obviously the most effective cause was the fact of the transportation service of the railroads.

The land grants did not build these railroads, but they furnished a basis of credit which made it possible for them to be built. So doing, they did what never had been done before—provided transportation ahead of settlement. The result is almost beyond measurement. It was to be found in a startling reduction in the cost of transportation, as is abundantly shown in the reports of the Quartermaster General of the Army during that period.[59] And a

[59] From letter from Quartermaster-General M. C. Meigs to Secretary of War William W. Belknap, Jan. 28, 1873 in *H.R. Ex. Doc. No. 169,* 42 Cong., 3 Sess., Vol. 9, relating to savings to the War Department in transportation costs from July 1, 1866, to Jan. 28, 1873, as a result of the building of the Union Pacific Railroad:

The average rates per mile for troops are, on through business, 5 2/10 cents; on local business, 8 cents, being an average of 6 3/5 cents per man per mile. The average rates per mile for troops by the Overland Stage Company were, on through business, 12½ cents; on local business, 15 cents, being an average of 13 3/4 cents per mile per man.

Assuming that all of these troops would have traveled by stage, in the absence of the railroad (which is by no means probable), the total estimated cost by stage is shown by the following, based on the averaged rates above stated:

Average rate per man per mile: rail	6 3/5 cents
Average rate per man per mile: stage	13 3/4 cents
Actual cost for troops at railroad rates	$1,446,262.25
Estimated cost at stage rates	$3,013,046.35

The average rates per 100 pounds per 100 miles charged for freight by the railroad during the period required are, on through business, 19 cents; on local business, 62 cents, being an average of 40½ cents per 100 pounds per 100 miles by railroad.

. . . the estimated cost of the transportation of the freight moved by the Union Pacific Railroad, including express charges as shown above, . . . would be as follows:

Rates per 100 pounds per 100 miles: railroad rates	40½ cents
Rates per 100 pounds per 100 miles: wagon rates	$1.46
Actual cost of freight at railroad rates	$1,896,589.57
Estimated cost at wagon rates	$6,837,088.32

Showing a total estimated cost for moving the troops and supplies by stage and wagon of	$9,850,134.67
Total actual cost by railroad	$3,342,851.82

Estimated difference . . . equivalent to about 66 per cent.	$6,507,282.85

result "beyond any estimate the Quartermaster General can make," as W. T. Sherman, then General-in-Chief of the Armies reported, was to be found in the "opening up to settlement of regions now wild, which would give homes and employment to . . . industrious people." [60] It was to be found in the value added to land and its products. It was to be found in the transformation of nontaxable resources into property which furnishes the principal tax-base, for the support of the state and local governments of half a continent.

More important even than these was the contribution of the land grant railroads to military security and national unity. Indeed, as General Sherman once wrote, at the time of its building the Pacific Railway was "looked upon as a military necessity and as the only thing positively essential to the binding together of the republic." [61]

Almost without exception, however, the history textbooks have failed to develop this major and essential fact that, whatever may have been its shortcomings, the land grant policy touched off national and individual energies which in a few short years accomplished the greatest engineering, construction, and colonization project ever undertaken up to that time, a project which transformed the West from a wilderness to a civilized community and welded the nation into one.

[60] Reports from General W. T. Sherman and the Quartermaster-General transmitted May 12, 1880, by Secretary of War Alexander Ramsey to Hon. R. M. McLane, Chairman, House of Representatives Committee on the Pacific Railroads. Original letters are on file in the Clerk's Office, House of Representatives. General Sherman's letter is reprinted in *Railway World*, May 22, 1880, pp. 492–3, as follows:

I have the honor to acknowledge the receipt, by reference, from you of the resolution of the House committee on Pacific railroads, calling for information as to the probable saving in money to the military authorities by the completion of the Northern Pacific Railroad from Bismarck westward, and its general effect on the military and Indian services in that quarter. . . . In a military sense, the immediate extension of this railroad from Bismarck to the Yellowstone, and up the valley of that river as high as the mouth of the Big Horn, will be beyond any estimate the Quartermaster-General can make, because this railroad will transport men and supplies for ten if not twelve months of the year, while the Missouri river and the Yellowstone are barely navigable by light draft boats for two or at most three months. . . . It is equally important to the military and civil interests of the whole country that Montana should fill up with hardy farmers, and this will be an immediate result of the extension westward of this northern railroad . . . I am unable to make even an approximate estimate of the saving in cost of transportation of men and military stores by the completion of this railroad, but this bears a small proportion to the great result of opening up to settlement regions now wild, which would give homes and employment to two or three millions of industrious people.

[61] Letter from General W. T. Sherman, dated Jan. 16, 1867, to Major-General Grenville M. Dodge, in *How We Built the Union Pacific Railway*, Senate Doc. No. 447, 61 Cong., 2 Sess., 14.

APPENDIX

FEDERAL LAND GRANTS TO RAILROADS [1]

State	Total Acreage [2]	Apparent area shown on Map No. 1 (p. 48) Acres	Per Cent of State Area	Actual area shown on Map No. 2 (p. 48) Acres [3]	Per Cent of State Area
Alabama	33,029,760	14,863,392	45	2,747,479	8.3
Arizona	72,901,760	34,263,827	47	7,695,203	10.6
Arkansas	33,985,280	12,574,554	37	2,586,970	7.6
California	101,563,520	40,625,408	40	11,585,393	11.4
Colorado	66,718,080	6,671,808	10	3,757,673	5.6
Florida	37,478,400	10,868,736	29	2,218,705	5.9
Idaho	53,476,480	8,021,472	15	1,320,591	2.5
Illinois	36,096,000	12,633,600	35	2,595,133	7.2
Indiana	23,226,240	2,322,624 [4]	10	—	—
Iowa	36,019,200	32,417,280	90	4,711,328	13.1
Kansas	52,656,640	32,647,117	62	8,234,013	15.6
Louisiana	31,054,720	20,496,115	66	1,375,000	4.4
Michigan	37,258,240	27,943,680	75	3,134,058	8.4
Minnesota	53,803,520	37,662,464	70	9,953,008	18.5
Mississippi	30,538,240	6,718,413	22	1,075,345	3.5
Missouri	44,591,360	12,485,581	28	2,328,674	5.2
Montana	94,168,320	44,259,110	47	14,736,919	15.6
Nebraska	49,431,680	13,840,870	28	7,272,623	14.7
Nevada	70,745,600	8,489,472	12	5,086,283	7.2
New Mexico	77,866,240	26,474,522	34	3,355,179	4.3
North Dakota	45,225,600	22,612,800	50	10,697,490	23.7
Oregon	62,067,840	24,827,136	40	3,655,390	5.9
South Dakota	49,310,080	2,465,504 [5]	5	—	—
Utah	54,346,240	4,347,699	8	2,230,085	4.1
Washington	43,642,880	29,240,730	67	9,582,878	22.0
Wisconsin	35,938,560	24,438,221	68	3,666,062	10.2
Wyoming	62,664,960	13,786,291	22	5,749,051	9.2
TOTAL	1,389,805,440	527,998,426	38	131,350,534	9.5

[1] As reported in U. S. General Land Office Information Bulletin, 1939 Series, No. 5, *Transportation.* . . .

[2] Table 1, *Report of Commissioner of General Land Office* . . . *June 30, 1943.*

[3] *Ibid.,* Tables 76 and 77.

[4] No Federal lands in Indiana were granted to railroads.

[5] 443,312 acres of the Winona & St. Peter R. R. extending into Dakota Territory (now part of South Dakota) are included with Minnesota by the General Land Office. No other railroad company received a land grant in South Dakota.

13

As HAS already been evident in many of the articles included in this collection, the most striking trend in contemporary writing of American history is the dissatisfaction with and therefore rejection of the once dominant economic interpretation. Sometimes, as in the case of Edmund Morgan's reinterpretation of the coming of the American Revolution, the attack on the old view has been mounted by political or social historians. But it is important to observe that the playing down of economic forces as the primary impetus to historical change has stemmed from more than simply an interest in other, noneconomic sources of human motivation. The truth is that dissatisfaction with the economic interpretation derives from a broader conception of human nature. The new view emphasizes not only the multiplicity of causes but also the breadth of human motivations, not only the complexity of civilized society but the complexity of man as a social being. In short, unfavorable criticism of the economic interpretation has come not from any disenchantment with economics but from a disenchantment with a flat and pallid conception of man. Another way of saying the same thing is to note that economic historians have often been in the vanguard of those who have found the old economic interpretation wanting in both subtlety and accuracy.

Coben's article is a good example of an economic historian's reasons for finding the economic interpretation inadequate. The working out of Reconstruction policy in the years after the close of the Civil War, as he makes clear, has long been seen through the eyes of the economic interpretation, particularly in the seminal work of Charles and Mary Beard. It was the late Howard K. Beale's *The Critical Year* (New York, 1930), though, which provided the flesh for the Beards' skeleton. At the very least, Coben's article is a frontal assault on Beale's conclusion that the inception of the program of the Congressional radicals derived from essentially economic considerations.

By and large, Coben's method in uncovering the roots of the radical Reconstruction policy is the same as Beale's, that is, amassing quotations from important political and business leaders of the time. Neither Beale nor Coben has been able to use statistical evidence to arrive at his conclusion simply because the question they both ask is not susceptible to such an approach. The number of people who helped to shape Reconstruction attitudes and policies were many, while the extant evidence is severely limited. Moreover, the question is obviously subtle, requiring close analysis of statements. These statements, votes in Congress, and so forth cannot be reduced to a simple counting of heads to ascertain what was the principal or predominant motive animating Congress or the business community.

Yet the determination of which of the two conclusions is to be accepted is not to be left to the flip of a coin or the inclination of the reader's own prejudices. There are rather persuasive—even objective—reasons why one is to be clearly preferred over the other. One such reason is the kinds of evidence employed by the two authors. The character of Coben's evidence, aside from the amount, is the more convincing. He draws his evidence almost entirely from the correspondence of businessmen and from the public pronouncements of business groups. Beale's evidence, on the other hand, is largely drawn from the Congressional debates and the correspondence of political figures, though the issue is the position of the business community. In short, Coben's sources are broader than Beale's. The most important reason, however, for accepting Coben's conclusions over Beale's is quite different. Beale has tried to show a preponderance of business opinion on one side of the Reconstruction debates. Simply by showing that the business community was seriously divided on the economic policies to be pursued, Coben is able to overturn Beale's conclusion.

That it has been overturned is clear from subsequent writings of historians on the era. Perhaps the best summary of current views is that of David Donald in his superb revision of James G. Randall's *Civil War and Reconstruction* (New York, 1961), p. 543, the standard work on the period. After reviewing the Beale thesis Donald writes that it seriously distorts the true picture of motivations for radical Reconstruction. "On the whole," he continues, "it is more accurate to view the economic struggles of the reconstruction period not so much as a clear-cut sectional or even class fight, but as 'a contest between opposing banking, investing, mercantile, industrial, labor and agricultural interests that was fought out on intra-sectional as well as inter-sectional lines.' "

Coben's article also illustrates another trend in modern American historiography. His study is actually just one of several that have emphasized the diversity of interests and aims within the business community in the Reconstruction and other periods. For the Reconstruction period, for example, Chester McArthur Destler, in the chapter "Legal and Sectional Aspects of the Pendleton Plan" in his *American Radicalism* (New London, 1946), argued much the same conclusion as Coben, though in connection with a narrower issue. More recently Robert P. Sharkey, in his *Money, Class, and Party* (Baltimore, 1959), has concluded that the supposed unanimity of business interests in support of the resumption of specie payments in the 1870s had little basis in fact. Some business groups, like manufacturers, almost unanimously opposed contraction of the currency, while bankers strongly supported contraction, which would have followed upon the resumption of specie payments. A similar conclusion has also been reached by Irwin Unger in his "Business Men and Specie Resumption" *Political Science Quarterly*, LXXIV (March 1959), 46–70. In his book *The Greenback Era: A Social and Political History of American Finance, 1865–1879* (Princeton, 1964), Unger goes further than simply a division of views within the business community; he sees ethical scruples influencing businessmen's attitudes and specifically singles out Charles Beard's naked economic interpretation of the era as inadequate.

For later periods other historians have been stressing the same diversity of interests among business groups. Lee Benson's *Merchants, Farmers, and Railroads* (Cambridge, Mass., 1955) has shown that the movement for railroad regulation in New York State, which culminated in the Interstate Commerce Act of 1887, derived from businessmen, merchants, and even railroad leaders as much as from the demands of farm groups, which have usually been described as the prime movers. Robert Wiebe's *Businessman and Reform: A Study of the Progressive Movement* (Cambridge, Mass., 1962) demonstrates that even during the reform years of 1901–1912 businessmen were divided in their goals and attitudes toward reform. Samuel Hays's *Conservation and the Gospel of Efficiency* (Cambridge, Mass., 1959) takes a similar approach to the conservation movement by demonstrating that it was more than simply a "people's" movement to keep the national resources out of the exploiting hands of business interests. Not only were some of the prominent conservationists deeply interested in the orderly exploitation of natural resources, but they also received substantial support for their conservation aims from certain business groups. On the other hand, some business groups opposed the conservation movement.

At the conclusion of his article Coben declares that if businessmen were not united in their support of radical Reconstruction, then "it seems clear that factors other than the economic interests of the Northeast must be used to explain the motivation and aims of Radical Reconstruction." This observation points up one of the principal dividends to be derived from the work of Coben, Sharkey, Destler, and Unger. Although Coben doesn't say so, it seems fair to say that at least one of the other factors is certainly a democratic and humanitarian concern for the Negro in the South.

One of the undesirable effects of the economic interpretation of Reconstruction has been the refusal of historians to take at anything like face value the tremendous interest in the Negro that runs all through the Congressional and public debates on Reconstruction policy. Because the concern for Negro rights could not be fitted into a scheme that stressed self-interest and economic gain, it was often played down as being only a smoke screen for other less noble motives or lightly dismissed as a propaganda issue to gain votes from a more gullible public. Now, it seems, the central concern of both public men and the people in the fate of the newly freed slaves in the years immediately after the war can receive the attention and emphasis to which its pre-eminence in the sources entitle it. That this emphasis is now being made is evident from a number of recent monographs that stress civil rights for Negroes as a substantive issue in the making of Reconstruction policy decisions. Notable examples of this new approach are Eric L. McKitrick, *Andrew Johnson and Reconstruction* (Chicago, 1960), La Wanda and John Cox, *Politics, Principle, and Prejudice, 1865-1866* (Glencoe, Ill., 1963), and W. R. Brock, *An American Crisis, Congress and Reconstruction, 1865–1867* (London, 1963). In all three of these works the so-called "radicals" are portrayed as sincerely concerned with what they said they were primarily interested in, namely, protection of the Negro's civil and political rights. Conversely, in the Coxes' book and in McKitrick's study Andrew Johnson's resistance to the radical program is specifically depicted as stemming largely from hostility to the idea of Negro equality. All of the three recent works, therefore, support a decided alteration in the traditional interpretation of Andrew Johnson.

Mr. Coben is assistant professor of history at Princeton University.

Northeastern Business and Radical Reconstruction: a Re-Examination

BY STANLEY COBEN

HISTORIANS have generally accepted the view that Radical Reconstruction "was a successful attempt by northeastern business, acting through the Republican party, to control the national government for its own economic ends: notably, the protective tariff, the national banks, [and] a 'sound' currency."[1] The Radical program is also said to have been "the method by which the 'Masters of Capital' . . . expected to exploit the resources of the southern states" behind federal protection.[2] Western hostility to these eastern business designs was avoided by large appropriations for rivers, harbors, railroads, free land, and pensions, and by use of the ever-potent "bloody shirt." This is supposed to have been prevented by a union of western and southern agrarian opposition to the industrial and financial masters of the East.[3]

This thesis has met with little serious challenge and has been subjected to only occasional qualification. It continues to influence studies of the political and economic history of the post-Civil War era.[4] Yet a closer examination of the important economic legislation

SOURCE: Reprinted by permission from the *Mississippi Valley Historical Review*, XLVI (June 1959). Copyright, 1959, by the Mississippi Valley Historical Association.

[1] This is the conclusion of the most recent survey of historians' attitudes toward Radical Reconstruction. T. Harry Williams, "An Analysis of Some Reconstruction Attitudes," *Journal of Southern History* (Baton Rouge), XII (November, 1946), 470. Williams calls this the "Beale thesis," because it has been most completely developed by Howard K. Beale in his *The Critical Year: A Study of Andrew Johnson and Reconstruction* (New York, 1930), and his "On Rewriting Reconstruction History," *American Historical Review* (New York), XLV (July, 1940), 807–27.

[2] William B. Hesseltine, "Economic Factors in the Abandonment of Reconstruction," *Mississippi Valley Historical Review* (Cedar Rapids), XXII (September, 1935), 191.

[3] Helen J. and T. Harry Williams, "Wisconsin Republicans and Reconstruction, 1865–1870," *Wisconsin Magazine of History* (Madison), XXIII (September, 1939), 17–39.

[4] For recent expressions of the "Beale thesis," see C. Vann Woodward, *Origins of the New South, 1877–1913* (Baton Rouge, 1951), 23–24; George R. Bentley, *A History of the Freedmen's Bureau* (Philadelphia, 1955), 34–36;

and congressional battles of the period, and of the attitudes of businessmen and influential business groups, reveals serious divisions on economic issues among Radical legislators and northeastern businessmen alike. Certainly neither business leaders nor Radicals were united in support of any specific set of economic aims. Considerable evidence also suggests that the divisions among businessmen often cut across sectional as well as industrial lines. Furthermore, evidence indicates that few northeastern business groups were interested in southern investments in the early postwar years, and that these few were hostile to Radical Reconstruction.

The evident need for new interpretations of the motivation of northern Radicals and of the economic history of the entire period is demonstrated by a re-examination of the most important of the "economic ends" usually agreed upon as motives for Radical Reconstruction: the tariff and the currency issues, and the charge that northern business interests sought federal protection for the exploitation of the South.

The tariff split northeastern businessmen more than any other issue.[5] So fierce was business competition in this era, and so eager were the antagonists to use every possible means of winning an advantage, that almost all important tariff schedules became battlegrounds between industries, as well as between firms within the same industry. The copper, iron, linseed, and woolen textile industries, for example, were bitterly divided on crucial tariff schedules. The most significant split, however, was between certain highly protectionist Pennsylvania interests on one side and influential low-tariff groups in New England and New York on the other. Pennsylvania coal mine operators feared the competition of rich Nova Scotia deposits, mined by low-wage labor, close to major

---

William B. Hesseltine, *Confederate Leaders in the New South* (Baton Rouge, 1950), 136; Arthur S. Link, *American Epoch: A History of the United States since the 1890's* (New York, 1955), 4–5; George R. Woolfolk, *The Cotton Regency: The Northern Merchants and Reconstruction, 1865–1880* (New York, 1958).

Earlier statements of the thesis may be found in Charles A. and Mary R. Beard, *The Rise of American Civilization* (2 vols., New York, 1927), II, Chap. XX; Louis M. Hacker, *The Triumph of American Capitalism* (New York, 1940), Chap. 25; Richard N. Current, *Old Thad Stevens: A Story of Ambition* (Madison, 1942), Introduction, Chap. IV, and pp. 226, 249, 260; Matthew Josephson, *The Politicos, 1865–1896* (New York, 1938), Chap. I. James S. Allen, *Reconstruction: The Battle for Democracy, 1865–1867* (New York, 1937), is a Marxist version of the thesis.

[5] For a very different point of view, see Howard K. Beale, "The Tariff and Reconstruction," *American Historical Review*, XXXV (January, 1930), 276–94.

American markets. Iron and steel manufacturers, the largest highly protected interest, were faced with the competition of long-established, technologically advanced English producers, whose wage scale was only a fraction of that of the Americans. Pennsylvania carpet, glass, and wool industries demanded protection for similar reasons. The Keystone State was the largest extractor of iron ore and coal, the largest manufacturer of every form of iron and steel, of carpets, glass, and chemicals. On the other hand, powerful opposition to the tariff objectives of the Pennsylvanians came from the cotton and many of the woolen textile manufacturers of New England, and from the intertwined importing, financial, and railroad interests of New York.

New Englanders had become strong advocates of lower tariffs in the 1850's. The sharp tariff reductions of 1857 were accomplished chiefly by southern and New England votes.[6] New England manufacturers, especially textile producers, desired cheap imported raw materials in order to lower the price of their finished goods on the international market. Furthermore, they agreed to reduced rates on manufactured goods to discourage the growth of domestic competition.[7] Among American manufacturers, New England producers as a group were farthest from domestic sources of raw materials, closest to sources of cheap foreign commodities. Cheap supplies of coal, lumber, flaxseed, building stone, fine wool, and other commodities were available in nearby Canada and Nova Scotia. Scottish and British iron, Indian linseed, and Russian and Philippine hemp were imported into Boston in large quantities for the benefit of manufacturers.[8] Hardly any wool for the finer grades of cloth was produced in America, either before or after the war; nor were the rough, lowest grades, used in carpets and blankets, available at

[6] Davis R. Dewey, *Financial History of the United States* (New York, 1903), 263. Dewey calculated the House vote for the 1857 tariff by section: New England 18 to 9 in favor, South 60 to 2 in favor, West 14 to 33 opposed, Middle States 24 to 28 opposed. There was no roll call on the final vote in the Senate, but see speeches by Senator Henry Wilson of Massachusetts, *Cong. Globe*, 34 Cong., 3 Sess., Appendix, 333–34 (February 26, 1857), and Senator Daniel Clark of New Hampshire, *ibid.*, 36 Cong., 2 Sess., 1023 (February 19, 1861). See also Richard Hofstadter, "The Tariff Issue on the Eve of the Civil War," *American Historical Review*, XLIV (October, 1938), 50–55.

[7] George W. Bond and George Livermore, *Report of the Boston Board of Trade on Wool for 1859* (Boston, 1860), 2; Frank W. Taussig, *The Tariff History of the United States* (8th ed., New York, 1931), 142; Melvin T. Copeland, *The Cotton Manufacturing Industry of the United States* (Cambridge, 1912), 14.

[8] See, for example, "Review of the Boston Market for the Year 1865," *Twelfth Annual Report of the Boston Board of Trade* (Boston, 1866), 72–95.

home.[9] By the end of the war, northeastern cotton manufacturers were importing cheap Indian Surat cotton already widely used in England.[10]

English textile manufacturers, rivals of the New Englanders both in world markets and in America, obtained their raw materials free of duty.[11] There were good reasons for northeastern producers to believe that only the American system of imposts kept them from equaling the British in world trade. By the 1850's, many American mills had been in operation for three generations. They had experienced managers and weavers, cheap and abundant credit, modern machinery and production methods. In cotton cloth manufacturing, for which machinery could be used most extensively, New England labor was the most productive in the world. By 1860, the average number of looms per weaver was four in America, two in Great Britain. French and German manufacturers lagged even farther behind in methods and machinery.[12]

In addition to high productivity which made their goods competitive in the world markets, and the need to import cheap raw materials, many New England manufacturers preferred low tariffs from a fear that high textile duties would foster the growth of new competitors at home. New producers might bring cutthroat competition and periodic chaos to the industry by their poor judgment of market conditions. A special committee of the Boston Board of Trade acknowledged in 1858 that New England textile manufacturers had potentially dangerous rivals, especially in Pennsylvania; but the committee concluded that the tariff reduction of 1857 removed any immediate threat. "Under the impulse of a high protective tariff they accomplished so little, that now, under a change of policy, there seems no present cause of alarm." [13] When

[9] Arthur H. Cole, *The American Wool Manufacture* (2 vols., Cambridge, 1926), II, 310, 319, 330; John L. Hayes, *Statement of Fact Relative to Canada Wools and the Manufacture of Worsted* (Boston, 1866), 10, 19.

[10] "It may soon become imperatively necessary to us to be able to obtain foreign cotton on even terms with English manufacturers if we expect to compete with them in other markets." *Boston Board of Trade: Report of a Committee upon the Cotton Tax* (Boston, 1867); *Ninth Annual Report of the Boston Board of Trade* (Boston, 1863), Appendix, 99.

[11] Shepard B. Clough and Charles W. Cole, *Economic History of Europe* (3rd ed., Boston, 1952), 472-76, 605-607.

[12] Copeland, *Cotton Manufacturing Industry*, 10. "What this country wants," Massachusetts cotton manufacturer Edward Atkinson wrote Senator Henry Wilson in 1866, "is cheap iron. Our cotton mills now cost to build $30 per spindle complete with looms, etc., etc., against $10 to $12 in England." Atkinson to Wilson, July 7, 1866, Harold F. Williamson, *Edward Atkinson: The Biography of an American Liberal* (Boston, 1934), 67.

[13] *Fifth Annual Report of the Boston Board of Trade* (Boston, 1859), 96-97.

the higher Morrill duties came before the House in 1860, Representative Alexander H. Rice of Massachusetts, speaking for the manufacturers of his state, declared that "excessive protection" would stimulate "ruinous and irresponsible competition at home." In the Senate, textile manufacturer Henry Wilson proclaimed: "A high protective policy . . . is calculated to raise up rivals at home, and is more injurious to us than foreign competition." [14]

After the war, fear of the growth of protected competition continued to influence New England tariff sentiment. Edward Atkinson, president of the Cotton Spinners of New England, and a director of the Boston Board of Trade, wrote to Henry Wilson in 1866: "The strongest men in the trade are more afraid of the unskillful competition built up at home by high duties than they are of foreign competition." [15] Enoch R. Mudge, one of the most influential New England textile men, told the organizing meeting of the National Association of Cotton Manufacturers and Planters in 1868: "When we speak of protection, I think it should be given only at the point where the cotton manufacturer requires it." [16] For well-established, efficient New England producers, of course, there were comparatively few points at which protection was necessary. They had seen evidence of the success of their low tariff theories in the few years the 1857 schedules were in force. "The operation of the tariff of 1857 has contributed largely to the prosperity of our woolen manufactures," one of Boston's largest wool dealers reported in 1859.[17] Exports of cotton cloth had risen steadily, from an average of $7,000,000 in the years 1851 through 1856, to almost $11,000,000 in 1860.[18]

The government's need for revenue allowed protectionists an almost unchallenged ascendancy during the Civil War,[19] but the battle between northeastern business groups over tariff schedules was resumed after Appomattox. For example, when a resolution for lower tariffs was placed before the National Board of Trade Convention in 1869, delegates from the Boston Board of Trade

[14] *Cong. Globe*, 36 Cong., 1 Sess., 1867 (April 26, 1860); *ibid.*, 36 Cong., 2 Sess., 1026 (February 19, 1861). Rice later became president of the Boston Board of Trade, then governor of Massachusetts.

[15] Atkinson to Wilson, July 7, 1866, Williamson, *Atkinson*, 67–68.

[16] *Proceedings of a Convention for the Purpose of Organizing the National Association of Cotton Manufacturers and Planters* (Boston, 1868), 13.

[17] Bond and Livermore, *Report on Wool*, 2.

[18] Copeland, *Cotton Manufacturing Industry*, 14; Taussig, *Tariff History*, 142.

[19] Dewey, *Financial History*, 265–67, 272, 301–304; Taussig, *Tariff History*, 150, 159–62; Edward Stanwood, *American Tariff Controversies in the Nineteenth Century* (2 vols., Boston, 1903), II, 130.

and Boston Corn Exchange voted 6 to 1 for the resolution; Philadelphia delegates voted 7 to 0 against it.[20] The Boston Board of
Trade also worked unsuccessfully to prevent abrogation of the
reciprocity treaty with Canada; Philadelphia's Board joined western
agricultural interests in demanding an end to reciprocity.[21]

These divisions within the business community were likewise reflected in the congressional debates and voting on important tariff
schedules. Cotton manufacturers resumed their prewar demands
for lower schedules, even for cotton textiles. Senator William
Sprague, whose sprawling Rhode Island mills were relatively inefficient, protested against the 25 per cent cut in cotton textile
duties proposed in 1867. He was answered by Senator William P.
Fessenden of Maine, sponsor of the measure: "I am informed by
the commissioner [Revenue Commissioner David A. Wells] that
these duties were fixed at a rate perfectly satisfactory to those
engaged in the manufacture of cottons, who appeared before
him. . . . The cotton interest of this country has got so that it can
stand of itself pretty much." [22]

Schedules on coal similarly came under attack. As power looms
replaced hand looms, and steam power replaced water power, New
England manufacturers became increasingly interested in lower
coal duties.[23] Under reciprocity and the low tariff of 1857, imports
of coal into Boston rose steadily from 88,531 tons in 1858, to
209,225 tons in 1865, most of this being cheap Nova Scotia fuel.[24]
Representative George S. Boutwell and Senator Charles Sumner
of Massachusetts tried in vain to prevent higher coal schedules from
being placed in the proposed tariffs of 1866 and 1867. Sumner
acknowledged that there was a lot of coal in Pennsylvania, West
Virginia, and the West. "But why," he asked, "should New England, which has a natural resource comparatively near at home,
be compelled at a great sacrifice to drag her coal from these distant
supplies?" Sumner's amendment was defeated 11 to 25, with eight

[20] *Proceedings of the Second Annual Meeting of the National Board of
Trade* (Boston, 1870), 321.

[21] *Eleventh Annual Report of the Boston Board of Trade* (Boston, 1865),
42; *Thirteenth Annual Report of the Boston Board of Trade* (Boston, 1867),
2–3; *Thirty-first Annual Report of the Philadelphia Board of Trade* (Philadelphia, 1864), 17.

[22] *Cong. Globe*, 39 Cong., 2 Sess., 709, 744 (January 24, 25, 1867).

[23] Copeland, *Cotton Manufacturing Industry*, 29; J. Herbert Burgy, *The
New England Cotton Textile Industry: A Study in Industrial Geography* (Baltimore, 1932), 24, 30, 34, 100.

[24] *Twelfth Annual Report of the Boston Board of Trade* (Boston, 1866),
75.

New Englanders, both New Yorkers, and one senator from Oregon comprising those favoring lower duties on coal.[25]

Many other schedules in the proposed bills of 1866 and 1867 were fought out by competing or conflicting business interests. Manufacturers, especially New Englanders, dependent upon cheap imported raw materials, were continually in opposition to the combined efforts of raw material producers and competing manufacturers closer to these native sources of supply. When Senator Benjamin F. Wade of Ohio moved to raise the duty on linseed, largely grown in the West, Fessenden of Maine accused him of asking the higher rate "for this simple, selfish reason: that the trade of crushing seed and manufacturing oil on the sea-coast may be utterly destroyed for the benefit of crushers of seed and the manufacturers of oil in the West." [26]

Rolling mills, chiefly eastern, which controlled the American Iron and Steel Association,[27] almost forced through an extremely low duty on scrap iron. Such a duty would allow the mills to import huge quantities of cheap European used rails, and to re-roll them in lieu of using domestic pig iron for new rails. Senator Zachariah Chandler, from the iron producing state of Michigan, demanded that the proposed duty on wrought scrap iron be quadrupled, and the duty on cast scrap be almost tripled. Lower schedules, he declared, would close the iron mines, put out every blast furnace, and mean "total ruin to the iron interests of the United States. . . . It is a bill gotten up to suit the railroad rolling-mills, and to sacrifice every other iron interest in the United States." The rolling mills won one Senate vote, but Chandler forced another, which was won by those sympathetic with the mine operators and pig iron producers. Almost all the western senators and both Pennsylvanians voted for higher duties on scrap metal. All but one senator from New England and New York voted for the low schedule.[28]

The only tariff adjustment besides the wool and woolens bill to

[25] *Cong. Globe*, 39 Cong., 1 Sess., 3569 (July 3, 1866); 39 Cong., 2 Sess., 830, 857 (January 29, 30, 1867).

[26] *Ibid.*, 39 Cong., 2 Sess., 705 (January 24, 1867). Linseed oil was important in the manufacture of paints, dyes, and varnishes.

[27] Pig iron producers, still the dominant segment of the iron and steel industry in the early 1870's, withdrew from the American Iron and Steel Association in 1871 and formed their own association, which by 1873 numbered two hundred firms. For the sharp division which this Association saw between itself and the American Iron and Steel Association, see *The American Pig Iron Manufacturing Association, Meeting Held in New York City, February 19, 1873* (Philadelphia, 1873), 32, 64.

[28] *Cong. Globe*, 39 Cong., 2 Sess., 799–801 (January 28, 1867), 860–62 (January 30, 1867).

become law in the early postwar years was a measure passed in 1869, greatly increasing the duties on copper. Eastern smelters, who used a combination of eastern and cheap South American ores, were forced out of business by this bill, passed for the benefit of Lake Superior mine operators, whose domestic ores did not require smelting. The Lake Superior mine owners, some of whom were eastern financiers, were thus given a monopoly of the American market. They were thereby enabled to charge much higher than world prices at home and to dump their surplus abroad at much lower prices.[29] Similar conflicts among business interests developed on tariff schedules for salt (used for scouring wool), zinc, lead, nickel, and building stones.[30]

The wool and woolens bill of 1867, which considerably raised most schedules, has been cited as a prime example of the co-operation of business interests, because it was devised in a conference between a committee of wool growers and representatives of the National Association of Wool Manufacturers. What has generally been overlooked is the fact that the manufacturers' association, like the American Iron and Steel Association, was dominated by a well-organized segment of the industry, in this case by worsted and carpet manufacturers, whose interests conflicted with those of other important groups within the woolen industry.

Most influential of the men who negotiated the agreement for the manufacturers were Erastus B. Bigelow, president and founder of the Association, and America's leading carpet manufacturer; John L. Hayes, permanent secretary of the Association; and J. Wiley Edmonds, treasurer of the giant Pacific Mills, a leading worsted producer. Hayes reported to the membership that "for six months Mr. Bigelow gave himself unremittingly to the great work ... [and to him they] must attribute the happy results of the conference." Before this "happy" conclusion, Hayes conceded, most woolen manufacturers "were becoming more and more disposed to look abroad for the chief supply of raw material ... and were inclined to advocate the British policy of free trade in raw materials, including wool." [31] Certainly the results of the conference were not

[29] Taussig, *Tariff History*, 219–21; *Letter of Henry Martin, Esq., President of the Baltimore Copper Company to the Senate of the United States in Opposition to the Bill Increasing the Duty on Imported Copper Ores* (Baltimore, 1869); Bliss Perry, *Life and Letters of Henry Lee Higginson* (Boston, 1921), 263–64; William B. Gates, *Michigan Copper and Boston Dollars* (Cambridge, 1951), 33–35, 45–47.

[30] *Cong. Globe*, 39 Cong., 2 Sess., 680, 765, 793, 798, 821 (January 23, 26, 28, 29, 1867).

[31] *Transactions of the National Association of Wool Manufacturers, Second Annual Report* (Boston, 1866), 12, 20. For interesting evidence of Edmonds'

so happy for manufacturers of woolen cloth, the largest item of domestic woolen output. These producers would be forced to pay much higher rates for imported raw wool than the worsted manufacturers with whom they competed. Carpet and blanket manufacturers would pay by far the lowest rates.[32]

The largest manufacturer of wool cloth taking part in the negotiations with the growers was Edward Harris of the Harris Manufacturing Company, Woonsocket, Rhode Island. Harris later declared that he had no part in deciding the schedules, and that his name had been appended to the agreement without his knowledge or consent.[33] Senator Henry Wilson of Massachusetts, a manufacturer of fine woolen cloth, told the Senate Finance Committee that if the new schedules were put into effect, he would have to close his factory. He subsequently declared in the Senate: "Some of the very ablest men in Massachusetts and in New England earnestly believe that this bill, so far as it concerns two thirds of the woolen manufacturers of the country, is not so good as the present tariff. [Only] the carpet manufacturers are abundantly satisfied." Wilson's statement was reinforced by other New England senators. William Sprague of Rhode Island, William P. Fessenden of Maine, and Lot M. Morrill of Maine reported similar opinions of the wool and woolens bill among the cloth manufacturers in their constituencies.[34] Nevertheless, there was no organized opposition in Washington to the energetic Hayes or to the large number of western congressmen who were anxious to honor an agreement which gave protection to wool growers. The wool and woolens bill passed easily despite adverse votes from men like Wilson, Sumner, and Sprague who had close associations with the New England woolen industry.[35]

---

part in this agreement, see speech by Senator Jonathan P. Dolliver, *Cong. Record*, 61 Cong., 1 Sess., 1717 (May 4, 1909). For the protectionist ideas of Bigelow and Hayes, see Erastus B. Bigelow, *Objects and Plan of the National Association of Wool Manufacturers* (Boston, 1865), 3–4; John L. Hayes, *The Fleece and the Loom: An Address before the National Association of Wool Manufacturers at the First Annual Meeting in Philadelphia, September 6, 1865* (Boston, 1866), 60.

[32] For more detailed discussion of the schedules, see Chester W. Wright, *Wool Growing and the Tariff* (Cambridge, 1910), 213–15; Haldor R. Mohat, *The Tariff on Wool* (Madison, 1935), 23–25; Taussig, *Tariff History*, 195–218.

[33] Edward Harris, *Memorial of Manufacturers of Woolen Goods to the Committee on Ways and Means* (Washington, 1872), 22.

[34] *Cong. Globe*, 39 Cong., 2 Sess., 909–11 (January 31, 1867).

[35] *Ibid.*, 1958 (March 2, 1867). A relatively small but well-informed and organized group within the woolen industry was able to write schedules to suit itself because they had to be phrased in complicated, technical language.

Northeastern opposition to the cloth schedules continued after the passage of the bill, and in the winter of 1869–1870, Edward Harris and forty-three other New England woolen manufacturers petitioned Congress to reduce the duties on wool for cloth as low as carpet wool duties, which were one-fifth as high. On reaching Washington with this petition, Harris was informed that the wool growers and John Hayes, who said he represented three hundred companies and individuals associated with the woolen industry, had first claim on congressmen's votes.[36] In 1889, the woolen cloth manufacturers obtained 530 signatures from wool manufacturers and dealers asking for lower duties—and again failed. Finally, in 1909, the cloth manufacturers formed a separate organization to do permanent battle in Washington with the worsted and carpet interests.[37]

For somewhat different reasons a low-tariff sentiment similar to that in New England was also strong in New York City, by far the largest importing and financial center in the country. New York merchants, shippers, and those who financed their activities opposed tariffs which might restrict imports, while the railroad financiers protested that under the proposed tariff of 1866 the Erie and the New York Central systems alone would have to pay out annually "about two million dollars by way of protection." [38] The New York Chamber of Commerce had opposed the Morrill bill of 1861 as "a radical change in the tariff policy of the country," but had patriotically refrained from strenuous protests as tariff rates steadily rose during the war.[39] In listing the organization's postwar objectives, however, Secretary John Austin Stevens declared: "The principles of free, unshackled trade, which it has ever upheld, must

---

See Senator Dolliver's comments on this subject, *Cong. Record*, 61 Cong., 1 Sess., 1715 (May 4, 1909). The major reason for passage, however, was the fact that the schedules pleased leading wool growers.

[36] Edward Harris, *The Tariff and How It Effects the Woolen Cloth Manufacture and Wool Growers* (Woonsocket, 1871), 14–15; *Carded Wool Bulletin* (Boston), I (May, 1910), 6; Edward Atkinson, *Reply to the Argument by Mr. John L. Hayes* (Woonsocket, 1872).

[37] Mohat, *Tariff on Wool*, 19; Taussig, *Tariff History*, 316–17.

[38] Statement of Representative Henry J. Raymond of New York, *Cong. Globe*, 39 Cong., 1 Sess., 3516 (June 30, 1866).

[39] *Fourth Annual Report of the Chamber of Commerce of the State of New York* (New York, 1862), 2–3; *Fifth Annual Report of the Chamber of Commerce of the State of New York* (New York, 1863), 4–5. Senator Edwin D. Morgan, a member of the Chamber, voted for tariff increases during the war, then reverted to fighting high schedules in 1866. James A. Rawley, *Edwin D. Morgan, 1811–1883: Merchant in Politics* (New York, 1955), 207–209.

be reaffirmed." [40] A few months after the war's end, the *Commercial and Financial Chronicle* observed: "Signs are not wanting that the subject of Free Trade will be made the text of the next political agitation in this country." The *Journal of Commerce* also began agitating for lower tariffs soon after the war; and the introduction of the first postwar tariff bill, providing for generally increased rates, naturally brought a strong protest from the New York Chamber of Commerce.[41]

Clearly, then, New England cotton manufacturers and many wool and other manufacturers preferred and worked for lower tariff schedules—as did most of New York's financial and mercantile community. This fact was obvious to contemporary protectionists, especially the fervent Pennsylvanians. They recognized the role New Yorkers and New Englanders played in reducing many schedules, and in defeating, by obstructionist tactics, bills of which they disapproved. A delegate from Philadelphia's Board of Trade complained to the National Board of Trade in 1869 that New England's industries had been built up behind tariff walls. "Now they are marked disciples of free trade. . . . They overlook the interests yet in their infancy. . . . Is this right? Is this just?" [42] Henry C. Carey, leading spokesman for Pennsylvania iron, coal, and other protected interests, charged in 1867 that for twenty years, on tariff questions, "It has pleased the representatives of Massachusetts to array themselves on the side of cotton planters, slave owners, railroad monopolists." [43]

---

[40] *Centennial Celebration of the Chamber of Commerce of the State of New York . . . : Report of Proceedings* (New York, 1868), 21; also, *Ninth Annual Report of the Chamber of Commerce of the State of New York* (New York, 1867), Part I, p. 5.

[41] *Commercial and Financial Chronicle* (New York), I (July 8, 1865), 38; New York *Journal of Commerce*, May 23, 1865; *Ninth Annual Report of the Chamber of Commerce of the State of New York*, Part I, pp. 29, 30, 60, 61. The Chamber's protest could not be ignored. The organization's membership included many of the largest campaign contributors to both parties, including, in 1866, such merchants and importers as Moses Grinnell, Alexander T. Stewart, William E. Dodge, Horace Claflin, and Senator Edwin D. Morgan; and such financiers as Henry Clews, Levi P. Morton, John Austin Stevens, Moses Taylor, John J. Cisco, and J. Pierpont Morgan.

[42] *Proceedings of the Second Annual Meeting of the National Board of Trade* (Boston, 1870), 312. For a justification of their low tariff policies, see the comments by New England textile men in *First Annual Meeting of the National Board of Trade* (Boston, 1869), 127–34.

[43] Henry C. Carey, *Reconstruction: Industrial, Financial and Political, Letters to the Hon. Henry Wilson, Senator from Massachusetts* (Philadelphia, 1867), 34. As Carey observed, votes on the complex tariff bills of 1866 and 1867 were not an accurate indication of tariff sentiment. Some additional insight into these bills is provided by Herbert R. Ferleger, *David A. Wells and*

Northeastern businessmen were thus far from united in support of high tariffs after the Civil War. Leading business interests of New England and New York believed that they lost more than they gained from high postwar tariffs. Had reconstruction politics allowed them a choice, it seems likely that these important groups would have preferred a return to the coalition which had produced the low tariff of 1857—a coalition which included the South. *Certainly they would not have opposed the return of southern representatives in order to retain high imposts.*

The business interests of the Northeast were divided into fiercely competing groups not only by the tariff issue, but by currency questions as well. These conflicts were brought into the open shortly after the Civil War by attempts to contract the swollen wartime currency. Secretary of the Treasury Hugh McCulloch's proposals for contraction, designed for quick resumption of specie payments, won a cordial response from many importers and financiers, who would gain materially from the elimination of the premium on gold and a consequent rise in the market value of government bonds.[44] Many businessmen longed for the currency stability they believed resumption would bring. But McCulloch met with warnings and protests from other important northeastern business groups. The Philadelphia Board of Trade immediately warned against hasty action, "lest by injudicious measures and rapid contraction," the people's interests should be sacrificed. A few weeks later, the *Commercial and Financial Chronicle,* a firm advocate of hard money, was forced to admit: "There is little doubt that the depression in public confidence, of which a proof will be found in our account of the week's fluctuation in the Stock Market, is closely connected with the anticipated effects of the contraction movement of the Secretary of the Treasury." [45]

---

the *American Revenue System, 1865–1870* (New York, 1942), 22–168; Williamson, *Atkinson,* 64–71; Taussig, *Tariff History,* 175–77. Carey was especially hurt by what he considered the apostasy of his friend, Revenue Commissioner Wells, who went over to the camp of the low-tariff New Englanders in 1866–1867.

[44] It should be noted that while immediate resumption would have raised the market value of federal bonds, it would also have reduced the value of interest payments, which were made in gold. Important dealers in government bonds, like Henry Clews and Jay Cooke, opposed contraction. Cooke wrote his brother in 1867, "As to getting back to specie payments, the least said about that the better, as it is the premium on gold that enables us to sell the 5-20's." Jay Cooke to Henry D. Cooke, September 20, 1867, Henrietta M. Larson, *Jay Cooke: Private Banker* (Cambridge, 1936), 204, 209–10.

[45] *Thirty-third Annual Report of the Philadelphia Board of Trade* (Philadelphia, 1866), 1. *Commercial and Financial Chronicle,* II (January 13, 1866), 31; *Iron Age* (New York), V (November 7, 1867), 2, 4.

Although only a moderate amount of currency was taken out of circulation, businessmen continued to fear that goods bought at high prices with inflated greenbacks might have to be sold at much lower prices if McCulloch were allowed to proceed with contraction. Wholesale prices fell sharply after January, 1866, confirming their fears.[46] As general price depreciation continued through 1866 and 1867, businessmen's objections to contraction became increasingly loud and widespread. The Commercial Exchange of Philadelphia adopted a resolution in January, 1867, "That premature resumption will prove a curse and not a blessing." A vice-president of the New York Chamber of Commerce, who approved contraction, recalled "living in the midst of the clamor against that process, where almost every man I met was denouncing the Secretary and predicting ruin upon all the interests of the country unless the policy was discontinued." [47]

Opposition to McCulloch's policy spread to Congress, where Representative William D. Kelley of Pennsylvania called it the "road to bankruptcy." [48] Finally, in January, 1868, Senator John Sherman of Ohio introduced legislation to end contraction. "We hear the complaint from all parts of the country," he said, "from all branches of industry . . . that industry for some reason is paralyzed and that trade and enterprise are not so well rewarded as they were. Many, perhaps erroneously, attribute all this to the contraction of the currency." [49]

Passage of Sherman's measure, however, did not end the conflict among northeastern businessmen over currency. Most seem to have favored a stable money supply, and to have opposed currency expansion and quick resumption alike. Many of the more conservative bankers, importers, and merchants, however, continued to support an early return to specie payments. There was also an influential and vocal group of businessmen which persistently called for currency inflation. This last group found adherents among those manufacturers and merchants who sought to take advantage of

[46] Wesley C. Mitchell, *Gold, Prices, and Wages under the Greenback Standard* (Berkeley, 1909), 26; "Review of the Boston Market for the Year 1866," *Thirteenth Annual Report of the Boston Board of Trade* (Boston, 1867), 43. Wholesale prices fell fastest, affecting manufacturers and the larger merchants and importers more than retailers. Both wholesale and retail prices fell faster than wages and farm prices.

[47] *Proceedings of the First Annual Meeting of the National Board of Trade* (Boston, 1869), 114, 173.

[48] "Contraction, the Road to Bankruptcy," reprinted in William D. Kelley, *Speeches, Addresses, and Letters on Industrial and Financial Questions* (Philadelphia, 1872), 210.

[49] *Cong. Globe*, 40 Cong., 2 Sess., 407, 537, 674 (January 9, 15, 22, 1868).

great postwar demand for their products, but who had difficulty obtaining capital for plant and inventory expansion, even at extremely high interest rates. Many of those who borrowed large sums for investments in factories, mines, and railroads, were apt to favor currency expansion, which they believed would lower interest rates, raise prices, and make debts easier to pay. Radical Senator Sprague, for example, in control of a Rhode Island empire of factories, real estate, utilities, and banks, complained to the Senate that "The interest paid by the borrower today is just double what it was at the close of the War." He placed the blame on "the power centralized in New York." [50]

It is significant that Jay Cooke, once an ardent hard money man, became something of an inflationist after he borrowed millions to build the Northern Pacific, and saw his corporation become a huge land speculator through government grants. In a letter to his brother and partner, written in 1868, Cooke called for moderate currency expansion which would keep pace "with the new habits and enlarged area of Country." "Why," he asked, "should this Grand and Glorious Country be stunted and dwarfed—its activities chilled and its very blood curdled by these miserable 'hard coin' theories—the musty theories of a by gone age?" [51]

Pennsylvania iron and steel men, through their representatives and periodicals, led eastern demands for an increased supply of currency. Their industry was expanding rapidly behind high tariff walls, stimulated by the postwar spurt in railroad building. Iron manufacturer Thaddeus Stevens was a leader in congressional schemes to inflate the currency. Both Stevens and Kelley of Pennsylvania supported textile manufacturer Benjamin F. Butler's resolution to pay the wartime bonds in paper rather than gold.[52] Representative Daniel J. Morrell, a bank president as well as former general manager of the giant Cambria Iron Works in Pennsylvania, called for more circulation, and contended that under a program of inflation "Capital would be less valuable, and a larger share of the increase in wealth would go to the enterprise and labor which created it." [53] Pennsylvania iron and steel periodicals took up the fight against the bankers. "In the seaboard cities," said

[50] *Ibid.*, 40 Cong., 1 Sess., 65, 361 (March 15, 30, 1867). Sprague's overextended empire went into bankruptcy in 1873 when his loans were called in. Zechariah Chafee, Jr., "Weathering the Panic of '73," *Dorr Pamphlets* (Providence), No. 4 (1942).

[51] Jay Cooke to Henry D. Cooke, November 23, 1869, Larson, *Jay Cooke*, 205.

[52] *Cong. Globe*, 40 Cong., 2 Sess., 212–13 (December 16, 1867).

[53] *Ibid.*, 41 Cong., 2 Sess., Appendix, 142 (March 10, 1870).

Iron Age in 1867, "the money power seeks to attain a position of irresistible control, and to subdue and subordinate to itself all the interests of industry." [54] The lines of battle were perhaps drawn most succinctly and cogently in a speech by Representative Kelley in January, 1867. "The contest," he said, "is between the creditor and the debtor class—the men of investments and the men of enterprise." [55]

The issue, however, was not as simple as Kelley put it. Most foreign goods were paid for with gold, not greenbacks. Customs duties were also payable in gold. As long as specie payments could be postponed, the premium on gold would remain. In the early postwar years, the premium fluctuated between 30 and 40 per cent. The effect was to raise the cost of foreign goods about one-third above what their cost would be if specie resumption should occur.[56] Monetary inflation would tend to raise the premium and consequently the price of imports even higher. This fact was not lost on the Pennsylvanians. As early as 1863, the Philadelphia Board of Trade noted that the "premium on foreign exchange adds greatly to tariff and transportation costs." [57] In 1864, Samuel J. Reeves, iron manufacturer and chairman of the executive committee of the American Iron and Steel Association, wrote the Commissioner of Internal Revenue: "The constant advance in the price of gold has acted as so much protection to the home manufacturer above the duty.... The iron manufacture now finds its safety only in the high cost of gold; what is to become of it when there will be no premium on gold?" [58] The answer, so far as many iron manufacturers were concerned, was to retain the premium on gold.

The significance of the Pennsylvanians' currency policies was obvious to importers, financiers, and many manufacturers in New York and New England. Most of these favored hard money and low tariffs. The Boston Board of Trade's "Wool Report" for 1863 noted the effect of the gold premium on the price of wool.[59] New

[54] *Iron Age*, V (October 24, 1867), 4; *ibid.* (November 7, 1867), 4; *Industrial Bulletin* (Philadelphia), VIII (November, 1871), 4.
[55] Kelley, *Speeches, Addresses, and Letters*, 226.
[56] See statement of costs of English rails in *Bulletin of the American Iron and Steel Association* (Philadelphia), No. 2 Supplement (February 6, 1867), 186. The Association's figures show the premium to have been a greater share of total cost than was the tariff duty.
[57] *Thirtieth Annual Report of the Philadelphia Board of Trade* (Philadelphia, 1863), 40.
[58] "Extracts from a letter to the Hon. Joseph J. Lewis . . . from Samuel J. Reeves," *Thirty-second Annual Report of the Philadelphia Board of Trade* (Philadelphia, 1865), 76.
[59] Bond and Livermore, *Report on Wool*, 3.

York merchants protested that the high price of gold seriously discouraged imports, and the city's Chamber of Commerce adopted a resolution charging that "Powerful interests are striving to perpetuate the existing depreciation of the currency." [60]

When contraction was abruptly ended and tariff reform failed, in 1867–1868, some businessmen in New York and New England felt that the government's policies were falling under the control of high tariff and paper money men. On the other hand, Henry C. Carey, spokesman for Pennsylvania protectionists, charged that New England, aided by New Yorkers, was attempting to create a monopoly in money and manufacturing. One instrument of the monopolists, said Carey, was a low tariff, which New England manufacturers could afford because of their low interest charges and modern machinery, and which they used to ruin domestic competition and to obtain cheap foreign raw materials to aid New England producers. A second instrument, he continued, was the banking system—"a great money monopoly for the especial benefit of the Trading States." Even with this monopoly, Carey complained, the traders wished to contract the currency, further reducing the pittance allowed Pennsylvania and further raising interest charges manufacturers would have to pay. Either the New Englanders would change their ways, he warned, or they would be compelled to do so by a combination of southern, western, and middle states, in which Pennsylvania would take the lead.[61] In reply, cotton manufacturer Edward Atkinson "rejoiced" at this analysis of New England's advantage, and assured Carey that henceforth the New England representatives would support the low tariff and hard money policies even more strongly. Instead of fearing the threatened combination of sections under Pennsylvania's leadership against those policies, he prophesied that New England would join with the South and the West in promoting them.[62]

[60] *Eighth Annual Report of the Chamber of Commerce of the State of New York* (New York, 1866), Part II, p. 90; *Memorial to the Honorable the Senate and House of Representatives* (New York, 1869), signed by A. A. Low and Samuel Babcock for the New York City Chamber of Commerce; remarks by A. A. Low in *Eighth Annual Report of the New York Chamber of Commerce* (New York, 1866), Part I, p. 28; and *Ninth Annual Report of the New York Chamber of Commerce* (New York, 1867), Part I, pp. 74, 76.

[61] Carey, *Reconstruction*, 4, 8, 21, 24–26, 50, 53–58, 67–68.

[62] Atkinson to Carey, November 11, 1867, Williamson, *Atkinson*, 79–80. For further details of this controversy see Henry Wilson to Carey, September 21, 1867; Carey to Wilson, September 25, 1867; George L. Ward to Carey, October 16, 1867; Carey to Ward, October 18, 1867; David A. Wells to Carey, November 1, 6, 1867; Carey to Atkinson, November 18, 1867, Henry C. Carey Papers, Edward Carey Gardiner Collection (Historical Society of Pennsylvania, Philadelphia).

Both Carey and Atkinson overstated the unity of New England manufacturers, oversimplified the varied and conflicting interests in the West, and conjectured about the probable political and economic alignments of the postwar South. Nevertheless, both were more realistic than historians who have explained northeastern leadership of Radical Reconstruction in terms of a unified northeastern business interest anxious to keep the South out of the Union in order to protect high tariffs and hard money.

Nor can the direction and support which northeastern representatives gave to Radical Reconstruction be accurately explained as an attempt to "make easy the road for northern economic penetration and exploitation of the South." [63] Few important northeastern capitalists had any desire to place their money in a war-torn, unsettled region. Eventually, northerners invested huge sums in southern factories, mines, railroads, and real estate; but it is significant that only a small number did so as long as Radicals controlled southern state legislatures.

Many southern leaders and periodicals recognized the need for northern capital after the Civil War, and numerous cordial invitations were extended.[64] That such invitations were futile was obvious to businessmen, North and South. "We want capital attracted to the South," said the *Commercial and Financial Chronicle* of New York City, "and this cannot be, so long as the States are under semi-military rule." And from the South *De Bow's Review* echoed, "It is idle to ask capital to venture until order is restored." South Carolina exempted manufacturers from all state and local taxation, but failed to attract northern capital partly because of the uncertainties of Reconstruction.[65] Thomas W. Conway, a former Freedmen's Bureau official, who toured the North in 1866 trying to induce businessmen to make southern investments, reported to the New York Chamber of Commerce, which had encouraged his mission: "The substantial men met by me in all parts of the country are sick of the delay in regard to the settlement of our national political difficulties." Until such settlement occurred, he predicted,

---

[63] Hesseltine, *Confederate Leaders in the New South*, 136.

[64] For example, see Petersburg (Va.) *News*, quoted in New York *Journal of Commerce*, May 20, 1865. A number of similar appeals for northern capital are cited in John F. Stover, *The Railroads of the South, 1865–1900: A Study in Finance and Control* (Chapel Hill, 1955), 54–55. See also Broadus Mitchell, *The Rise of Cotton Mills in the South* (Baltimore, 1921), 237.

[65] *Commercial and Financial Chronicle*, II (February 17, 1866), 198; *De Bow's Review* (Nashville), After the War Series, Vol. IV (November, 1867), 451; Francis B. Simkins and Robert H. Woody, *South Carolina during Reconstruction* (Chapel Hill, 1932), 290–91.

there would be continued uncertainty and violence in the South, and poor prospects for northern investment.[66]

Even Pennsylvania's Representative William D. Kelley, who was both a Radical leader and an enthusiastic advocate of northern investments in the postwar South, soon found that Radical Reconstruction interfered with southern industrial growth. In March, 1868, Kelley demanded immediate readmission of Alabama—a potential economic paradise, he said, whose wealth was "paralyzed" while Reconstruction ran its violent course. Thaddeus Stevens, less interested in southern industrial development than was Kelley, fought against his colleague's haste, insisting that Alabama must first guarantee the suffrage rights of Negroes.[67]

New England cotton manufacturers, dealers, and shippers feared that northerners' refusal to send their capital south would result in an insufficient cotton crop. Edward S. Tobey, Boston cotton merchant and manufacturer, recommended that the Freedmen's Bureau be authorized to take over the role of private capital in organizing Negro labor for cotton cultivation. The South's deficiency of capital, Tobey told the Boston Board of Trade in a famous speech in November, 1865, was proved by "frequent applications from Southern men to Northern capitalists to invest in cotton lands at low prices." It would be ideal if private investors could supply this want; but capital, Tobey observed, "is seldom placed by its possessors where society is disorganized and life and property comparatively unprotected by a stable and efficient government." The Board approved Tobey's suggestion.[68]

A few months after Tobey's speech, however, the New Englander's plans were changed by a sudden shift in the cotton market. The southern cotton crop was larger than expected. Furthermore, the English, with new machinery and methods for manufacturing with cheap Indian Surat cotton, had become increasingly less dependent upon American producers. New England manufacturers and dealers were caught with large supplies of cotton as the price dropped almost 40 per cent in the first four months of 1866.[69] The momentary interest New England businessmen had shown in reconstruc-

[66] Thomas W. Conway, "Introduction of Capital and Men into the Southern States of the Union," *Ninth Annual Report of the Chamber of Commerce of the State of New York* (New York, 1867), Part II, pp. 8–13.

[67] *Cong. Globe*, 40 Cong., 2 Sess., 2139–41 (March 26, 1868). For another significant conflict between Kelley and Stevens see *ibid.*, 39 Cong., 1 Sess., 3687–88 (July 9, 1866).

[68] Edward S. Tobey, *The Industry of the South . . . : A Speech Delivered before the Boston Board of Trade, November 27, 1865* (Boston, 1878). See also *Twelfth Annual Report of the Boston Board of Trade* (Boston, 1866), 57.

[69] *Thirteenth Annual Report of the Boston Board of Trade* (Boston, 1867), 47.

tion legislation dropped with the price of cotton. The Boston Board of Trade's "Review of the Boston Market for the Year 1867," declared: "Business men, generally, are loud in their complaints against the course of legislation for two years past. Important interests have been neglected by Congress, and too much time has been wasted on questions which only led to discord and bad feeling in the different branches of the Government." [70]

Most large northern investors, instead of being concerned over the difficulties of investing in the South, turned their attention to the many lucrative opportunities elsewhere—in Minnesota timberlands, Michigan iron and copper mines, Pennsylvania coal and oil, and railroads in almost every state. Significantly, the Pennsylvania Railroad, with abundant capital and great influence in Congress, did not attempt to create its "Southern empire" until Radical Reconstruction was nearing its conclusion. Until 1871, the Pennsylvania preferred to take advantage of investment opportunities in the Northwest. When Thomas A. Scott, who guided the railroad's expansion, decided to move south, he dealt with Conservative governors and legislators in the South as successfully as he had with Democrats and Republicans in the North and West.[71]

Only one important northeastern business group was strongly attracted by investment opportunities in the South immediately after the war: New York financiers, the true "masters of capital," who had long-standing commercial ties with the South, and had sufficient funds to risk large amounts in a turbulent area. New York merchants, shippers, and financiers were as interested as Bostonians in large postwar cotton crops, but they emphatically disagreed with the Boston proposal to use the Freedmen's Bureau to grow cotton. When Tobey's plan was put before the executive committee of the New York Chamber of Commerce, the committee reported: "Our best reliance for attaining the desired end is to present to capitalists this most inviting field." [72]

[70] *Fourteenth Annual Report of the Boston Board of Trade* (Boston, 1868), 122. For further evidence of the New Englander's rapid change of heart, see Williamson, *Atkinson*, 59–61, and *Boston Board of Trade, Report of a Committee upon the Cotton Tax* (Boston, 1867).

[71] Stover, *Railroads of the South*, 99–121. According to Stover, "While many southerners in the postwar years eagerly sought northern capital for their stricken railways, their entreaties up to 1870 had rarely resulted in more than visits of railroad carpetbaggers." John F. Stover, "The Pennsylvania Railroad's Southern Rail Empire," *Pennsylvania Magazine of History and Biography* (Philadelphia), LXXXI (January, 1957), 28.

[72] *Eighth Annual Report of the Chamber of Commerce of the State of New York* (New York, 1866), Part I, p. 70. One of the few influential New Englanders interested in "exploiting" the South was former abolitionist, Governor John A. Andrew of Massachusetts. His small American Land Company and Agency was forced out of business in 1866. Andrew was not sympathetic to

In so far as northern capital was invested in southern railroads, both before and immediately after the war, most of it was provided by New Yorkers. A recent study shows, for example, that of some 280 directors of twenty-five major southern lines in 1867–1868 only eleven were northerners, and ten of these were from New York.[73] Two important New York investors in southern railroads were elected to Congress and were thus in a position to speak publicly about reconstruction legislation. One of the two was William E. Dodge, metal importer, iron manufacturer, land speculator, railroad investor, and president of the New York Chamber of Commerce; the other was William W. Phelps, director of four large banks and eight railroads.[74] The evidence suggests that the opinions these men expressed of Radical Reconstruction were typical of those held by New York's financial leaders.

When Thaddeus Stevens' bill for dividing the South into military districts reached the floor of the House in January, 1867, Dodge voted against it; and in explaining his vote he told his Republican colleagues: "I claim to be as loyal as any other man ... [but] if these southern states are still to be kept year after year in this state of disquietude we at the North, sympathizing with them in our social and business relations, must to a certain extent suffer with them." Furthermore, said Dodge, businessmen believed that this bill would result in continued high taxation to support an army of occupation in ten states.[75] And in the debate on Butler's civil rights bill in 1875, Phelps—one of three Republicans to vote against it in the House—expressed sentiments long held in the New York financial community. "You are trying to do," he said, "what seems to me this House everlastingly tries in one form or another to do—to legislate against human nature. You are trying to legislate against human prejudice, and you cannot do it. . . . Let us end this cruel policy." [76]

---

the Radicals' program, and favored turning southern state governments over to the old leaders of southern society—businessmen, politicians, former Confederate officers. Henry G. Pearson, *The Life of John A. Andrew* (2 vols., Boston, 1904), II, 267, 270, 273.

[73] Stover, *Railroads of the South*, 38.

[74] For one example of southern railroad investments by Dodge and Phelps see Hugh M. Herrick (comp.), *William Walter Phelps: His Life and Public Service* (New York, 1904), 31–32. The other two men who took part in this investment were Moses Taylor, president of the National City Bank, and John J. Cisco, investment banker and treasurer of Credit Mobilier. Both Taylor and Cisco also opposed Radical Reconstruction.

[75] *Cong. Globe*, 39 Cong., 2 Sess., 627–29 (January 21, 1867).

[76] *Ibid.*, 43 Cong., 2 Sess., 1002 (February 4, 1875). For similar earlier statements see *Commercial and Financial Chronicle*, I (August 26, 1865), 260; New York *Journal of Commerce*, May 25, 1865.

Many New York financiers made public their support of President Andrew Johnson in his battle against the Radicals. When Johnson vetoed the bill for the continuation of the Freedmen's Bureau, in Feburary, 1866, a mass meeting to celebrate the veto was arranged by the city's business leaders, and a committee was sent to Washington to offer the President New York's aid. Among those on the committee were Moses Taylor, dean of New York bankers, and William B. Astor, known as the "landlord of New York." [77] Six months later, when Johnson visited New York as part of his "swing around the circle," a grand dinner was given for him at Delmonico's. Chairman of arrangements was Alexander T. Stewart, the "dry goods king"; treasurer for the dinner was Henry Clews, probably second only to Jay Cooke as a dealer in government bonds, and second to none as a dealer in southern railroad securities. A large number of New York's leading businessmen attended the dinner.[78] This was followed on September 17, 1866, by a giant National Union celebration to demonstrate the city's support of the President at the height of his crucial campaign against the Radicals. The reception committee for this impressive meeting included Stewart, Taylor, Clews, Edwards, Pierrepont, and August Belmont. Among those who gave public notice of their approval of Johnson's policies by allowing their names to be listed as vice-presidents of the meeting were such well-known financiers as William H. Aspinwall, Cornelius Vanderbilt, John J. Cisco, and Henry Grinnell, as well as numerous important merchants and manufacturers.[79]

[77] New York *Morning Herald*, February 23, 1866. Among the organizers of the meeting were Dodge; banker and brokerage house president George Opdyke; Dodge's predecessor as Chamber of Commerce president, A. A. Low; and financier and merchant Moses Grinnell. See also George Fort Milton, *The Age of Hate: Andrew Johnson and the Radicals* (New York, 1930), 289–96.

[78] *Dinner to the President of the United States in Honor of His Visit to the City of New York, August 29, 1866*, printed program in Samuel J. Tilden Papers (New York Public Library); also Henry Clews to Samuel J. Tilden, September 6, 1866, Tilden Papers. In Philadelphia, banker Anthony J. Drexel met with other leading businessmen in the Merchant's Exchange and planned Johnson's welcome to the city. Philadelphia *Age*, August 28, 1866. For evidence of Jay Cooke's disgust with Radical Reconstruction, see Ellis P. Oberholtzer, *Jay Cooke: Financier of the Civil War* (2 vols., Philadelphia, 1907), II, 22.

[79] *National Union Celebration at Union Square, September 17, 1866* (New York, 1866). After the 1866 election, when it was apparent that Johnson could not be reelected in 1868, these men began to switch their support to Grant, who was known to be safe and sound on the currency, and who seemed most likely to bring peace to the South. Many northern businessmen were antagonized by Johnson's undignified campaign. New York *Tribune*, December 5, 1867.

Similar indications of support or approval of the presidential reconstruction program rather than that of Congress also came from the New York Chamber of Commerce and from the financial press. In 1866 the Chamber of Commerce adopted a resolution, introduced by the banker brother of Radical leader Roscoe Conkling, which expressed the hope that Reconstruction "may be everywhere signalized by magnanimity and clemency and that it may nowhere be stained by a single act which will be condemned as needlessly harsh or revengeful." A copy of this resolution was sent to Washington as encouragement to the President.[80] As early as July, 1865, *Hunt's Merchants Magazine* and the *Commercial and Financial Chronicle*—two of the leading business journals of the period—had applauded Johnson's program for the speedy restoration of the seceded states. As the Radicals gathered their forces in the fall of 1865, the *American Railroad Journal* announced that Reconstruction "is going on as well as could be hoped. The President ... sets the example of kindness and benignity and a large majority of both parties ... are evidently disposed to support his policy." And in January, 1866, the *Journal of Commerce* proclaimed its support of Johnson.[81]

From evidence such as this, the reconstruction program of the Radicals cannot be explained as an organized attempt by the business interests of the Northeast either to preserve and promote their own economic advantages or to obtain protection for economic exploitation of the South. Actually, northeastern businessmen had no unified economic program to promote. Important business groups within the region opposed each other on almost every significant economic question, and this lack of a common interest was likewise reflected in the economic views of Radical congressmen. Thaddeus

---

[80] *Eighth Annual Report of the Chamber of Commerce of the State of New York* (New York, 1866), Part I, p. 4.

[81] *Hunt's Merchants Magazine and Commercial Review* (New York), LIII (July, 1865), 28–30, 43; *Commercial and Financial Chronicle*, I (July 1, 1865), 3, 5; (July 29, 1865), 133; *American Railroad Journal* (New York), XXXIII (October 7, 1865), 949; New York *Journal of Commerce*, January 9, 1866.

Although lack of space necessitated the omission from this article of discussions of government bonds and national banks, the antagonism to Radical Reconstruction of the great financiers, their organizations and periodicals, is perhaps the best evidence of the remote relationship between these financial issues and congressional reconstruction policies. For the negative attitude of the New York bankers toward the national banking system, both during the Civil War, see Fritz Redlich, *The Molding of American Banking: Men and Ideas* (2 vols., New York, 1951), II, 105, 106, 108, 121, 140–46; Larson, *Jay Cooke*, 140–42.

Stevens, for example, dominant Radical leader in the House, was a fervent protectionist and a proponent of paper money inflation; Charles Sumner, Senate Radical leader, spoke and voted for lower tariff schedules and for resumption of specie payments. With both the businessmen and the legislators thus divided on economic issues, and with the New York merchants and financiers—who were in a position to gain most from economic exploitation of the South—definitely critical of the Radicals' program, it seems clear that factors other than the economic interests of the Northeast must be used to explain the motivation and aims of Radical Reconstruction.

14

FOR the past quarter century historians of the South have been steadily—and, by now, devastatingly—chipping away at the monolithic conception of Reconstruction in the South. (The process has a much longer lineage among Negro historians, but it was not until white historians began to join them in the 1940s that the revisionist view gained a hearing within the profession. A. A. Taylor's studies of Reconstruction in South Carolina [Washington, 1924] and in Virginia [Washington, 1926], and W. E. B. DuBois's *Black Reconstruction* [New York, 1935] were pathbreaking works by Negro scholars.) Today the view that Reconstruction was unrelieved suppression of whites and a riotous bacchanalia for Negroes has been discarded. In its place there has emerged a much more complex picture of a society undergoing social revolution as a new order struggled to life over the ruins of defeat. One measure of the widespread acceptance of the new approach is that in 1960 the Southern Historical Association awarded its prize for the best article published in its journal during 1959 to Bernard Weisberger's "The Dark and Bloody Ground of Reconstruction Historiography" *Journal of Southern History*, XXV (November 1959), 427–447. Weisberger's article, which is already somewhat out-of-date because of the rapidity with which this area of study is growing, is undoubtedly the best critical introduction to the literature on Reconstruction. More than that, it is itself a devastating attack on the old view of Reconstruction.

David Donald's article is one of the first to upset the stereotype of Reconstruction by a re-examination of the relevant evidence. (An earlier study, Francis B. Simkins and Robert Woody, *South Carolina During Reconstruction* [Chapel Hill, 1932], probably deserves the palm for priority among both articles and books.) Donald's article, to be sure, re-examines only a single facet of the Reconstruction story, but it is an important one, for the role of the southern white man is crucial in the myth of Reconstruction, as Donald points out in the opening paragraphs of his article.

Since Donald's article appeared, there has been little reason to change its fundamental conclusions. In only one respect can his article be described as "dated." Writing in 1940, probably under the influence of Howard K. Beale's seminal book *The Critical Year* (New York, 1930), he emphasized the *economic* attitudes of the old Whigs. Today the Unionist sentiment of Whigs would almost certainly have been added in listing their motives for opposing Democrats and finding the Republican party congenial. A work that thoroughly documents the devotion to the Union of thousands of large planters, most of whom were old Whigs, is Frank W. Klingberg's *The Southern Claims Commission* (Berkeley, 1955). Indeed, since Donald's article appeared, a whole minor literature has sprung up that emphasizes the persistence of Whig attitudes into the Reconstruction period. Notable in this connection is C. Vann Woodward's *Reunion and Reaction* (Boston, 1951) on the Compromise of 1877, and Thomas B. Alexander's articles "Whiggery and Reconstruction in Tennessee," *Journal of Southern History*, XVI (August 1950), 291–305, and "Persistent Whiggery in Alabama and the Lower South, 1860–67," *Alabama Review*, XII (January 1959), 35–52.

There is little reason to doubt Donald's conclusion that by 1875 the overwhelming majority of white men in Mississippi, including the old Whigs, were voting the Democratic ticket. His further conclusion, though, that the upsurge in Democratic votes derived from the accession of old Whigs cannot be so easily accepted. For one thing, by his own figures there were never enough whites within the Republican party in Mississippi to account for the enormous growth recorded in 1875. He sees a maximum of twenty thousand white Republicans in 1873, while the increase in Democrats cited in his footnote 74 is of the order of fifty thousand. The real source of Democratic increase in voters seems rather to be the result of the excitement and enthusiasm aroused in favor of finally overthrowing radical rule. This agitation brought out Democrats who had not bothered to vote before. The same source was also tapped successfully in other states, like South Carolina in 1876, where, as in Mississippi, Negroes were a majority of the population. In his recent revision of James G. Randall's standard textbook *Civil War*

and Reconstruction (*Boston*, 1961) Donald has abandoned his belief that the changeover of the Whigs to the Democrats accounts for
the Democratic victory in Mississippi in 1875. On p. 684 of that
book, in describing the "Mississippi Plan," he writes: "One part
of the scheme had to do with arousing enthusiasm among the Democratic masses and with coercing the few remaining scalawags into
leaving the Republican party. Its principal purpose, however, was
to intimidate the Negroes." But his portrayal of the scalawag as
often being an old Whig—with intelligence, responsibility, and a
respectable past—has stood the test of time.

In a sense, though, Donald's article can be misleading if one
generalizes from the example of Mississippi to the whole South.
To speak of "old Whigs" is to lump under one political rubric two
quite different social groups. It is true, as Donald has shown for
Mississippi, that the Whigs of the deep southern states (Alabama,
Louisiana, and to some extent Georgia, in addition to Mississippi)
were often large planters. But in states like Tennessee and North
Carolina, which also returned heavy Whig votes in the ante-bellum
years, the social character of the Whig party was quite different.
There its leaders and membership were often small farmers. Thus
in these states the persistence of Whiggery brought into the new
Republican party not great and respected planters but small farmers,
who were often not even slaveholders and rarely large ones. Yet
as Thomas B. Alexander in *Political Reconstruction in Tennessee*
(Nashville, 1950) shows, these men, too, were frequently men of
ability rather than disreputable incompetents.

Recently Donald's portrayal of the substantial planters as important participants in the southern Republican party during Reconstruction has come under criticism. Allen William Trelease in
an elaborate and imaginative statistical analysis, "Who Were the
Scalawags?," *Journal of Southern History*, XXIX (November
1963), 445–468, has argued that the great majority of native
white southern Republicans were small farmers. His analysis, though,
rather than proving his contention, actually does no more than substantiate the well-known point that the western counties of North
Carolina and the eastern counties of Tennessee, where slavery had
been weakly established, were important centers of Republican
voting during Reconstruction. For as David Donald correctly points
out in a criticism of Trelease's analysis, *Journal of Southern History*, XXX (May 1964), 253–256, the method used is so conceived
that it can *only* reveal substantial numbers of Republicans in areas
in which Negroes were few in number. Hence it cannot tell us any-

thing about the strength of white Republicanism in the so-called "black counties," that is, where the kind of old Whigs that Donald writes about in Mississippi would be expected to be found.

David Donald is Henry C. Black Professor of American History at The Johns Hopkins University.

The Scalawags in Mississippi Reconstruction

BY DAVID H. DONALD

T HE scalawag is the forgotten man of Reconstruction history. In spite of the excellent work of recent revisionists,[1] the old stereotypes as to the political course of Reconstruction in the South have remained largely undisturbed. On the one hand, it is said, were the Democrats, the vast majority of the white population, battling valiantly for the creed of the Old South, and on the other the Republicans, black in morals as in skin. The Republican party, so the story goes, consisted of the great body of uneducated Negroes, dominated by carpetbaggers from the North or—worst of all—by a few renegade Southerners [2] opprobriously termed scalawags. These were, it is usually considered, the very lowest dregs of mankind; they were "southern white men . . . [who] sold themselves for office";[3] they were the veritable Esaus of the Caucasian race.[4]

SOURCE: David H. Donald, "The Scalawag in Mississippi Reconstruction," *Journal of Southern History*, X (November 1944), 447–60. Copyright 1944, by the Southern Historical Association. Reprinted by permission of the Managing Editor.

[1] For an excellent summary of these new points of view, see Howard K. Beale, "On Rewriting Reconstruction History," in *American Historical Review* (New York, 1895–), XLV (1940), 807–27.

[2] An illustration of this idea in college textbooks may be found in Samuel E. Morison and Henry S. Commager, *Growth of the American Republic*, 2 vols. (New York, 1942), II, 46. For other secondary accounts conveying the same ideas, see James Ford Rhodes, *History of the United States from the Compromise of 1850*, 7 vols. (New York, 1892–1906), VI, 91; Walter L. Fleming, *The Sequel of Appomattox* (New Haven, 1919), 153; E. Merton Coulter, *A Short History of Georgia* (Chapel Hill, 1933), 347; Claude G. Bowers, *The Tragic Era* (Cambridge, 1929), 199; and many others.

[3] *Senate Reports*, 44 Cong., 1 Sess., No. 527 (2 vols.), II, 1071.

[4] John S. McNeilly, "War and Reconstruction in Mississippi, 1863–1890," in *Mississippi Historical Society Publications* (Oxford-Jackson, 1898–1925), Centenary Series, II (1918), 425–26.

A fresh study of the Reconstruction era in Mississippi, however, casts some doubt on the conventional interpretation of the scalawag's role in that troubled time. Republicans ruled Mississippi for five years after its readmission in 1870, and during this period one-third of the congressmen, one of the governors, two of the three supreme court justices, and about one-third of both houses of the state legislature were southern-born white Republicans.[5] Further analysis shows that almost every one of these officeholders had before the war been an old-line Whig and a bitter opponent of the Democrats.[6]

Surprisingly little attention has been paid to the postwar attitudes of southern Whig leaders. That party, after all, had been numerous. In 1852 its candidate in Mississippi had defeated no less a person than Jefferson Davis for the United States Senate. As Unionists the Whigs had cast a respectable vote for John Bell in 1860.[7] And, as late as 1863, they had secured a majority in the Mississippi legislature, selected a Whig for Confederate senator, and elected a former Whig as governor.[8] They were the wealthiest and best educated element in the state.

It has generally been assumed that after the war southern Whigs immediately joined with the Democrats to combat carpetbag and Negro rule. Actually this was far from the case. Some few Whig leaders did from the beginning urge the disbanding of the old party in favor of such an alignment,[9] but their efforts came at a time when the Democratic party itself was virtually defunct, and when influential southern newspapers were urging a dissolution of that party.[10] But Whigs were not attracted by the Democratic policies or leadership anyway. "[W]ould it not be absurd," questioned one, "for Whigs to abandon their high conservative position, and aid in the

[5] For example, of the 83 attending members of the state constitutional convention of 1868, 48 were southern-born white Republicans or "conservatives." James W. Garner, *Reconstruction in Mississippi* (New York, 1901), 187–88. Of Mississippi's 22 representatives in Congress during the period, 8 were southern white Republicans. On the supreme court justices, see Dunbar Rowland, *Courts, Judges, and Lawyers of Mississippi, 1798–1935* (Jackson, 1935), 97–99.

[6] This is certainly true of all the congressmen, of Governor James L. Alcorn, and of Chief Justice Ephraim G. Peyton. There is some uncertainty as to Justice Horatio F. Simrall's political affiliations before the war.

[7] Percy L. Rainwater, *Mississippi: Storm Center of Secession, 1856–1861* (Baton Rouge, 1938), 18–19, 199.

[8] John K. Bettersworth, *Confederate Mississippi* (Baton Rouge, 1943), 52–53.

[9] Raymond (Miss.) *Hinds County Gazette*, October 12, 26, 1870.

[10] Columbus *Index*, quoted in *ibid.*, November 27, 1872. See the letter of Albert G. Brown in Raymond *Hinds County Gazette*, April 10, 1872, and James B. Ranck, *Albert Gallatin Brown: Radical Southern Nationalist* (New York, 1937), 252ff.

reorganization of the Democratic party?"[11] Much of the prewar bitterness between parties still remained, and the editor of one of the best papers in the state asserted: "Men who think that 'the war' knocked all of the old Whig spirit out of the Whigs are just ... fatally mistaken." [12]

Throughout the Reconstruction period, therefore, there were efforts to reorganize the party. Again and again Whig leaders called on the Democrats to abandon their party and join other moderates in battling both Radical Republicans and radical secessionists.[13] A general "Consultation" was held in 1870 so that Whig leaders over the state could agree on policies. The action of this group, termed by hostile Democrats "the grandest fizzle of the age," [14] reflects the difficulties in the way of a third party in the South. Finding too much resentment connected with all the old party names, these men decided that a union of conservatives should be formed, "composed of Whigs, Democrats [and] Republicans," [15] but as a commentator noted, the new party was to be "upon a Whig basis." [16] No very tangible results were to come from such efforts to revive the Whig party. The appeal was, after all, to a limited class of conservative planters and businessmen, and popular feeling was too strong for most Southerners to repudiate Democracy.

Many Whigs had realized these difficulties from the beginning and had joined the Republicans. Within two years after readmission to the Union they were joined by most of their party. Although any statistics for this difficult period must be regarded skeptically, it has been estimated that from twenty-five to thirty per cent of the Mississippi white voters had by 1873 joined the Republican party,[17] and nearly all of these were former Whigs.[18] Such action is not

---

[11] Raymond *Hinds County Gazette*, October 19, 1870.

[12] *Ibid.*, October 5, 1870. The editor was Major George W. Harper, who had been very prominent before the war as a Whig, and whose paper was now one of the most influential in the state.

[13] See, for example, the Boonville *Recorder*, quoted in Raymond *Hinds County Gazette*, October 5, 1870.

[14] Vicksburg *Herald*, quoted in Raymond *Hinds County Gazette*, December 7, 1870.

[15] Raymond *Hinds County Gazette*, November 30, 1870.

[16] *Ibid.*, October 26, 1870.

[17] John R. Lynch, *The Facts of Reconstruction* (New York, 1913), 106. Lynch, a Negro, was speaker of the state house of representatives. For another, similar estimate, see Vernon L. Wharton, "The Negro in Mississippi, 1865–1890" (Ph.D. dissertation, University of North Carolina, 1939), 285, who believes that the Republican party "included at times from fifteen to twenty thousand of the seventy to eighty thousand white votes."

[18] W. H. Braden, "Reconstruction in Lee County," in *Mississippi Historical Society Publications*, X (1909), 139; *Senate Miscellaneous Documents*, 44 Cong., 2 Sess., No. 45, p. 746.

hard to understand. The Whigs were wealthy men—the large planters and the railroad and industrial promoters—who naturally turned to the party which in the state as in the nation was dominated by business interests.

A glance at the leadership of the scalawag element in Mississippi confirms these generalizations. Most important of all was James Lusk Alcorn, elected first governor of the reconstructed state in 1869 and later chosen United States senator. One of the wealthiest plantation owners in the rich Mississippi delta, a large slaveholder, and a Whig opposed to secession, he had reluctantly gone with his state in 1861 and had served briefly in the Confederate army. After the war he was one of the first to admit that secession had been wrong, indeed, treasonable.[19] Now a Republican leader, his program was basically a simple one: "I propose," he declared, "to vote with ... [the Negro]; to discuss political affairs with him; to sit, if necessary, in political counsel with him." [20] By recognizing the legal equality of the Negroes, Alcorn hoped to gain their political support for his own policies.

Alcorn's legislative program shows plainly the direction in which the Whig element hoped to lead the Republican party. First of all, the Negroes had to be conciliated by the adoption of civil rights measures.[22] On economic questions the governor naturally favored the planter class, urging the rebuilding of levees, reduction of land taxes, leasing of convicts to secure a steady labor supply,[23] and state aid in the reconstruction of railroads.[24] The powers of the state government were to be expanded in order to exercise close control over county finances. It was, of course, a program of class legislation, but it was not corrupt. The administration was both intelligent and honest, and it has not been found that any of Alcorn's followers misused their state offices for personal profit.[25] There

[19] Garner, *Reconstruction in Mississippi*, 180. For a biographical sketch of Alcorn, see Dunbar Rowland (ed.), *Encyclopedia of Mississippi History*, 2 vols. (Madison, Wis., 1907), I, 62–71.
[20] Wharton, "The Negro in Mississippi," 258.
[21] "His plan" a close personal friend testified, was "to unite the old whigs . . . and through them control the negro." Frank A. Montgomery, *Reminiscences of a Mississippian in Peace and War* (Cincinnati, 1901), 275.
[22] Garner, *Reconstruction in Mississippi*, 285–86.
[23] Wharton, "The Negro in Mississippi," 435–52, gives a study of the convict leasing arrangements.
[24] Garner, *Reconstruction in Mississippi*, 288–89.
[25] *Ibid.*, 322–23. Professor Garner noted that "The only large case of embezzlement among the state officers during the post-bellum period was that of the Democratic state treasurer in 1866. The amount of the shortage was $61,962."

is much to be said for their program of guaranteeing civil rights, improving schools, and expanding the judiciary.

The Alcorn-Whig program was not to be carried through to completion. It met with difficulties on all sides. The Democrats, of course, objected violently, partly from politics, partly from principle. It was believed that the economic policies of the Alcorn administration tended to discriminate against the predominantly Democratic hill regions in favor of the Whiggish delta bottoms. The rallying point of the Democrats was opposition to Alcorn's plan of granting the Negro legal equality. A prominent Mississippi newspaper, doubtless voicing the sentiments of its readers, felt that "Nigger voting, holding office and sitting in the jury box are all wrong, and against the sentiment of the country." [26] For recognizing Negro rights Alcorn became known as "an open and avowed enemy of his race." [27] It was asserted that "the name of Benedict Arnold ought to occupy a more exalted and honorable . . . position in the annals of american history than that of J. L. Alcorn." [28] A Democrat had rather be called a horse thief than a scalawag.[29]

Carpetbaggers were also bitter against Alcorn and the southern Republicans. One Northerner declared that the governor was "an old whig and in some of his appointment he has put in his style of whig d—m rebels . . . and . . . he is fixing up a party of his own (whig) and using the negro for a blind." [30] The basic trouble was that, though he might advocate legal equality and civil rights as a measure of expediency, the southern planter could not bring himself to accede to the Negro's demand for social equality.[31] Many of the carpetbaggers had come to the South with preconceived and doctrinaire ideas concerning race relations in their adopted section and felt that the Negro's rights were not secure. More, perhaps, were disgruntled when well paid offices were filled by men of southern birth. These factors, intensified by Alcorn's known dislike of Northerners,[32] caused an early break between the Whig and carpetbag factions of the Republican party. When the governor

[26] Columbus *Democrat*, quoted in Wharton, "The Negro in Mississippi," 334.
[27] McNeilly, "War and Reconstruction in Mississippi," in *loc. cit.*, 424.
[28] Eldridge McArthur to James L. Alcorn, April 21, 1871, James L. Alcorn MSS. (Mississippi Department of Archives and History, Jackson).
[29] Vicksburg *Herald*, quoted in Raymond *Hinds County Gazette*, May 8, 1872.
[30] Beatty to Shill, June 21, 1870, Alcorn MSS. This is a copy, in which the given names and initials of both men have been omitted, and it has not been possible to identify them further.
[31] Wharton, "The Negro in Mississippi," 319.
[32] *House Reports*, 42 Cong., 2 Sess., No. 22, p. 450. Note, however, that Alcorn himself was born in the North.

failed to call in federal troops after a minor disturbance in 1871, a Radical Republican charged that he was trying to gain "power and favor from the democracy at the price of . . . the blood of his friends." [33] After two years of rule by Alcorn, another was convinced that "old line whigs are worse men to-day than any whipped (in the war) Democrats." [34]

The Negroes, too, were dissatisfied with the Alcorn regime. Increasingly conscious of the importance of their votes, they demanded a share of the offices proportional to their numerical strength. The freedmen cared little about the Whigs' economic policies, but they distrusted their former owners and, prompted by the carpetbag leaders, were inclined to demand social and civil equality. [35]

The opposition of any one of these elements would have been formidable, and the chances for men of Alcorn's views to succeed were from the start very slight. But—contrary to the version of the Democratic state historians—these three groups worked closely together to bring about Alcorn's defeat. As early as 1871 the Democrats approached the carpetbag group for a political alliance. [36] This alignment was strikingly revealed the following year when Democrats and Radical Republicans joined forces to prevent a Whig paper from securing the lucrative state printing contract. [37] Hoping to break the governor's control of the colored vote, the Democrats encouraged the political aspirations of the Negroes, [38] while carpetbaggers were more successful in organizing the blacks into Union Leagues.

The real test of the Whig program occurred in 1873, when Alcorn —who had resigned to take a seat in the United States Senate, leaving a faithful disciple in his place at Jackson—decided to run again for governor. His opponent for the Republican nomination was Adelbert Ames, a carpetbagger born in Maine and a son-in-law of Benjamin F. Butler of Massachusetts. Ames—variously characterized by the Democrats as "Addle-pate" Ames or "onion headed" Ames [39] —was a man of real ability and had a sincere belief in his duty to protect Negro rights, which he felt Alcorn was neglecting. [40] When the carpetbagger secured the Republican nomination, Alcorn bolted

---

[33] Garner, *Reconstruction in Mississippi*, 291, note 4.
[34] Jackson *Pilot*, quoted in Raymond *Hinds County Gazette*, August 23, 1871.
[35] Garner, *Reconstruction in Mississippi*, 293.
[36] *Senate Reports*, 44 Cong., 1 Sess., 527, I, 21.
[37] Raymond *Hinds County Gazette*, February 7, 21, 28, April 24, May 1, 1872.
[38] Charles Nordhoff, *The Cotton States in the Spring and Summer of 1875* (New York, 1876), 76.
[39] Hazelhurst *Mississippi Democrat*, September 1, 1875.
[40] Garner, *Reconstruction in Mississippi*, 290.

and formed a new party of his own, composed almost entirely of former Whigs.[41] Though this group had the nominal endorsement of the Democrats,[42] many Democratic leaders voted for the carpetbagger rather than for the delta planter.[43] Ames was elected by a huge majority.[44] While conservative papers blamed Alcorn's defeat on the indifference of the Democrats, it might also be attributed to the growing realization by the Negro of his political power.

This election of 1873 marked the end of a period. Former Whigs had joined and then dominated the Republican party in Mississippi. They had sponsored a legislative program that would attract to their party sound and conservative men regardless of former political affiliation. Now, repudiated by the Negro and carpetbag sections of the Republican party and rejected by the more fanatical element of the Democrats, they were thoroughly defeated. They had no choice but to make their way slowly and reluctantly over to the Democratic camp.

The exciting next two years are the best known portion of the state's Reconstruction story. The account of the final restoration of "home rule" in Mississippi has been told many times by historians attracted by the drama of the carpetbag debacle. It was a time when party feelings ran high and when race relations were at a critical point. Old residents of the state still recall vividly the tension and excitement of these years. Mississippi was torn between two hostile political camps, and there was no longer a place for middle-of-the-road, Whig policies.

Beginning in 1874 the Democrats made definite plans to carry the elections of the following year, by persuasion if possible, by force if necessary. This is the entire content of the Mississippi Plan of 1875.[45] Objecting on many grounds to the corruption and excesses of the Radicals, they made the drawing of a color-line the central theme of their campaign—the universal opposition of all white men to any Negro participation in politics.[46] In order to secure the goal of white supremacy—meaning, of course, a Democratic victory— it was necessary first to rally all Democrats to the party standard, then to persuade the scalawags to vote on the color-line, to harry

[41] McNeilly, "War and Reconstruction in Mississippi," in *loc. cit.*, 462–63.

[42] Lynch, *The Facts of Reconstruction*, 76.

[43] McNeilly, "War and Reconstruction in Mississippi," in *loc. cit.*, 466. Among these was a future governor of the state, John M. Stone.

[44] *Appleton's American Annual Cyclopedia* (New York, 1862–1903), XIII (1873), 515. Ames received 74,307 votes; Alcorn, 52,904.

[45] Frederic Bancroft, *A Sketch of the Negro in Politics* . . . (New York, 1885), 61.

[46] A good statement of the color-line creed can be found in *House Reports*, 43 Cong., 2 Sess., No. 263, p. iii.

carpetbaggers out of the state, and to frighten the Negroes from the polls.

At the same time the Republican party was becoming a well-oiled political machine. Under the shrewd carpetbag leadership the Negroes were herded into the notorious Union Leagues and voted in droves as their leaders dictated. Both state and federal patronage were used to bolster a weakening regime. To an increasing extent the Republican party stressed the necessity for social and civil equality for its black members. And to an increasing extent southern-born white leaders were discarded for carpetbaggers or Negroes.

In this crisis Mississippi Whigs had to choose between open support of color-line policies and a program which they firmly believed would lead to racial amalgamation. While to some it was Hobson's choice, there could never have been any doubt as to the course the majority would eventually take. As men of wealth and property they were indignant over extravagances of the carpetbag government, which were reflected in high taxes; they disliked the Northerners as aliens and resented their control over the Negroes; they were alarmed by the facility with which federal troops could be called in whenever the Republicans seemed about to lose an election. But is was the Negro that was the deciding factor. For the southern planter who had never been able to accept ideas of racial equality, the present political power and organization of the colored vote, accompanied by Radical proscription of conservative white leaders, made opposition to the Republicans inescapable.

Under these pressures the former Whigs gradually drifted into an alliance with their Democratic foes of previous years. Even former Governor Alcorn participated in color-line meetings in his county, and he publicly declared that he was not and really never had been a "negro Republican." [47] On the few recalcitrants tremendous social and economic pressure was exerted. Democratic papers carried conspicuously the names of white Republicans who must no longer be spoken to on the street and whose attentions must be scorned by "every true woman." [48] The scalawag who persisted in his obduracy was publicly labeled "a beast in man's clothing" or "a traitor to his country." [49] Those who failed to renounce their Republican affiliations faced ostracism.[50] "No white man," a former

[47] Wharton, "The Negro in Mississippi," 333; Peter J. Hamilton, *Reconstruction* (*The History of North America*, edited by Guy Carleton Lee, XVI, Philadelphia, 1905), 549.
[48] Canton *Mail*, quoted in Wharton, "The Negro in Mississippi," 336.
[49] *Senate Miscellaneous Documents*, 44 Cong., 2 Sess., No. 54, p. 648.
[50] Nordhoff, *The Cotton States*, 81.

Republican wrote, "can live in the South in the future and act with any other than the Democratic party." [51]

Heartened by Whig support, the Democrats waged a lively campaign. There were political demonstrations in every town: parades two miles long,[52] fireworks and Confederate cannon,[53] floats and transparencies of spectacular size,[54] barbecues, picnics, and interminable speeches.[55] Half the villages in the state claimed the local rally as "The Grandest Affair of the Campaign." [56] The more martial elements, donning the red-shirt badge of southern manhood, formed armed rifle companies and drilled and marched in public. These were no secret Ku Kluxers; they wanted the Negro and his friends to know that the entire white population of Mississippi was against continuance of Republican rule.[57]

Most of the color-liners were convinced that efforts to win the colored votes would fail, and it was felt that the best policy was to keep the Negroes from the polls. Republican meetings were disturbed by red-shirt horsemen who remarked loudly that "maybe they might kill a buck that day." [58] When Confederate cannon were fired in the immediate vicinity of Negro rallies, the terrified freedmen believed the war had begun again.[59] There were countless tales of torchlight processions, of disrupted Republican rallies, of nocturnal raids, of whippings, and worse.[60] Whenever the Negroes tried to retaliate, there occurred a race riot. At least a dozen of these conflicts happened during the campaign, and in every case the result was the same. Trained bands of white men were able to defeat the badly-led Negroes; dozens of blacks were killed, few if any whites injured.[61]

[51] Quoted in Lynch, *The Facts of Reconstruction*, 122.
[52] Susan Dabney Smedes, *A Southern Planter* (London, 1889), 229–30.
[53] Garner, *Reconstruction in Mississippi*, 374, note 2.
[54] Hazelhurst *Mississippi Democrat*, October 13, 1875.
[55] Ernest F. Puckett, "Reconstruction in Monroe County," in *Mississippi Historical Society Publications*, XI (1910), 145–46.
[56] Hazelhurst *Mississippi Democrat*, October 13, 1875.
[57] For a thorough discussion of the rifle clubs, see Ross H. Moore, "Economic and Social Conditions during Reconstruction in Mississippi" (Ph.D. dissertation, Duke University, 1938).
[58] *Senate Reports*, 44 Cong., 1 Sess., No. 527, I, 757.
[59] *Ibid.*, I, 88–90.
[60] Among many examples, the following articles in the *Mississippi Historical Society Publications* may be cited: John U. Kyle, "Reconstruction in Panola County," XIII (1913), 71; Fred M. Witty, "Reconstruction in Carroll and Montgomery Counties," X (1909), 127; and Julia C. Brown, "Reconstruction in Yalobusha and Grenada Counties," XII (1912), 252.
[61] The following articles in the *Mississippi Historical Society Publications* contain important accounts of race riots: Fred Z. Browne, "Reconstruction in Oktibbeha County," XIII (1913), 289–91; Robert Bowman, "Reconstruction in

Every race riot brought two results. The whites were more solidly united than ever. Whig and Democrat, secessionist and unionist, and even Confederate and Federal joined hands against what they regarded as aggression from the carpetbag-Negro combination. And on the other hand, the Republican party was completely demoralized. The Negroes were terrified;[62] President Grant refused to send additional troops;[63] and Governor Ames, to prevent a race war, virtually surrendered to the Democratic leaders.[64] The Republican regime in Mississippi was doomed.

The important elections of 1875 were ominously quiet.[65] As one observer put it, the Negroes were afraid to make any trouble and the whites did not need to.[66] Election frauds, in spite of a number of hair-raising tales,[67] seem not to have been unusually large. The result was a sweeping Democratic success. Virtually all the counties now passed under the control of color-line administrations. The whites gained heavy majorities in both houses of the legislature and elected all but one of the congressmen, while in the only general race the Democratic candidate for state treasurer had a lead of over thirty thousand votes.[68]

The sequel of the election may be noted very briefly. The Republican governor, Ames, and the lieutenant governor were impeached when the new legislature met. The former, although there was no real case against him, resigned, and the latter was convicted.[69] By 1876 "home rule" was officially restored, and Mississippi has ever since been a Democratic state.

The combination of force and intimidation known as the Mississippi Plan received much attention in other southern states, where

---

Yazoo County," VII (1903), 127–219; Charles H. Brough, "The Clinton Riot," VI (1902), 53–63. See also, Wharton, "The Negro in Mississippi," 350ff

[62] See the letters from various Negro leaders to Governor Ames, in *Senate Reports*, 44 Cong., 1 Sess., No. 527, II, Doc. Ev., 89ff.

[63] The President was reported to have said that "the whole public are tired out with these annual autumnal outbreaks in the South." *Appleton's American Annual Cyclopedia*, XV (1875), 516.

[64] Frank Johnston, "The Conference of October 15th, 1875, between General George and Governor Ames," in *Mississippi Historical Society Publications*, VI (1902), 65–77.

[65] Garner, *Reconstruction in Mississippi*, 392.

[66] *Senate Reports*, 44 Cong., 1 Sess., No. 527, II, 1200.

[67] *Ibid.*, I, 496; Bowman, "Reconstruction in Yazoo County," in *loc. cit.*, 130; Braden, "Reconstruction in Lee County," in *loc. cit.*, 143; Witty, "Reconstruction in Carroll and Montgomery Counties," in *loc. cit.*, 128; and many others.

[68] *Appleton's American Annual Cyclopedia*, XV (1875), 517.

[69] Garner, *Reconstruction in Mississippi*, 401–410.

Democratic leaders imitated the Mississippi tactics.[70] Much of the political history of the South in the decades after 1875 was centered about the idea that white supremacy could be maintained only by preventing the Negro from voting. This point of view is closely connected with the customary explanation of the success of the Mississippi Plan. It has been held by every student of Reconstruction since William A. Dunning that white supremacy in the South was secured through the intimidation of the Negro. "The real Mississippi plan," it is contended, "was to play upon the easy credulity of the negroes and inspire them with terror so that they would . . . stay away from the polls." [71]

This explanation seems to be an over-simplification of the problem. The difficulties of making an adequate study of a Reconstruction election in the South have seldom been realized. First of all, it is impossible to secure accurate statistics of population, since the 1870 census is almost worthless, even as an estimate. In most cases the number of potential and registered voters cannot be discovered. The disfranchised Confederate element is another unknown. It cannot be determined with any degree of accuracy what proportion of the vote each race cast, and it is even more impossible to ascertain how many Negroes were herded to the polls by Democratic landlords or by Republican politicians. Finally, the amount of actual election fraud, always considerable during the period, adds another indeterminable variable. The whole situation is one of the utmost complexity, and any sweeping generalizations must be received with caution.

But even in the face of these difficulties it can be determined that the conventional explanation of the success of the Mississippi Plan is not satisfactory. If the Negroes were kept from voting, there should have been fewer Republican ballots cast than in former years. This is not the case.[72] Actually the Republicans were nearly as strong as in previous elections, and if it is admitted that most whites had by 1875 left the Republican fold, the election returns show that in reality *more* Negroes voted than ever before.

It seems safe to conclude that in the Mississippi election of 1875 the Negroes as a general rule voted the Republican ticket. But there

[70] Alfred B. Williams, *Hampton and his Red Shirts* (Charleston, 1935), especially 21–35.

[71] Rhodes, *History of the United States*, VII, 134. This is the view of all the general studies of the Reconstruction period, as well as of the more specialized studies, such as Garner, Moore, Wharton, and McNeilly, cited above.

[72] The total Republican vote was only about 3,000 less than it had been in 1873, the year of the Ames landslide. *Senate Reports*, 44 Cong., 1 Sess., No. 527, II Doc. Ev., 144–45.

are exceptions even to this assertion. In certain counties anti-Ames Negro Republicans joined the Democrats to fight the administration's candidates, and "fusion" tickets were elected. In some five delta counties, moreover, the Democratic vote was so large as to justify the belief that wealthy landowners "voted" their colored tenants for the Democratic party.[73]

With the white population, the picture is somewhat clearer. To the old Democratic nucleus there were now added many recruits.[74] Southern white men who since the war had felt that the political situation was hopeless [75] now saw a chance for their principles to triumph and returned to support their party. But the greatest accession of Democratic strength came from the thousands of so-called scalawags—mostly former Whigs—who now denounced the Republican party and voted on the color-line.[76]

It appears, therefore, that a number of misconceptions concerning the course of Reconstruction need revision. The southern political scene in this postwar period was never simple. In Mississippi the importance of the former Whigs has generally been neglected. Toward the beginning of Reconstruction most of these joined the Republican party. Their moderate program of gradual adjustment to the realities of Reconstruction was defeated by a combination of extremists from all parties. By 1875 these Whigs, disgusted by Radical excesses and attracted by color-line principles, had gradually changed political allegiance and joined the Democratic party. Not until this shift was completed did the Democrats win an election. The triumph of the Democratic color-line policies, known as the Mississippi plan of 1875, would seem to be due to the successful union of all southern whites into one party rather than to the intimidation of the Negro.

[73] These were Grenada, Hinds, Holmes, Tallahatchie, and Warren counties, all of which are partly in the Delta, and in all of which the Negroes were a heavy majority of the population. On "fusion," see John S. McNeilly, "Climax and Collapse of Reconstruction in Mississippi, 1874–1896," in *Mississippi Historical Society Publications*, XII (1912), 381ff.

[74] In 1873 the Democratic candidate for state treasurer—also the Alcorn candidate—had received but 47,486 votes. In 1875 the color-line candidate obtained 98,715 votes. *Senate Reports*, 44 Cong., 1 Sess., No. 527, II, Doc. Ev., 144–45.

[75] Edward Mayes, *The Life, Times, and Speeches of Lucius Q. C. Lamar* (Nashville, 1896), 170–72.

[76] "The naked truth is, less than a baker's dozen of the [former] . . . Republican leaders . . . were supporters of Governor Ames in . . . 1875." Garner, *Reconstruction in Mississippi*, 398.

15

"THE business of America," said Calvin Coolidge in his usual laconic fashion, "is business." But this truism, like most others, obscures rather than illuminates the character of business in modern America. From the beginning, to be sure, the buying and selling of goods and services has been an important part of the economic life of the people. But business organization and function changed greatly toward the end of the nineteenth century. Not until after the Civil War did American business take on its modern lineaments. During the late nineteenth century the United States astounded itself as well as the rest of the world with the enormous increase in the size and productive capacity of its industrial enterprises. As Mr. Chandler points out in this article, as late as 1870 a very substantial proportion of economic enterprises, whether in agriculture or in industry, were small. Yet thirty years later the problem of how to control "trusts," "monopolies," and giant holding companies was on the lips of millions of ordinary citizens as well as being the object of concern of political parties and publicists. It was this popular anxiety over the new and rapidly achieved power of big business that provided the occasion and the audience for the so-called "muckraking" literature of the Progressive era at the opening of the twentieth century.

The question that Chandler set himself is, how did business in the United States become "big"? (The question, of course, has contemporary relevance, too, for "bigness" is the most obvious characteristic of modern business enterprise.) What exactly is meant by "big" business as distinguished from earlier business enterprises? Although big business, almost by definition, employs great numbers of employees and requires large amounts of capital, these are only the most obvious measures of the way in which it differs from business in the years prior to 1870. For business in the late nineteenth century, like that today, was *corporate* in legal form, *oligopolistic* in its interfirm relationship, *integrated* in its structure, and *bureaucratic* in its administration. Since these four terms appear throughout Chandler's article, they are briefly defined here.

Corporate. Before the 1870s the typical manufacturing company was either a single owner or a partnership in legal form. Corporations, which issued stock to a multitude of "owners," were largely confined to railroads and canals. But the corporation, with its limited liability and its consequent attractiveness to large amounts of capital, soon became the typical legal form of the big business, as it has remained to this day.

Oligopolistic. This word, derived from the Greek words for "few sellers" (the same root as in "monopoly," "one seller"), means that the goods in a particular industry are produced by such a small number of firms that true competition does not prevail. Hence prices can be and are determined by the actions of a few firms rather than being set by competition among many producers, or "supply" and demand." As Chandler makes clear in his article, in oligopolistic industries a few, large firms achieved their control over production and the market in a variety of ways and for a variety of reasons. But whatever the means or motives, the result was to weaken, if not to end, the competition among many firms, which was the basis for a market economy of many small producers.

Integrated. This is the economist's word for the bringing together of several companies under a single firm's control. Integration can assume two forms, both of which may be used by the same corporation. "Vertical" integration exists where a producer, say, of automobiles owns not only the plant for manufacturing the actual cars but also the plants that manufacture the glass or the tires. Complete vertical integration would mean that it might own rubber plantations, coal fields, ore mines, steel mills, the intermediate manufacturing processes, and the factories in which the cars were finally assembled. In short, the completely vertically integrated firm owns or controls all of the materials and processes that go into the manufacture of its product "from the bottom to the top"—hence, "vertical" integration. In "horizontal" integration, as can be surmised, a corporation controls many otherwise competing firms in the same industry, thus spreading its control "across" the field—hence, "horizontal" integration.

Bureaucratic. All big businesses, simply because they employ large numbers of workers and control many producing units that are spread across a large national market, require a large staff to keep records, audit accounts, sell goods, administer the business, and gather information for the making of decisions. The individual owner or a few partners of the small firm are now replaced by a myriad of accountants, secretaries, salesmen, and minor and major executives, all of whom are dependent upon one another.

Before the late 1940s virtually all of the historical writing on the rise of big business in America was hostile. (The often sycophantic or laudatory histories of industrial enterprises, which were frequently commissioned by the firms themselves, did not seriously influence the writing of general American history.) Much of this hostility derived from the fear of the power of large-scale enterprises that was reflected in the programs of political parties during the era of the Populists and the Progressive years. Often the writing of business history was highly moralistic, emphasizing the exploitation of workers and the defrauding of consumers, and frequently personal, as in Gustavus Myers's *History of the Great American Fortunes* (Chicago, 1910). The lust for power and profits on the part of the men who created the great industrial combines, emphasized in books like Charles and Mary Beard's *Rise of American Civilization* (New York, 1927) and Matthew Josephson's *Robber Barons* (New York, 1934), fashioned a view of late nineteenth-century business that has remained standard until very recently.

Since the 1940s an increasing number of historians of business have been cutting a new path in the examination of the so-called "age of the robber barons." A pioneer of such studies was Allan Nevins's *John D. Rockefeller: The Heroic Age of American Enterprise* (New York, 1940), which has been revised as *Study in Power: John D. Rockefeller, Industrialist and Philanthropist* (New York, 1953). In the same pattern is Harold C. Passer's *Electrical Manufacturers* (Cambridge, Mass., 1953) and Ralph and Muriel Hidy's *Pioneering in Big Business, 1882–1911* (New York, 1955). Chandler's article goes a step beyond these studies of an individual firm or industry by using them as well as the results of his own research to explain the growth of big business as a whole.

Unlike the general treatments written before the Second World War, Chandler's purpose is not to blame or to pick out moral deficiencies in the industrial leaders but to see businessmen and their enterprises as making adjustments to broad currents of social, technological, and economic change. The search for profits, instead of being somehow immoral or reprehensible, is seen simply as the goal of any business and the ultimate source of its survival. On the other hand, his approach is not sycophantic, as so many of the earlier histories of individual companies were. In short, the great merit of Chandler's article, like that of the new school of business historians in general, is to envision business organization and practice as a functioning part of American life. He applies to them the standards of historical research and displays the same detachment that is being applied to other American institutions like political parties, labor unions, and reform movements.

One of the hallmarks of the new approach to business history is its recognition that business firms differ, that it is not realistic to treat them as if all had a single history or were molded by identical aims. (Stanley Coben's article, No. 13, above, has already suggested this from a different angle of vision.) Thus Chandler draws distinctions between the development of consumers' industries (those selling directly to the public) and producers' industries (those selling to other manufacturers). He also notices differences in the behavior and adjustments of "old" and more recent producers. Finally, it should be observed that he sees a variety of motives for consolidation, not simply the desire to avoid competition, which had been the staple explanation of the older writers on business history.

Chandler's essay is also noteworthy because in analyzing business enterprises he has not dealt with them in a social vacuum. By pointing out the interaction between the rise of cities and the growth of big business he has demonstrated what is in fact a symbiotic relationship between the two most important social and economic developments of the late nineteenth century. For this reason his article is not only an important contribution to the history of American business but also a major addition to understanding the role of the city in the making of modern America.

Mr. Chandler is professor of history at The Johns Hopkins University. His most recent study of the development of American business is *Strategy and Structure: Chapters in the History of Industrial Enterprise* (Cambridge, Mass., 1962).

The Beginnings of "Big Business" in American History*

BY ALFRED D. CHANDLER, JR.

CRITERIA FOR SELECTION AND ANALYSIS

THE historian, by the very nature of his task, must be concerned with change. What made for change? Why did it come when it did, and in the way it did? These are characteristically historians' questions. For the student of American business history, these basic questions can be put a little more precisely. What in the American past has given businessmen the opportunity or created the need for them to change what they were doing or the way they were doing it? In other words, what stimulated them to develop new products, new markets, new sources of raw materials, new ways of procuring, processing, or marketing the goods they handled? What encouraged them to find new methods of financing, new ways of managing or organizing their businesses? What turned them to altering their relations with their working force, their customers and competitors, and with the larger American public?

The question of what constitutes the dynamic factors in American business history, dynamic in the sense of stimulating change and innovation, can be more clearly defined if the country's land, natural resources, and cultural patterns are taken as given. Land and resources were the raw materials with which the businessmen had to work, and the cultural attitudes and values helped set the legal and ethical rules of the game they had to play. Within this cultural and geographic environment a number of historical developments appear to have stimulated change. These provide a framework around which historical data can be compiled and analyzed.

SOURCE: Reprinted by permission of the Harvard Graduate School of Business Administration from *The Business History Review*, XXXIII (Spring 1959). Copyright, 1959, by the President and Fellows of Harvard College.
* This study was supported by the Sloan Research Fund of The School of Industrial Management and the Center for International Studies, Massachusetts Institute of Technology.

The following major dynamic forces are visible in the American business economy since 1815: the western expansion of population; the construction and initial operation of the national railroad network; the development of a national and increasingly urban market; the application of two new sources of power: the internal combustion engine and electricity, to industry and transportation; and the systematic application of the natural and physical sciences, particularly chemistry and physics, to industry through the institutionalizing of research and development activities.

The first, the westward expansion, appears to have provided the primary impetus, except possibly in New England, to business innovation in the years from 1815 to about 1850; the building of the railroads appears to have been the major factor from the 1850's to the late 1870's; the growth of the national and urban market from the 1880's until a little after 1900; the coming of electricity and the internal combustion engine from the early 1900's to the 1920's; and, finally, the growth of systematic and institutionalized research and development since the 1920's.

These five factors are essentially aspects of fundamental population changes and technological advances. There were, of course, other factors that encouraged business innovation and change. The coming of the new machines and mechanical devices may have been a more important stimulant to innovation in New England than the growth of her markets and sources of supply in the expanding South and West. Wars usually precipitated change. The business cycle, flow of capital, government policy and legislation all played a significant part in business innovation. But such political and financial developments appear to have intensified or delayed the more basic changes encouraged initially by fundamental population shifts and technological achievements.

The purpose of making such a list is, however, not to argue that one development was more dynamic than the other. Nor are these five factors to be considered as "causes" for change; nor are they "theses" to be argued as representing reality, nor "theories" to provide an over-all explanation of change or possibly of predicting change. They are, rather, a framework on which historical information can be tied and inter-related. They provide a consistent basis upon which meaningful questions can be asked of the data.

This framework and these questions are, it should be emphasized, concerned only with fundamental changes and innovation in the business economy. They do not deal with the day-to-day activities to which businessmen must devote nearly all of their time. They are not concerned with the continuous adaptation to the constant variations of the market, sources of supply, availability of capital, and technological developments. Nor do they consider why some businesses and businessmen responded quickly and creatively to the basic population and technological changes and others did not. But an understanding of the continuous response and adjustment would seem to require first an awareness of the meaning of the more fundamental or "discontinuous" changes.

Since historical compilation and analysis must be selective, it is impossible to undertake any historical study without some criteria either implicit or explicit for selection. Further study and analysis, by indicating the defects of this approach and framework, will suggest more satisfactory ones. In the process, an analysis and interpretation of change in the American business past should come a little nearer to reality.

The purpose of this article then is, by using the framework of basic, dynamic forces, to look a little more closely at the years that witnessed the beginnings of big business in American industry. What types of changes came during these years in the ways of marketing, purchasing, processing, and in the forms of business organization? Why did these changes come when they did in the way they did? Was the growth of the national market a major prerequisite for such innovation and change? If not, what then was? How did these innovations relate to the growth of the railroad network or the coming of electricity and the internal combustion engine?

In addition to secondary works on this period, the data used in seeking answers to these questions have been annual and other corporation reports, government documents, articles in periodicals, histories, and biographies concerning the 50 largest industrial companies in the country in 1909. Nearly all these companies, listed in Table I, had their beginnings in the last years of the nineteenth century.

MAJOR CHANGES IN AMERICAN INDUSTRY
AT THE END OF THE NINETEENTH CENTURY

Between the depression of the 1870's and the beginning of the twentieth century, American industry underwent a significant transformation. In the 1870's, the major industries serviced an agrarian economy. Except for a few companies equipping the rapidly expanding railroad network, the leading industrial firms processed agricultural products and provided farmers with food and clothing. These firms tended to be small, and bought their raw materials and sold their finished goods locally. Where they manufactured for a market more than a few miles away from the factory, they bought and sold through commissioned agents who handled the business of several other similar firms.

By the beginning of the twentieth century, many more companies were making producers' goods, to be used in industry rather than on the farm or by the ultimate consumer. Most of the major industries had become dominated by a few large enterprises. These great industrial corporations no longer purchased and sold through agents, but had their own nation-wide buying and marketing organizations. Many, primarily those in the extractive industries, had come to control their own raw materials. In other words, the business economy had become industrial. Major industries were dominated by a few firms that had become great, vertically integrated, centralized enterprises.

In the terms of the economist and sociologist a significant sector of American industry had become bureaucratic, in the sense that business decisions were made within large hierarchical structures. Externally, oligopoly was prevalent, the decision-makers being as much concerned with the actions of the few other large firms in the industry as with over-all changes in markets, sources of supplies, and technological improvements.

These basic changes came only after the railroads had created a national market. The railroad network, in turn, had grown swiftly primarily because of the near desperate requirements for efficient transportation created by the movement of population westward after 1815.[1] Except for the Atlantic seaboard between Boston and Washington, the construction of the American railroads was stimulated almost wholly by the demand for better transportation to move crops, to bring farmers supplies, and to open up new territories to commercial agriculture.

By greatly expanding the scope of the agrarian economy, the railroads quickened the growth of the older commercial centers, such as New York, Philadelphia, Cincinnati, Cleveland, and St. Louis, and helped create new cities like Chicago, Indianapolis, Atlanta, Kansas City, Dallas, and the Twin Cities. This rapid urban expansion intensified the demand for the products of the older consumer goods industries—particularly those which processed the crops of the farmer and planter into food, stimulants, and clothing.

[1]The factors stimulating the growth of the American railroad network and the impact of the earlier construction and operation of this network on the American business economy and business institution is suggested in Chandler, *Henry Varnum Poor—Business Editor, Analyst, and Reformer* (Cambridge, 1956), especially chaps. 4, 6–9.

At the same time, railroad construction developed the first large market in this country for producers' goods. Except for the making of relatively few textile machines, steamboat engines, and ordnance, the iron and nonferrous manufacturers had before 1850 concentrated on providing metals and simple tools for merchants and farmers. Even textile machinery was usually made by the cloth manufacturers themselves. However, by 1860, only a decade after beginning America's first major railroad construction boom, railroad companies had already replaced the blacksmiths as the primary market for iron products, and had become far and away the most important market for the heavy engineering industries. By then, too, the locomotive was competing with the Connecticut brass industry as a major consumer of copper. More than this, the railroads, with their huge capital outlay, their fixed operating costs, the large size of their labor and management force, and the technical complexity of their operations, pioneered in the new ways of oligopolistic competition and large-scale, professionalized, bureaucratized management.

The new nation-wide market created by the construction of the railroad network became an increasingly urban one. From 1850 on, if not before, urban areas were growing more rapidly than rural ones. In the four decades from 1840 to 1880 the proportion of urban population rose from 11 per cent to 28 per cent of the total population, or about 4 per cent a decade. In the two decades from 1880 to 1900 it grew from 28 per cent to 40 per cent or an increase of 6 per cent a decade. Was this new urban and national market, then, the primary stimulant for business innovation and change, and for the coming of big business to American industry?

CHANGES IN THE CONSUMERS' GOODS INDUSTRIES

The industries first to become dominated by great business enterprises were those making consumer goods, the majority of which were processed from products grown on the farm and sold in the urban markets. Consolidation and centralization in the consumers' goods industries were well under way by 1893. The unit that appeared was one which integrated within a single business organization the major economic processes: production or purchasing of raw materials, manufacturing, distribution, and finance.

Such vertically integrated organizations come in two quite different ways. Where the product tended to be somewhat new in kind and especially fitted for the urban market, its makers created their businesses by first building large marketing and then purchasing organizations. This technique appears to have been true of the manufacturers or distributors of fresh meat, cigarettes, high-grade flour, bananas, harvesters, sewing machines, and typewriters. Where the products were established staple items, horizontal combination tended to precede vertical integration. In the sugar, salt, leather, whiskey, glucose, starch, biscuit, kerosene, fertilizer, and rubber industries a large number of small manufacturers first combined into large business units and then created their marketing and buying organizations. For a number of reasons the makers of the newer types of products found the older outlets less satisfactory and felt more of a need for direct marketing than did the manufacturers of the long-established goods.

Integration via the Creation of Marketing Organization

The story of the changes and the possible reasons behind them can be more clearly understood by examining briefly the experience of a few innovating firms. First, consider the experience of companies that grew large through the creation of a nation-wide marketing and distributing organization. Here the story of Gustavus F. Swift and his brother Edwin is a significant one. Gustavus F. Swift, an Easterner, came relatively late to the Chicago meat-packing business. Possibly because he was from Massachusetts, he appreciated the potential market for fresh western meat in the eastern cities.[2] For after the Civil War, Boston, New York, Philadelphia, and other cities were rapidly outrunning their local meat supply. At the same time, great herds of cattle were gathering on the western plains. Swift saw the possibilities of connecting the new market with the new source of supply by the use of the refrigerated railroad car. In 1878, shortly after his first experimental shipment of refrigerated meat, he formed a partnership with his younger brother, Edwin, to market fresh western meat in the eastern cities.

For the next decade, Swift struggled hard to carry out his plans, the essence of which was the creation, during the 1880's, of the

[2] Swift's story as outlined in Louis F. Swift in collaboration with Arthur Van Vlissingen, *The Yankee of the Yards—the Biography of Gustavus Franklin Swift* (New York, 1928). The United States Bureau of Corporations, *Report of the Commissioner of Corporations on the Beef Industry, March 3, 1905* (Washington, 1905), is excellent on the internal operations and external activities of the large meat-packing firms. There is additional information in the later three-volume *Report of the Federal Trade Commission on the Meat Packing Industry* (Washington, 1918–1919). R. A. Clemen, *The American Livestock and Meat Industry* (New York, 1923) has some useful background data.

nation-wide distributing and marketing organization built around a network of branch houses. Each "house" had its storage plant and its own marketing organization. The latter included outlets in major towns and cities, often managed by Swift's own salaried representatives. In marketing the product, Swift had to break down, through advertising and other means, the prejudices against eating meat killed more than a thousand miles away and many weeks earlier. At the same time he had to combat boycotts of local butchers and the concerted efforts of the National Butchers' Protective Association to prevent the sale of his meat in the urban markets.

To make effective use of the branch house network, the company soon began to market products other than beef. The "full line" soon came to include lamb, mutton, pork, and, some time later, poultry, eggs, and dairy products. The growing distributing organization soon demanded an increase in supply. So between 1888 and 1892, the Swifts set up meat-packing establishments in Kansas City, Omaha, and St. Louis, and, after the depression of the 1890's, three more in St. Joseph, St. Paul, and Ft. Worth. At the same time, the company systematized the buying of its cattle and other products at the stockyards. In the 1890's, too, Swift began a concerted effort to make more profitable use of by-products.

Before the end of the 1890's, then, Swift had effectively fashioned a great, vertically integrated organization. The major departments —marketing, processing, purchasing, and accounting—were all tightly controlled from the central office in Chicago. A report of the Commissioner of Corporations published in 1905 makes clear the reason for such control: [3]

> Differences in quality of animals and of their products are so great that the closest supervision of the Central Office is necessary to enforce the exercise of skill and sound judgement on the part of the agents who buy the stock, and the agents who sell the meat. With this object, the branches of the Selling and Accounting Department of those packing companies which have charge of the purchasing, killing, and dressing and selling of fresh meat, are organized in the most extensive and thorough manner. The Central Office is in constant telegraphic correspondence with the distributing houses, with a view to adjusting the supply of meat and the price as nearly as possible to the demand.

As this statement suggests, the other meat packers followed Swift's example. To compete effectively, Armour, Morris, Cudahy, and Schwarzschild & Sulzberger had to build up similar integrated organizations. Those that did not follow the Swift model were des-

[3] *Report of Commissioner of Corporations on the Beef Industry*, p. 21.

tined to remain small local companies. Thus by the middle of the 1890's, the meat-packing industry, with the rapid growth of these great vertically integrated firms had become oligopolistic (the "Big Five" had the major share of the market) and bureaucratic; each of the five had its many departments and several levels of management.

This story has parallels in other industries processing agricultural products. In tobacco, James B. Duke was the first to appreciate the growing market for the cigarette, a new product which was sold almost wholly in the cities.[4] However, after he had applied machinery to the manufacture of cigarettes, production soon outran supply. Duke then concentrated on expanding the market through extensive advertising and the creation of a national and then world-wide selling organization. In 1884, he left Durham, North Carolina, for New York City, where he set up factories, sales, and administrative offices. New York was closer to his major urban markets, and was the more logical place to manage an international advertising campaign than Durham. While he was building his marketing department, Duke was also creating the network of warehouses and buyers in the tobacco-growing areas of the country.

In 1890, he merged his company with five smaller competitors in the cigarette business to form the American Tobacco Company. By 1895 the activities of these firms had been consolidated into the manufacturing, marketing, purchasing, and finance departments of the single operating structure Duke had earlier fashioned. Duke next undertook development of a full line by handling all types of smoking and chewing tobacco. By the end of the century, his company completely dominated the tobacco business. Only two other firms, R. J. Reynolds & Company and P. Lorillard & Company had been able to build up comparable vertically integrated organizations. When they merged with American Tobacco they continued to retain their separate operating organizations. When the 1911 antitrust decree split these and other units off from the American company, the tobacco industry had become, like the meat-packing business, oligopolistic, and its dominant firms bureaucratic.

What Duke and Swift did for their industries, James S. Bell of the Washburn-Crosby Company did during these same years in the making and selling of high-grade flour to the urban bakeries

---

[4] Some information on James B. Duke and the American Tobacco Company can be found in John W. Jenkins, *James B. Duke, Master Builder* (New York, 1927), chaps. 5–7, 10. More useful was the United States Bureau of Corporations, *Report of the Commissioner of Corporations on the Tobacco Industry* (Washington, 1909).

and housewives, and Andrew J. Preston achieved in growing, transporting, and selling another new product for the urban market, the banana.[5] Like Swift and Duke, both these men made their major innovations in marketing, and then went on to create large-scale, departmentalized, vertically integrated structures.

The innovators in new consumer durables followed much the same pattern. Both Cyrus McCormick, pioneer harvester manufacturer, and William Clark, the business brains of the Singer Sewing Machine Company, first sold through commissioned agents. Clark soon discovered that salaried men, working out of branch offices, could more effectively and at less cost display, demonstrate, and service sewing machines than could the agents.[6] Just as important, the branch offices were able to provide the customer with essential credit. McCormick, while retaining the dealer to handle the final sales, came to appreciate the need for a strong selling and distributing organization, with warehouses, servicing facilities, and a large salaried force, to stand behind the dealer.[7] So in the years following the Civil War, both McCormick and Singer Sewing Machine Company concentrated on building up national and then world-wide marketing departments. As they purchased their raw materials from a few industrial companies rather than from a mass of farmers, their purchasing departments were smaller, and required less attention than those in the firms processing farmers' products. But the net result was the creation of a very similar type of organization.

Integration via Horizontal Combination

In those industries making more standard goods, the creation of marketing organizations usually followed large-scale combinations of a number of small manufacturing firms. For these small firms, the coming of the railroad had in many cases enlarged their markets but simultaneously brought them for the first time into competition with many other companies. Most of these firms appear to have expanded production in order to take advantage of the

[5] The story of Bell is outlined in James Gray, *Business Without Boundary, the Story of General Mills* (Minneapolis, 1954), and of Preston in Charles M. Wilson, *Empire in Green and Gold* (New York, 1947).

[6] The early Singer Sewing Machine experience is well analyzed in Andrew B. Jack, "The Channels of Distribution for an Innovation: the Sewing Machine Industry in America, 1860–1865," *Explorations in Entrepreneurial History*, Vol. IX (Feb., 1957), pp. 113–141.

[7] William T. Hutchinson, *Cyrus Hall McCormick* (New York, 1935), Vol. II, pp. 704–712.

new markets. As a result, their industries became plagued with overproduction and excess capacity; that is, continued production at full capacity threatened to drop prices below the cost of production. So in the 1880's and early 1890's, many small manufacturers in the leather, sugar, salt, distilling and other corn products, linseed and cotton oil, biscuit, petroleum, fertilizer and rubber boot and glove industries, joined in large horizontal combinations.

In most of these industries, combination was followed by consolidation and vertical integration, and the pattern was comparatively consistent. First, the new combinations concentrated their manufacturing activities in locations more advantageously situated to meet the new growing urban demands. Next they systematized and standardized their manufacturing processes. Then, except in the case of sugar and corn products (glucose and starch), the combinations began to build large distributing and smaller purchasing departments. In so doing, many dropped their initial efforts to buy out competitors or to drive them out of business by price-cutting. Instead they concentrated on the creation of a more efficient flow from the producers of their raw materials to the ultimate consumer, and of the development and maintenance of markets through brand names and advertising. Since the large majority of these combinations began as regional groupings, most industries came to have more than one great firm. Only oil, sugar, and corn products remained long dominated by a single company. By World War I, partly because of the dissolutions under the Sherman Act, these industries had also become oligopolistic, and their leading firms vertically integrated.

Specific illustrations help to make these generalizations more precise. The best-known is the story of the oil industry, but equally illustrative is the experience of the leading distilling, baking, and rubber companies.

The first permanent combination in the whiskey industry came in 1887 when a large number of Midwestern distillers, operating more than 80 small plants, formed the Distillers' and Cattle Feeders' Trust.[8] Like other trusts, it adopted the more satisfactory legal form

---

[8] The major sources of information on combination and consolidation in the distilling industry are Jeremiah W. Jenks, "The Development of the Whiskey Trust," *Political Science Quarterly*, Vol. IV (June, 1889), pp. 296–319; J. W. Jenks and W. E. Clark, *The Trust Problem* (rev. ed.; New York, 1917), pp. 141–149. The annual reports of the Distilling and Cattle Feeding Company and its various successors provide some useful additional data, as does the Industrial Commission, *Preliminary Report on Trusts and Industrial Combinations* (Washington, 1900), Vol. I, pp. 74–89, 167–259, 818–848, and Victor

of a holding company shortly after New Jersey in 1889 passed the general incorporation law for holding companies. The major efforts of the Distillers Company were, first, to concentrate production in a relatively few plants. By 1895 only 21 were operating. The managers maintained that the large volume per plant permitted by such concentration would mean lower costs, and also that the location of few plants more advantageously in relation to supply and marketing would still reduce expenses further. However, the company kept the price of whiskey up, and since the cost of setting up a distillery was small, it soon had competition from small local plants. The company's answer was to purchase the new competitors and to cut prices. This strategy proved so expensive that the enterprise was unable to survive the depression of the 1890's.

Shortly before going into receivership in 1896, the Distillers Company had begun to think more about marketing. In 1895, it had planned to spend a million dollars to build up a distributing and selling organization in the urban East—the company's largest market. In 1898, through the purchase of the Standard Distilling & Distributing Company and the Spirits Distributing Company, it did acquire a marketing organization based in New York City. In 1903, the marketing and manufacturing units were combined into a single operating organization under the direction of the Distillers Securities Company. At the same time, the company's president announced plans to concentrate on the development of brand names and specialties, particularly through advertising and packaging.[9] By the early years of the twentieth century, then, the Distillers Company had become a vertically integrated, departmentalized, centralized operating organization, competing in the modern manner, more through advertising and product differentiation than price.

The experience of the biscuit industry is even more explicit. The National Biscuit Company came into being in 1898 as a merger of three regional combinations: the New York Biscuit Company formed in 1890, the American Biscuit and Manufacturing Company, and the United States Biscuit Company founded a little later.[10] Its initial objective was to control price and production, but as in the case of the Distillers Company, this strategy proved too expensive. The

---

S. Clark, *History of Manufactures in the United States* (New York, 1929), Vol. II, pp. 505–506. Changes in taxes on liquors also affected the company's policies in the early 1890's.

[9] *Annual Report of the President of the Distillers Securities Company* for 1903.

[10] The information on National Biscuit comes largely from its annual reports.

Annual Report for 1901 suggests why National Biscuit shifted its basic policies: [11]

> This Company is four years old and it may be of interest to shortly review its history. . . . When the Company started, it was an aggregation of plants. It is now an organized business. When we look back over the four years, we find that a radical change has been wrought in our methods of business. In the past, the managers of large merchandising corporations have found it necessary, for success, to control or limit competition. So when this company started, it was thought that we must control competition, and that to do this we must either fight competition or buy it. The first meant a ruinous war of prices, and a great loss of profit; the second, a constantly increasing capitalization. Experience soon proved to us that, instead of bringing success, either of those courses, if persevered in, must bring disaster. This led us to reflect whether it was necessary to control competition. . . . we soon satisfied ourselves that within the Company itself we must look for success.
>
> We turned our attention and bent our energies to improving the internal management of our business, to getting full benefit from purchasing our raw materials in large quantities, to economizing the expenses of manufacture, to systematizing and rendering more effective our selling department; and above all things and before all things to improve the quality of our goods and the condition in which they should reach the customer.
>
> It became the settled policy of this Company to buy out no competition. . . .

In concentrating on distribution, the company first changed its policy from selling in bulk to wholesalers to marketing small packages to retailers. It developed the various "Uneeda Biscuit" brands, which immediately became popular. "The next point," the same Annual Report continued, "was to reach the customer. Thinking we had something that the customer wanted, we had to advise the customer of its existence. We did this by extensive advertising." This new packaging and advertising not only quickly created a profitable business, but also required the building of a sizable marketing organization. Since flour could be quickly and easily purchased in quantity from large milling firms, the purchasing requirements were less complex, and so the company needed a smaller purchasing organization. On the other hand, it spent much energy after 1901 in improving plant layout and manufacturing processes in order to cut production costs and to improve and standardize quality. Throughout the first decade of its history,

[11] *Annual Report of the National Biscuit Company for the Year Ending December, 1901,* January 3, 1902. References to centralizing of manufacturing facilities appear in several early annual reports. As this was written before Theodore Roosevelt had started to make the Sherman Act an effective antitrust instrument and Ida Tarbell and other journalists had begun to make "muck raking" of big business popular and profitable, the Biscuit Company's shift in policy could hardly have been the result of the pressure of public opinion or the threat of government action.

National Biscuit continued the policy of "centralizing" manufacturing operations, particularly in its great New York and Chicago plants.

In the rubber boot, shoe, and glove industries, the story is much the same. Expansion of manufacturing facilities and increasing competition as early as 1874, led to the formation, by several leading firms, of the Associated Rubber Shoe Companies—an organization for setting price and production schedules through its board of directors.[12] This company continued until 1886. Its successor, the Rubber Boot and Shoe Company, which lasted only a year, attempted, besides controlling prices and production, to handle marketing, which had always been done by commissioned agents. After five years of uncontrolled competition, four of the five firms that had organized the selling company again combined, this time with the assistance of a large rubber importer, Charles A. Flint. The resulting United States Rubber Company came, by 1898, to control 75 per cent of the nation's rubber boot, shoe, and glove output.

At first the new company remained a decentralized holding company. Each constituent company retained its corporate identity with much freedom of action, including the purchasing of raw materials and the selling of finished products, which was done, as before, through jobbers. The central office's concern was primarily with controlling price and production schedules. Very soon, however, the company began, in the words of the 1896 Annual Report, a policy of "perfecting consolidation of purchasing, selling, and manufacturing." [13] This was to be accomplished in four ways. First, as the 1895 Annual Report had pointed out, the managers agreed "so far as practicable, to consolidate the purchasing of all supplies of raw materials for the various manufactures into one single buying agency, believing that the purchase of large quantities of goods can be made at more advantageous figures than the buying of small isolated lots." [14] The second new "general policy" was "to under-

[12] The background for the creation of the United States Rubber Company can be found in Nancy P. Norton, "Industrial Pioneer: the Goodyear Metallic Rubber Shoe Company" (Ph.D. thesis, Radcliffe College, 1950), Constance McL. Green, *History of Naugatuck, Connecticut* (New Haven, 1948), pp. 126–131, 193–194, and Clark, *History of Manufactures,* Vol. II, pp. 479–481, Vol. III, pp. 235–237. The company's annual reports provide most of the information on its activities.

[13] *The Fifth Annual Report of the United States Rubber Company, March 31, 1897*, pp. 6–7.

[14] This and the following quotations are from the *Fourth Annual Report of the United States Rubber Company, May 25, 1896*, pp. 4–5, 7–8.

take to reduce the number of brands of goods manufactured, and to consolidate the manufacturing of the remaining brands in those factories which have demonstrated superior facilities for production or advantageous labor conditions. This course was for the purpose of utilizing the most efficient instruments of production and closing those that were inefficient and unprofitable." The third policy was to consolidate sales through the formation of a "Selling Department," which was to handle all goods made by the constituent companies in order to achieve "economy in the distribution expense." Selling was now to be handled by a central office in the New York City headquarters, with branch offices throughout the United States and Europe. Of the three great new departments, actually manufacturing was the slowest to be fully consolidated and centralized. Finally, the treasurer's office at headquarters began to obtain accurate data on profit and loss through the institution of uniform, centralized cost accounting.

Thus United States Rubber, National Biscuit, and the Distillers Securities Company soon came to have organizational structures paralleling those of Swift and American Tobacco. By the first decade of the twentieth century, the leading firms in many consumers' goods industries had become departmentalized and centralized. This was the organizational concomitant to vertical integration. Each major function, manufacturing, sales, purchasing, and finance, became managed by a single and separate department head, usually a vice president, who, assisted by a director or a manager, had full authority and responsibility for the activities of his unit. These departmental chiefs, with the president, coordinated and evaluated the work of the different functional units, and made policy for the company as a whole. In coordinating, appraising, and policy-making, the president and the vice presidents in charge of departments came to rely more and more on the accounting and statistical information, usually provided by the finance department, on costs, output, purchases, and sales.

CHANGES IN THE PRODUCERS' GOODS INDUSTRIES

Bureaucracy and oligopoly came to the producers' goods industries somewhat later than to those making products for the mass market. Until the depression of the 1890's, most of the combinations and consolidations had been in the consumers' goods industries. After that, the major changes came in those industries selling to other businesses and industrialists. The reason for the time difference seems to be that the city took a little longer to become a major market for producers' goods. Throughout the 1880's, railroad construction and operation continued to take the larger share of the output of steel, copper, power machinery, explosives, and other heavy industries. Then in the 1890's, as railroad construction declined the rapidly growing American cities became the primary market. The insatiable demand for urban lighting, communication, heat, power, transportation, water, sewerage, and other services directly and indirectly took over ever growing quantities of electric lighting apparatus, telephones, copper wire, newsprint, streetcars, coal, and iron, steel, copper, and lead piping, structures and fixtures; while the constantly expanding urban construction created new calls on the power machinery and explosives as well as the metals industries. Carnegie's decision in 1887 to shift the Homestead Works, the nation's largest and most modern steel plant, from rails to structures, symbolized the coming change in the market.[15]

Also the new combinations and consolidations in the consumers' goods industries increased the demand for producers' products in the urban areas. Standard Oil, American Tobacco, Swift and other meat packers, McCormick's Harvesting Machinery and other farm implement firms, American Sugar, Singer Sewing Machine, and many other great consumer goods companies concentrated their production in or near major cities, particularly New York and Chicago.

The changes after 1897 differed from the earlier ones not only in types of industries in which they occurred but also in the way they were promoted and financed. Combinations and vertical integration in the consumer goods industries before 1897 had been almost all engineered and financed by the manufacturers themselves, so the stock control remained in the hands of the industrialists. After 1897, however, outside funds and often outside promoters, who were usually Wall Street financiers, played an increasingly significant role in industrial combination and consolidation. The change reflected a new attitude of investor and financier who controlled capital toward the value of industrial securities.[16] Before the depres-

---

[15] Clark, *History of Manufactures*, Vol. II, chap. 19.

[16] The story of the shift from rails to industrials as acceptable investments is told in Thomas R. Navin and Marian V. Sears, "The Rise of the Market for Industrial Securities, 1887–1902," *Business History Review*, Vol. XIX (June, 1955), pp. 105–138. Government securities were, of course, important in the years before 1850 and during and after the Civil War, but in the late 1870's and 1880's as in the 1850's, railroads dominated the American security exchanges. As Navin and Sears point out, some coal and mining firms were traded on the New York Exchange, but the only manufacturing securities,

sion of the 1890's investment and speculation had been over-whelmingly in railroad stocks and bonds. The institutionalizing of the American security market in Wall Street had come, in fact, as a response to the needs for financing the first great railroad boom in the 1850's.

The railroads, however, had made a poor showing financially in the middle years of the 1890's when one-third of the nation's trackage went through receivership and financial reorganization. The dividend records of some of the new large industrial corporations, on the other hand, proved unexpectedly satisfactory. Moreover, railroad construction was slowing, and the major financial and administrative reorganizations of the 1890's had pretty well stabilized the industry. So there was less demand for investment bankers and brokers to market new issues of railroad securities.

Industrials were obviously the coming field, and by 1898 there was a rush in Wall Street to get in on this new business. The sudden availability of funds stimulated, and undoubtedly overstimulated, industrial combination. Many of the mergers in the years after 1897 came more from the desire of financiers for promotional profits, and because combination had become the thing to do, and less from the special needs and opportunities in the several industries. Moreover, as the financiers and promoters began to provide funds for mergers and expansion, they began to acquire, for the first time, the same type of control over industrial corporations that they had enjoyed in railroads since the 1850's.

The changes in the producers' goods industries were essentially like those in the consumer goods firms before the depression. Only after 1897 the changes came more rapidly, partly because of Wall Street pressures; and the differences that did develop between the two types of industries reflected the basic differences in the nature of their businesses. Like the companies making consumer goods, those manufacturing items for producers set up nation-wide and often world-wide marketing and distributing organizations, consolidated production into a relatively few large plants and fashioned purchasing departments. Because they had fewer customers, their sales departments tended to be smaller than those in firms selling to the mass market. On the other hand, they were more concerned with

---

outside of those of the Pullman Company, were some textile stocks traded on the local Boston Exchange. The connections between the railroad expansion and the beginnings of modern Wall Street are described in detail in Chandler, *Poor*, chap. 4.

obtaining control over the sources of their supply than were most of the consumer goods companies.

Here a distinction can be made between the manufacturers who made semi-finished products from raw materials taken from the ground, and those who made finished goods from semi-finished products. The former, producing a uniform product for a few large industrial customers, developed only small sales departments and concentrated on obtaining control of raw materials, and often of the means of transporting such materials from mine to market. The latter, selling a larger variety of products and ones that often required servicing and financing, had much larger marketing and distributing organizations. These makers of finished goods, except for a brief period around 1900, rarely attempted to control their raw materials or their semi-finished steel and other metal supplies. They did, however, in the years after 1900, begin to buy or set up plants making parts and components that went into the construction of their finished products.

Except in steel, integration usually followed combination in the producers' goods industries. And for both makers of semi-finished and finished goods, integration became more of a defensive strategy than it was in the consumers' goods industries processing agricultural products. In the latter the manufacturers had an assured supply of raw materials from the output of the nation's millions of farms. In the former, on the other hand, they had to consider the threatening possibility of an outsider obtaining complete control of raw materials or supplies.

Integration and Combination in the Extractive Industries

By the early twentieth century nearly all the companies making semi-finished product goods controlled the mining of their own raw materials. The industries in which they operated can, therefore, be considered as extractive. This was also true of two consumers' goods industries: oil and fertilizer. The experience of these two provides a good introduction to the motives for integration and the role it played in the coming of "big business" in steel, copper, paper, explosives and other businesses producing semi-finished goods.

In both the oil and fertilizer industries, control over raw materials came well after combination and consolidation of groups of small manufacturing firms. The Standard Oil Trust, after its formation in 1882, consolidated its manufacturing activities and then created a domestic marketing organization. Only in the late 1880's, when the new Indiana field began to be developed and the older Pennsylvania ones began to decline, did the Trust consider going into the production of crude oil. Both Allan Nevins in his biography of John D. Rockefeller and the Hidys in their history of Standard Oil agree that the need to be assured of a steady supply of crude oil was the major reason for the move into production.[17] Other reasons, the Hidys indicate, were a fear that the producers might combine and so control supplies, and the desire of the pipeline subsidiaries to keep their facilities operating at full capacity. Although neither Nevins nor the Hidys suggest that the desire to obtain a more efficient flow of oil from the well to the distributor was a motive for this integration, both describe the committees and staff units that were formed at the central office at 26 Broadway to assure more effective coordination between production, refining, and marketing.

What little evidence there is suggests somewhat the same story in the fertilizer industry. Shortly after its organization in the mid-1890's, the Virginia-Carolina Chemical Company, a merger of many small southern fertilizer firms, began, apparently for the same defensive reasons, to purchase phosphate mines. Quickly its major competitor, the American Agricultural Chemical Company, a similar combination of small northeastern companies formed in 1893, responded by making its own purchases of mines. As the latter company explained in a later annual report: "The growth of the business, as well as the fact that available phosphate properties were being fast taken up, indicated that it was the part of wisdom to make additional provision for the future, and accordingly . . . available phosphate properties were purchased, and the necessary plants were erected and equipped, so the company now has in hand a supply of phosphate rock which will satisfy its growing demand for 60 years and upwards." [18] However, neither of these companies appeared to have set up organizational devices to guide the flow of materials from mine to plant to market; nor did the managers of a third

[17] Ralph W. Hidy and Muriel E. Hidy, *Pioneering in Big Business, 1882–1911* (New York, 1955), pp. 176–188. Allan Nevins, *Study in Power, John D. Rockefeller, Industrialist and Philanthropist* (New York, 1953), Vol. II, pp. 1–3. Nevins adds that another reason for the move into production was "partly to limit the number of active wells and reduce the overproduction of crude oil," Vol. II, p. 2, but he gives no documentation for this statement.

[18] *Annual Report of the American Agricultural Chemical Company, August 14, 1907;* also the same company's *Annual Report* dated August 25, 1902. In addition to the annual reports of the two companies, Clark, *History of Manufactures,* Vol. III, pp. 289–291, provides information. There is a brief summary of the story of the International Agricultural Corporation in William Haynes, *American Chemical Industry—A History* (New York, 1945), Vol. III, p. 173.

large integrated fertilizer company, the International Agricultural Corporation, formed in 1909.

Defensive motives were certainly significant in the changes in the steel industry. Here the story can be most briefly described by focusing on the history of the industry's leader, the Carnegie Steel Company.[19] That company's chairman, Henry C. Frick, had in the early 1890's consolidated and rationalized the several Carnegie manufacturing properties in and about Pittsburgh into an integrated whole. At the same time, he systematized and departmentalized its purchasing, engineering, and marketing activities. The fashioning of a sales department became more necessary since the shift from rails to structures had enlarged the number of the company's customers.

Then in 1896 the Carnegie company made a massive purchase of ore lands when it joined with Henry W. Oliver to buy out the Rockefeller holdings in the Mesabi Range. As Allan Nevins points out, the depression of the 1890's had worked a rapid transformation in the recently discovered Mesabi region.[20] By 1896, the ore fields had become dominated by three great interests: the Oliver Mining Company, the Minnesota Mining Company, and Rockefeller's Consolidated Iron Mines. A fourth, James J. Hill's Great Northern Railroad, was just entering the field. Frick's purchases, therefore, gave the Carnegie company an assured supply of cheap ore, as well as providing it with a fleet of ore ships. Next, Frick and Carnegie bought and rebuilt a railroad from Lake Erie to Pittsburgh to carry the new supplies to the mills.

Yet the steel company's managers did little to coordinate systematically the mining, shipping, and manufacturing units in their industrial empire. These activities did not become departments controlled from one central office but remained completely separate companies under independent managements, whose contact with one another was through negotiated contracts. This was the same sort of relation that existed between the Frick Coke Company and Carnegie Steel from the time Frick had joined Carnegie in 1889. If the Carnegie company's strategy had been to provide a more effective flow of materials as well as to assure itself of not being caught without a supply of ore and the means to transport it, then Frick

[19] The information on the Carnegie Steel Company is taken from Burton J. Hendrick, *The Life of Andrew Carnegie*, 2 vols. (New York, 1932), George Harvey, *Henry Clay Frick, the Man* (New York, 1928), James H. Bridge, *The Inside Story of the Carnegie Steel Company* (New York, 1903.)
[20] Nevins, *Rockefeller*, Vol. II, p. 252.

and Carnegie would have created some sort of central coordinating office.

The steel industry responded quickly to the Carnegie purchases.[21] In 1898, Chicago's Illinois Steel Company, with capital supplied by J. P. Morgan & Company, joined the Lorain Steel Company (with plants on Lake Erie and in Johnstown, Pennsylvania) to purchase the Minnesota Mining Company, a fleet of ore boats, and railroads in the Mesabi and Chicago areas. Again, little attempt was made to coordinate mining and shipping with manufacturing and marketing. In the same year, many iron and steel firms in Ohio and Pennsylvania merged to form the Republic and National Steel Companies. Shortly thereafter, a similar combination in the Sault Sainte Marie area became the Consolidated Lake Superior Company. These three new mergers began at once to set up their marketing organizations and to obtain control by lease and purchase of raw materials and transportation facilities. In 1900, several small firms making high-grade steel did much the same thing by the formation of the Crucible Steel Company of America. In these same years, the larger, established steel companies, like Lackawanna, Cambria, and Jones & Laughlin obtained control of more supplies of ore, coke, and limestone and simultaneously reorganized their manufacturing and marketing organizations. Like Carnegie and Federal, they at first made little effort to bring their mining and coke operations under the direct control of the central office.

In copper, defensive motives for integration appear to have been somewhat less significant. In the 1890's, mining, smelting and refining were combined on a large scale. During the 'eighties the railroad had opened up many western mining areas, particularly in Montana and Arizona; a little later the new electrical and telephone businesses greatly increased the demand for copper. Mining firms like Anaconda, Calumet & Hecla, and Phelps Dodge moved into smelting and refining, while the Guggenheims' Philadelphia Smelt-

[21] The experience of the other steel firms comes primarily from their annual reports and from prospectuses and other reports in the Corporation Records Division of Baker Library. A company publication, *J & L—The Growth of an American Business* (Pittsburgh, 1953) has some additional information on that company. Also, books listed in footnote 26 on the United States Steel Corporation have something on these companies. Two other steel companies listed in Table I made major changes somewhat before and after the period immediately following 1898. One, the Colorado Fuel & Iron Co., established in 1892, quickly became an integrated steel company in the Colorado area. The Bethlehem Steel Corporation was formed in 1904 when Charles F. Schwab, formerly of the Carnegie company and the United States Steel Corporation, reorganized the finances, corporate structure, and administrative organization of the bankrupt United States Shipbuilding Company.

ing & Refining Company began to buy mining properties.[22] In the copper industry, the high cost of ore shipment meant that smelting and—after the introduction of the electrolytic process in the early 1890's—even refining could be done more cheaply close to the mines. Of the large copper firms, only Calumet & Hecla and the Guggenheims set up refineries in the East before 1898, and both made use of direct water transportation.

After 1898, several large mergers occurred in the nonferrous metals industries. Nearly all were initially promoted by eastern financiers. Of these, the most important were Amalgamated Copper, engineered by H. H. Rogers of Standard Oil and Marcus Daly of Anaconda, the American Smelting and Refining Company which the Guggenheims came to control, and United Copper promoted by F. Augustus Heinze. United Copper remained little more than a holding company. Amalgamated set up a subsidiary to operate a large refinery at Perth Amboy and another, the United Metals Selling Company, with headquarters in New York City, to market the products of its mining and processing subsidiaries. The holding company's central offices in New York remained small and apparently did comparatively little to coordinate the activities of its several operating companies. The Guggenheims formed a much tighter organization with direct headquarters control of the company's mining, shipping, smelting and marketing departments. On the whole, there appears to have been somewhat closer coordination between mining and processing in the large copper than in the major steel companies.

Lowering of costs through more effective coordination appears to have been a major motive for consolidation and combination in three other businesses whose raw materials came from the ground: explosives, paper, and coal.[23] The mergers that created the Pitts-

---

[22] Information on the mining companies came from their annual reports and from Isaac P. Marcosson's two books, *Magic Metal—the Story of the American Smelting and Refining Company* (New York, 1949), and *Anaconda* (New York, 1957), also Clark, *History of Manufactures* Vol. II, pp. 368–369.

[23] The story of the leading explosives, paper, salt and coal companies comes from annual reports and also from Charles E. Beachley, *History of the Consolidation Coal Company 1864–1934* (New York, 1934), George H. Love, *An Exciting Century in Coal* (New York, 1955), the company-written, *The International Paper Company, 1898–1948* (n.p., 1948), William S. Dutton, *DuPont —One Hundred and Forty Years* (New York, 1940), and *U. S. v. E. I. DuPont de Nemours & Company et al. in Circuit Court of the United States for the District of Delaware, #280 in Equity (1909), Defendants' Record Testimony*, Vol. I, and for the paper industry, Clark, *History of Manufactures*, Vol. III, pp. 245–252. The American Writing Paper Company, though less successful, had many parallels to International Paper.

burgh Coal Company in 1899 and greatly enlarged the Consolidation Coal Company in 1903 were followed by a reorganization and consolidation of mining properties and then by the creation of large marketing departments which operated throughout most of the country. The merger of close to 30 paper companies, forming the International Paper Company in 1899, was followed first by consolidation and reorganization of the manufacturing plants, next by the formation of a national marketing organization with headquarters in New York City, and then by the purchase of large tracts of timber in Maine and Canada. These three activities were departmentalized under vice presidents and controlled from the New York office. In all these cases, the central office was responsible for the flow of materials from mine or forest to the customer or retailer.

The explosive industries underwent a comparable sweeping change in 1902 and 1903. Since the 1870's, price and production schedules had been decided by the industry's Gunpowder Trade Association, and almost from its beginning, that Association had been controlled by one firm, the E. I. DuPont de Nemours & Company. However, the member concerns had retained their own corporate identities and managements. In 1902, the DuPonts bought out a large number of these independent companies through exchanges of stock, and then consolidated them into a single centralized organization. In the process, plants were shut down, others enlarged, and new ones built. A nation-wide selling organization was created, and centralized accounting, purchasing, engineering and traffic departments formed. Once the new organization was completed, then the company's executives obtained control of their raw materials through the purchase of nitrate mines and deposits in Chile.

Except possibly in paper, the control of price and production does not appear to have been a major motive for the initial combinations in the extractive industries making producers' goods. In steel before 1901, and in nonferrous metals and coal, there were several combinations, but none acquired as much as 20 per cent of the market. Nor is there any evidence that the creators of the different mergers, while they were forming their organizations, were arranging with one another to set over-all price and production schedules. In explosives, control of competition could not have been a significant reason for the 1902 changes since the DuPont company had enjoyed such control since the 1870's. In coal and explosives, and possibly in copper, the major motive for combination, consolidation, and the integration of supply with the manufacturing and marketing processes seems to have been an expectation of lowered costs through the creation of a national distributing organization, the consolidation of manufacturing activities, and the effective coordination of the different industrial processes by one central office. In steel and possibly copper, the desire for an assured supply of raw materials appears to have been more significant in encouraging combination and integration.

Changes and Integration in the Finished Producers' Goods Industries

Control of price and production was, on the other hand, much more of an obvious motive for combination and resulting consolidation in the industries manufacturing finished products or machinery from the semi-finished materials produced by the extractive firms. Concern over supply, however, was also a cause for change, for after 1898 the users of steel, copper, coal, and other semi-finished materials felt threatened by the growing number of combinations among their suppliers. In any case, between 1898 and 1900 there was a wave of mergers in these industries, largely Wall Street financed, which led to the formation of American Tin Plate, American Wire & Steel, American Steel Hoop, National Tube, American Bridge, American Sheet Metal, Shelby Steel Tube, American Can, National Enameling & Stamping Company and a number of other combinations among steel-fabricating firms.[24] At the same time, there were many amalgamations in the power machinery and implement businesses, such as American Car & Foundry, American Locomotive, Allis-Chalmers, International Steam Pump, and International Harvester. The largest combination among the copper users, the American Brass Company, came a little later, in 1903, after the Guggenheims, Rogers, and Heinze had completed the major copper mergers.

Nearly all these combinations quickly consolidated their constituent companies into a single operating organization. Manufacturing facilities were unified and systematized, over-all accounting procedures instituted, and national and often world-wide distributing organizations formed. Many set up central traffic and purchasing departments; some even began to assure themselves control over supply by building up their own rolling mills and blast furnaces. As American Wire & Steel and National Tube began to make their own steel, they cancelled contracts with Carnegie and other semi-

[24] The best brief summary of these mergers and the formation of the United States Steel Corporation is in Eliot Jones, *The Trust Problem in the United States* (New York, 1924), pp. 189–200. The companies' annual reports and prospectuses provide additional material.

finished steel producers. This development, in turn, led Carnegie to develop plans for fabricating his own finished products.[25]

The resulting threat of overcapacity and price-cutting led to the formation of the United States Steel Corporation.[26] This giant merger, which included Carnegie, Federal and National Steel, and the first six of the fabricating companies listed above, continued on as a combination. Although the activities of the various subsidiaries were re-formed and redefined, there was no consolidation. United States Steel remained a holding company only, and the central office at 72 Broadway did comparatively little to coordinate the operations of its many subsidiary companies.

After 1901, the fabricators and the machinery manufacturers made little attempt to produce their own steel or copper. Nor did the makers of semi-finished products try, for some years to come, to do their own fabricating. Possibly the metal users realized that even with the formation of United States Steel they were fairly certain of alternative sources of supply. Also they may have found that once they had combined they had enough bargaining power to assure themselves of a supply of steel and other materials more cheaply than they could make it themselves.

While such firms no longer sought to control their basic materials, many, particularly the machinery makers like General Electric, Westinghouse, American Car & Foundry, International Harvester and, a little later, General Motors, began to purchase or set up subsidiaries or departments to make parts and components.[27] Here again the motive was essentially defensive. Since much of their manufacturing had now become mainly assembling, they wanted to be sure to have a supply of parts available at all times. The lack of a vital part could temporarily shut down a plant. However, they expected to take only a portion of the output; a major share was sold to outsiders. One outstanding exception to this pattern was Henry Ford. He came to control his raw materials as well as his parts and components, and rarely sold such parts to outside companies. But Ford's insistence on having a completely integrated organization from mine to marekt, concentrated largely in one huge

[25] Hendrick, *Carnegie*, Vol. II, pp. 116–119.

[26] The beginnings and the operation of the United States Steel Corporation are outlined in Abraham Berglund, *The United States Steel Corporation: A Study of Growth and Combination in the Iron and Steel Industry* (New York, 1907), Arundel Cotter, *The Authentic History of the United States Steel Corporation* (New York, 1916), Ida M. Tarbell, *The Life of Elbert H. Gary, the Story of Steel* (New York, 1925).

[27] This generalization is based on the annual reports of the several companies.

plant, proved to be one of the most costly mistakes in American business history.

Control of parts and accessory units led to a diversification of the types of products these manufacturing companies made and sold. Such diversification brought, over time, important changes in business organization. Even more significant for stimulating product diversification was the new "full line" strategy adopted by a number of these recently consolidated concerns. Such a policy, initiated largely to help assure the maximum use of the new departments, encouraged technological as well as organizational change.

Pioneers in developing "full lines" in the producers' goods industries were the two great electrical companies: General Electric and Westinghouse. Unlike almost any other of the leading American industrial companies in 1900, these two had begun as research and development rather than manufacturing organizations. Because of their origins, they had the skilled personnel and the necessary equipment to move, in the mid-1890's, from making lighting equipment alone to manufacturing many lines of electric traction and power machinery products.[28] Allis-Chalmers, International Steam Pump, and American Locomotive began, shortly after their formation and subsequent consolidations, to develop new lines using electric and gasoline engines.[29] International Harvester, building up a number of farm implement lines, also started to experiment with the use of the gasoline engine for machinery on the farm. In this same first decade of the twentieth century, rubber, explosive, and chemical companies began to turn to industrial chemistry in their search to develop broader lines of products.

Continuing diversification came, however, largely in industries where science, particularly chemistry and physics, could be most easily applied. And it was in these industries, and in those which were directly affected by the coming of two new sources of power, electricity and the internal combustion engine, that the major innovations in American industry came after 1900. The chemical, automotive, power machinery, rubber, and petroleum industries led the way to the development of new processes and products, new ways

---

[28] As is well described in Harold C. Passer, *The Electrical Manufacturers* (Cambridge, 1953).

[29] The development of new lines by Allis-Chalmers, International Steam Pump, and American Locomotive is mentioned in their annual reports in the first decade of the twentieth century. International Harvester's similar "full line" policies are described in Cyrus McCormick, *The Century of the Reaper* (New York, 1931), chaps. 6–9, and United States Bureau of Corporations, *The International Harvester Co., March 3, 1913* (Washington, 1913), especially pp. 156–158.

of internal organization and new techniques of external competition as the new century unfolded. The metals industries and those processing agricultural goods have, on the other hand, changed relatively little since the beginning of the century. In these industries, the same firms make much the same products, use much the same processes, and compete in much the same manner in the 1950's as they did in the 1900's. For them the greatest period of change came in the last decade of the nineteenth century.

CONCLUSION: THE BASIC INNOVATIONS

The middle of the first decade of the new century might be said to mark the end of an era. By 1903, the great merger movement was almost over, and by then the metals industries and those processing agricultural products had developed patterns of internal organization and external competition which were to remain. In those years, too, leading chemical, electrical, rubber, power machinery and implement companies had initiated their "full line" policy, and had instituted the earliest formal research and development departments created in this country. In this decade also, electricity was becoming for the first time a significant source of industrial power, and the automobile was just beginning to revolutionize American transportation. From 1903 on, the new generators of power and the new technologies appear to have become the dominant stimuli to innovation in American industry, and such innovations were primarily those which created new products and processes. Changes in organizational methods and marketing techniques were largely responses to technological advances.

This seems much less true of the changes during the 20 to 25 years before 1903. In that period, the basic innovations were more in the creation of new forms of organization and new ways of marketing. The great modern corporation, carrying on the major industrial processes, namely, purchasing, and often production of materials and parts, manufacturing, marketing, and finance—all within the same organizational structure—had its beginnings in that period. Such organizations hardly existed, outside of the railroads, before the 1880's. By 1900 they had become the basic business unit in American industry.

Each of these major processes became managed by a corporate department, and all were coordinated and supervised from a central office. Of the departments, marketing was the most significant. The creation of nation-wide distributing and selling organizations was the initial step in the growth of many large consumer goods companies. Mergers in both the consumer and producer goods industries were almost always followed by the formation of a centralized sales department.

The consolidation of plants under a single manufacturing department usually accompanied or followed the formation of a national marketing organization. The creation of such a manufacturing department normally meant the concentration of production in fewer and larger plants, and such consolidation probably lowered unit costs and increased output per worker. The creation of such a department in turn led to the setting up of central traffic, purchasing, and often engineering organizations. Large-scale buying, more rational routing of raw materials and finished products, more systematic plant lay-out, and plant location in relation to materials and markets probably lowered costs still further. Certainly the creators of these organizations believed that it did. In the extractive and machinery industries integration went one step further. Here the motives for controlling raw materials or parts and components were defensive as well as designed to cut costs through providing a more efficient flow of materials from mine to market.

These great national industrial organizations required a large market to provide the volume necessary to support the increased overhead costs. Also, to be profitable, they needed careful coordination between the different functional departments. This coordination required a steady flow of accurate data on costs, sales, and on all purchasing, manufacturing, and marketing activities. As a result, the comptroller's office became an increasingly important department. In fact, one of the first moves after a combination by merger or purchase was to institute more effective and detailed accounting procedures. Also, the leading entrepreneurs of the period, men like Rockefeller, Carnegie, Swift, Duke, Preston, Clark, and the DuPonts, had to become, as had the railroad executives of an earlier generation, experts in reading and interpreting business statistics.

Consolidation and departmentalization meant that the leading industrial corporations became operating rather than holding companies, in the sense that the officers and managers of the companies were directly concerned with operating activities. In fact, of the 50 companies with the largest assets in 1909, only United States Steel, Amalgamated Copper, and one or two other copper companies remained purely holding companies. In most others, the central office included the heads of the major functional departments, usually the president, vice presidents, and sometimes a chairman of the board and one or two representatives of financial interests. These men made major policy and administrative decisions and evaluated the performance of the departments and the corporation as a whole. In the extractive industries a few companies, like Standard Oil (N.J.) and some of the metals companies, were partly holding and partly operating companies. At Standard Oil nearly all important decisions were made in the central headquarters, at 26 Broadway, which housed not only the presidents of the subsidiaries but the powerful policy formulating and coordinating committees.[30] But in some of the metals companies, the subsidiaries producing and transporting raw materials retained a large degree of autonomy.

The coming of the large vertically integrated, centralized, functionally departmentalized industrial organization altered the internal and external situations in which and about which business decisions were made. Information about markets, supplies, and operating performance as well as suggestions for action often had to come up through the several levels of the departmental hierarchies, while decisions and suggestions based on this data had to be transmitted down the same ladder for implementation. Executives on each level became increasingly specialists in one function—in sales, production, purchasing, or finance—and most remained in one department and so handled one function only for the major part of their business careers. Only he who climbed to the very top of the departmental ladder had a chance to see his own company as a single operating unit. Where a company's markets, sources of raw materials, and manufacturing processes remained relatively stable, as was true in the metals industries and in those processing agricultural goods, the nature of the business executive's work became increasingly routine and administrative.

When the internal situation had become bureaucratic, the external one tended to be oligopolistic. Vertical integration by one manufacturer forced others to follow. Thus, in a very short time, many American industries became dominated by a few large firms, with the smaller ones handling local and more specialized aspects of the business. Occasionally industries like oil, tobacco, and sugar, came to be controlled by one company, but in most cases legal action by the federal government in the years after 1900 turned monopolistic industries into oligopolistic ones.

Costs, rather than interfirm competition, began to determine prices. With better information on costs, supplies, and market con-

---

[30] Hidys, *Pioneering in Big Business*, chap. 3 and pp. 323-388.

ditions, the companies were able to determine price quite accurately on the basis of the desired return on investment. The managers of the different major companies had little to gain by cutting prices below an acceptable profit margin. On the other hand, if one firm set its prices excessively high, the other firms could increase their share of the market by selling at a lower price and still maintain a profit. They would, however, rarely cut to the point where this margin was eliminated. As a result, after 1900, price leadership, price umbrellas, and other evidences of oligopolistic competition became common in many American industries. To increase their share of the market and to improve their profit position, the large corporations therefore concerned themselves less with price and concentrated more on obtaining new customers by advertising, brand names, and product differentiations; on cutting costs through further improvement and integration of the manufacturing, marketing, and buying processes; and on developing more diversified lines of products.

The coming of the large vertically integrated corporation changed more than just the practices of American industrialists and their industries. The effect on the merchant, particularly the wholesaler, and on the financier, especially the investment banker, has been suggested here. The relation between the growth of these industrial units and the rise of labor unions has often been pointed out. Certainly the regulation of the large corporation became one of the major political issues of these years, and the devices created to carry out such a regulation were significant innovations in American constitutional, legal, and political institutions. But an examination of such effects is beyond the scope of this paper.

Reasons for the Basic Innovations

One question remains to be reviewed. Why did the vertically integrated corporation come when it did, and in the way it did? The creation by nearly all the large firms of nation-wide selling and distributing organizations indicates the importance of the national market. It was necessary that the market be an increasingly urban one. The city took the largest share of the goods manufactured by the processors of agricultural products. The city, too, with its demands for construction materials, lighting, heating and many other facilities, provided the major market for the metals and other producers' goods industries after railroad construction slowed. Without the rapidly growing urban market there would have been little need and little opportunity for the coming of big business in American industry. And such a market could hardly have existed before the completion of a nation-wide railroad network.

What other reasons might there have been for the swift growth of the great industrial corporation? What about foreign markets? In some industries, particularly oil, the overseas trade may have been an important factor. However, in most businesses the domestic customers took the lion's share of the output, and in nearly all of them the move abroad appears to have come after the creation of the large corporation, and after such corporations had fashioned their domestic marketing organization.

What about the investor looking for profitable investments, and the promoter seeking new promotions? Financiers and promoters certainly had an impact on the changes after 1897, but again they seem primarily to have taken advantage of what had already proved successful. The industrialists themselves, rather than the financiers, initiated most of the major changes in business organization. Availability of capital and cooperation with the financier figured much less prominently in these industrial combinations and consolidations than had been the case with the earlier construction of the railroads and with the financing of the Civil War.

What about technological changes? Actually, except for electricity, the major innovations in the metals industries seem to have come before or after the years under study here. Most of the technological improvements in the agricultural processing industries appear to have been made to meet the demands of the new urban market. The great technological innovations that accompanied the development of electricity, the internal combustion engine, and industrial chemistry did have their beginning in these years, and were, indeed, to have fundamental impact on the American business economy. Yet this impact was not to be really felt until after 1900.

What about entrepreneurial talent? Certainly the best-known entrepreneurs of this period were those who helped to create the large industrial corporation. If, as Joseph A. Schumpeter suggests, "The defining characteristic [of the entrepreneur and his function] is simply the doing of new things, and doing things that are already done, in a new way (innovation)," Rockefeller, Carnegie, Frick, Swift, Duke, McCormick, the DuPonts, the Guggenheims, Coffin of General Electric, Preston of United Fruit, and Clark of Singer Sewing Machine were all major innovators of their time.[31]

[31] Joseph A. Schumpeter, "The Creative Response in Economic History," *Journal of Economic History*, Vol. VII (May, 1947), p. 151, and also his *Theory of Economic Development*, trans, Redvers Opie (Cambridge, 1934), pp. 74–94.

TABLE I
The Fifty Largest Industrials
(Numbers indicate relative size according to 1909 assets)

Consumers' Goods Companies

Agricultural Processing	*Extractive*	*Manufacturing*
3. Am. Tobacco	2. Standard Oil	4. Int'l. Harvester
8. Armour & Co.	26. Va.-Carolina Chem.	10. U. S. Rubber
9. American Sugar	35. American Agri. Chem.	12. Singer Mfg. Co.
13. Swift & Co.		
30. Nat'l. Biscuit		
33. Distillers' Securities		
50. United Fruit		

Producers' Goods Companies

Agricultural Processing	*Extractive*	*Manufacturing*
6. Central Leather	1. U. S. Steel	7. Pullman
18. Corn Products Co.	5. Amalgamated	15. Gen. Elec.
21. Am. Woolens	(Anaconda) Copper	16. Am. Car & Foundry
	11. Am. Smelting &	19. Am. Can
	Refining	22. Westinghouse
	14. Pittsburgh Coal	24. DuPont
	17. Colo. Fuel & Iron	29. Am. Locomotive
	20. Lackawanna	36. Allis-Chalmers
	23. Consolidation Coal	44. Int. Steam Pump
	25. Republic Steel	46. Western Electric
	27. Int'l. Paper	
	28. Bethlehem Steel	
	31. Cambria Steel	
	33. Associated Oil	
	34. Calumet & Hecla	
	37. Crucible Steel	
	38. Lake Superior Corp.	
	39. U. S. Smelting & Ref.	
	40. United Copper	
	41. National Lead	
	42. Phelps Dodge	
	43. Lehigh Coal	
	45. Jones & Laughlin	
	48. Am. Writing Paper	
	49. Copper Range	

And their innovations were not in technology, but rather in organization and in marketing. "Doing a new thing," is, to Schumpeter a "creative response" to a new situation, and the situation to which these innovators responded appears to have been the rise of the national urban market.

There must be an emphasis here on the words "seem" and "appear." The framework used is a preliminary one and the data itself, based on readily available printed material rather than on business records are hardly as detailed or accurate as could be desired. More data, more precise and explicit questions, and other types and ranges of questions will modify the generalizations suggested here. For the moment, however, I would like to suggest, if only to encourage the raising of questions and the further compilation and analysis of data, that *the* major innovation in the American economy between the 1880's and the turn of the century was the creation of the great corporations in American industry. This innovation, as I have tried to show, was a response to the growth of a national and increasingly urban market that was created by the building of a national railroad network—the dynamic force in the economy in the quarter century before 1880. After 1900 the newly modified methods of interfirm and intrafirm administration remained relatively unchanged (as did the location of major markets and sources of raw materials) except in those industries directly affected by new sources of power and the systematic application of science to industry. In the twentieth century electricity, the internal combustion engine, and systematic, institutionalized research and development took the place of the national urban market as the dynamic factor in the American industrial economy.[32]

---

[32] This point has only been considered briefly here, but has been developed at some length in my "Development Diversification and Decentralization," to be published in a book of essays tentatively titled *The Postwar American Economy* under the sponsorship of the Department of Economics, Massachusetts Institute of Technology.

16

It is not to be wondered that nativism, or fear of and hostility toward foreign influences, figures prominently in the history of the United States. Americans are a people self-created in the full glare of modern, recorded history. They began as displaced peoples from other lands in an age when a man's primary identity was increasingly derived from his nation rather than from his locality or his church. The break from English nationality in the eighteenth century confronted Americans with the necessity of creating a new national identity. Sometimes this search for identity expressed itself in mild, cultural forms, as in Noah Webster's dictionary and spellers and in Emerson's famous lecture "The American Scholar." But the insistent need to erect a new identity resulted also in violent acts, as in the verbal and physical attacks on "foreigners" and "foreign" ideas. Only those unsure of their identity fear losing it. Americans have rarely been sure. Even today no democratic society has a legislative body comparable in name to the Un-American Activities Committee of the United States House of Representatives.

But as Higham observes in this article, the sources of nativism lie deeper than the newness of the society. They are also to be found in another peculiar attribute of American society: its great competitiveness, which is at once a cause of its prosperity and a result of its economic well-being. It is in demonstrating the influence of social competition that Higham's article represents a turning point in the historical examination of the nativist impulse in the American experience.

If on the one hand Americans have given vent to nativist fears, they have, on the other, regretted and then derided the nativist movements of their history. For nativism, almost by definition, is out of place in a society dedicated to opportunity for all and slavery for none. Instinctively Americans recognize, as President Franklin Roosevelt puckishly told a meeting of the Daughters of the American Revolution, that we are all "fellow immigrants." As a consequence modern, liberal-minded historians have usually simply rejected nativism as born out of bigotry by thoughtless prejudice. What Higham suggests in this article is that close analysis of the roots of nativism reveals not only important insights into nativism but important facts about American social development and thought.

From a historiographical point of view Higham's article is not the first to take a deeper look into the social sources of nativism. Breaks began to appear in the solid front of scholary condemnation of nativism as long ago as 1924. That year, in the October issue of the *South Atlantic Quarterly*, William G. Bean published an article entitled "An Aspect of Know-Nothingism—the Immigrant and Slavery." The article pointed out that in the 1850s one of the reasons for popular support of the Know-Nothing party in Massachusetts was the Irish immigrants' hostility to the antislavery movement rather than simply their foreign origin. Ten years later in another article, "Puritan versus Celt, 1850–1860," *New England Quarterly*, VII (March 1934), 70–89, Bean further documented his argument. Still later, Harry J. Carman and Reinhard H. Luthin in "Some Aspects of the Know-Nothing Movement Reconsidered," *South Atlantic Quarterly*, XXXIX (April 1940), 213–234, continued the re-examination by calling attention to the variety of forms that the Know-Nothing movement assumed in different parts of the country. W. Darrell Overdyke in his *Know-Nothing Party in the South* (Baton Rouge, 1950) documented the same point by showing that in the South Know-Nothingism frequently abandoned anti-Catholicism, if only because of the large and well-established Catholic populations in Louisiana and Maryland. Oscar Handlin's *Boston's Immigrants* (Cambridge, Mass. 1941) summed up the Massachusetts story in masterly fashion. Higham's article, then, is a culmination of a quarter century of critical reappraisal of nativism.

The point of the several studies prior to Higham's was that foreigners or immigrants, in a limited sense, at least, evoke the antagonisms directed against them. Generally, as Handlin showed in his book on the Boston Irish, the cause is the conservativism of the immigrants, which stood like a monolith in the path of reforms desired by many nativeborn citizens. Higham has taken this conclusion, broadened it to include other immigrant groups, and applied it to a later period and on a wider geographical scale. Rather

than seeing nativism as simply an irrational belaboring of the out-
group, he sees it as resulting from more objective factors, notably
the struggle for a better place or social status on the part of the
immigrant and the Roman Catholicism of many immigrants in the
midst of a largely Protestant nativeborn population. Since Higham
wrote, religious differences have continued to be emphasized by
historians in explaining political and social conflict in America. Lee
Benson, for example, in his *Concept of Jacksonian Democracy*
(Princeton, 1961) emphasizes religion as one of the chief attributes
differentiating Whigs and Democrats in New York State. Actually
religion alone is so potent a divisive force that there is reason to
believe that Higham's lumping together of anti-Catholicism and opposition to immigrants may obscure real differences between anti-
Catholic and anti-immigrant groups. Donald L. Kinzer, for example,
in his recent *An Episode in Anti-Catholicism: The American Protective Association* (Seattle, 1964) points out that the APA officially and in practice welcomed non-Catholic immigrants in its
crusade against the pope. And David Brion Davis in two articles
has observed that opposition to some religious groups served a
real function for those who displayed such hostilities (see his
"Themes of Counter-Subversion: An Analysis of Anti-Masonic,
Anti-Catholic and Anti-Mormon Literature," *Mississippi Valley Historical Review*, XLVII [September 1960], 205–224, and "Some
Ideological Functions of Prejudice in Ante-Bellum America," *American Quarterly*, XV [Summer 1963], 115–125). Like Higham, Davis
in his studies goes deeper than simply deploring intolerance toward
minority groups. Unlike Higham, however, he sees the deeper meaning in the ideology of the persecuting groups rather than in the
actions of the groups under attack.

A further merit of Higham's article is its directing our attention
to the varying responses of the nativeborn to the many different
nationalities who entered the United States. Although historians
generally speak of the hostility to immigrants, the fact is, as Higham
shows, that not all immigrant groups attracted hostility to the same
degree. Some, like the English, for example, evoked very little, while
the Irish, the Chinese, and the Jews aroused considerable. By asking
why some and not other immigrant nationalities evoked nativist
responses, Higham makes it difficult to believe that mere foreign
origin was sufficient to account for nativist concern. By another
observation he further calls into question simple foreignness as a
factor. Nativist response to immigrants varied, depending upon
how well established the newcomers were. Thus early arrivals, like

the Jews in San Francisco, escaped the kind of hostility that later-arriving Jews confronted in eastern cities.

In short, the study of nativism today is more than the story of bigotry, though it is certainly that, too; it is the examination of the painful process whereby the diversity of American life became accepted. For that diversity, after all, is more fundamentally American than the attempt to impose uniformity. Perhaps nativism is best seen as a response to the immigrant's participation in the American belief in social competition and glorification of material success.

Mr. Higham is professor of history at the University of Michigan. His book *Strangers in the Land* (New Brunswick, 1955) is now the standard study of nativism for the years between 1860 and 1925.

Another Look at Nativism *

BY JOHN HIGHAM

MY assignment this afternoon is probably not as treacherous as it appears to me to be; yet I embark upon it with acute trepidation. To deliver a paper on a subject *after* having written a book about it invites a kind of double jeopardy. There is, to be sure, an easy way out. I might sum up, more persuasively if possible, the story that is already copyrighted, with, perhaps, a special effort to lay low the critics. But they have been too indulgent for that, and anyway re-iteration seldom sheds much light. Another possible way of proceeding is to flatter oneself that others may wish to go further in more or less the same direction that the author has taken, and to point out to them some parts of the terrain which he has only sketch-ily mapped and which they might well fill in. This strategem meets the need for innovation half-way while safeguarding the author's intellectual capital. Any activity that may result, however, is more likely to be trivial than significant. Moreover, to make such a sum-

SOURCE: Reprinted by permission from *The Catholic Historical Review*, XLIV (July 1958). Copyright, 1958, by the Catholic University of America.

* In its original form this article was read as a paper at the joint session of the American Catholic Historical Association and the American Historical Association, New York, December 29, 1957.

mons requires a presumptuous self-assurance that is not always be-coming.

Shall I, then, fall back upon a perilous, third alternative? Shall I acknowledge the expectation and hope, which historians are sup-posed to cherish, that new research will depart from present con-clusions in the very act of appropriating them? Shall I confess that nativism now looks less adequate as a vehicle for studying the strug-gles of nationalities in America, than my earlier report of it, and other reports, might indicate? I am nerved to do so by the reflec-tion that historical inquiry does not advance so much by reversal and disavowal as it does by a widening of focus. At its best it achieves a fruitful tension between perspectives that do not cancel, but rather complement one another.

In some such spirit, I propose that research on the conflicts asso-ciated with foreign elements in American society should take a new line. The nativist theme, as defined and developed to date, is imagi-natively exhausted. Scholars who would do more than fill in the out-lines of existing knowledge must make a fresh start from premises rather different from those that have shaped the studies of the last twenty years. To explain what I mean will require some considera-tion of the literature on nativism that is now extant, and it will be convenient for me to speak particularly of the interests and assump-tions from which my own book derived.

The very term "nativism" has influenced profoundly our angle of vision in studying anti-foreign and anti-Catholic forces. The word is an "ism." It came into being in the middle of the nineteenth cen-tury to describe the principles advanced by a political party. Etymo-logically and historically, therefore, it refers to a set of attitudes, a state of mind. In contrast to words like assimilation, segregation, marginality, and the like, "nativism" does not direct attention pri-marily to an actual social process or condition. Those who study the phenomenon want to know why certain ideas emerge when and where they do, and how those ideas pass into action. Consequently, the histories of nativism have not tried, except incidentally, to clarify the structure of society. Instead, they trace an emotionally charged impulse.

While the word itself almost inevitably pulls our interest toward subjective attitudes, our contemporary culture has pushed us further in that direction. Since the 1930's the intellect and the conscience of America have been in revolt against what is call "prejudice," viz., the ill-treatment of ethnic and religious minorities. Now, prejudice is by definition subjective—a pre-judgment not grounded in factual experience. Nativism, of course, commonly qualifies as prejudice; and students regard it not only as a state of mind but as one which badly distorts the true nature of things. A good historian will certainly not consider nativism entirely as a set of prejudices; but since no one writes about it unless he shares the current revulsion against ethnic injustice, the subjective irrationality of nativism leaps to the historian's eye. He wants to know how we have mistaken one another and, perhaps too, he wishes to assure us that the mistkes were, indeed, mistakes in the sense that they arose from no compelling social need.

Along with the crusade against prejudice, another aspect of modern thought has affected the study of nativism. We live in an age that has an almost superstitious awe and distrust of ideologies. That is to say, we dread the power of ideas that are weapons in the hands of "hidden persuaders." Karl Mannheim, George Orwell, and others have taught us to see, behind the inhumanity of our day, the coercion of ideas which interpret life in terms functional to someone's bid for power. Disseminated by the agitator and the propagandist, ideologists distort reality, attack the foundations of belief, and threaten the independence and integrity of the human mind.[1] Historians and social scientists alike have been fascinated by ideologies and have labored to expose their dynamics. There is a consequent tendency to fix upon ideology as the critical factor in many a social problem, in the perhaps tenuous hope that the problem will yield to a reasonable solution once the ideological magic is exorcised.

The relevant consideration here is that the concern over ideologies reflects, more systematically, the same assumption that underlies the concept of prejudice. Both owe a great deal to our distinctively modern emphasis on the irrational depths of human nature. The modern mind dwells on the unconscious savagery lurking in its own dark corners. At the springs of human action the irrationalist historian, novelist, or social psychologist is not likely to find realistic motives of solidarity or calculated self-interest; nor is he likely to find high ideals. Instead, he discovers a fog of myths, prejudices, stereotypes, and power-hungry ideologies. If he looks at the American past he may notice this miasma overhanging many scenes, but nowhere does he find it more densely exhibited than in nativism. Nativism displays all the terrors that beset his own sensibility. It is an ideology: a rigid system of ideas, manipulated by propagandists seeking power, irrationally blaming some external group for

[1] In using the elusive term "ideology" in the hostile sense in which Mannheim employed it, I intend to designate a point of view toward ideas, not to endorse that point of view.

the major ills of society. It mobilizes prejudices, feeds on stereotypes, radiates hysteria, and provokes our outrage against ethnic
injustice.

I have said enough, I hope, about the general frame of reference
within which nativism is studied to indicate that interpretation of it
almost inevitably stresses subjective, irrational motives. Whenever
a contemporary point of view gives so much encouragement to a
certain historical approach, should we not suspect that our angle
of vision screens out a good deal? Specifically, should we not suspect
that the nativist theme does little justice to the objective realities of
ethnic relations? To answer this question concretely, let me turn
to my own experience in studying the subject.

Nativism, I felt sure, would not submit to effective analysis unless
it could be identified consistently as an idea. Its meaning must in-
here in a set of beliefs protean enough to apply to a variety of ad-
versaries yet definite enough to show the form and direction of its
history. To unravel the strands of nativist ideology became, therefore, a central problem. I discovered that the main strands ran more
or less independently of one another. There were, in fact, several
nativisms, each of which fixed upon some internal alien influence
as a gravely divisive threat to national unity. Generically, nativism
was a defensive type of nationalism, but the defense varied as the
nativist lashed out sometimes against a religious peril, sometimes
against a revolutionary peril, sometimes against a racial peril. Although on occasion nativists rallied against other kinds of disloyalty
too, these persistent anxieties provided a framework for studying
the nativistic mentality.

Notice what I was *not* doing by pursuing the subject in this way.
I was not trying to explain the total complex of ethnic tensions in
American society. I was not focusing upon the institutional rivalries
of Protestant and Catholic or upon their religious beliefs. I was not
dealing fundamentally with the living standards of Italian and
Yankee or with the party affiliations of Irish and German. All these
crowded the background, for all of them helped to shape the nativist
temper. Yet such basic components of the American ethnic scene
could not occupy the foreground of my picture without blurring the
clarity and significance of nativism as an idea. The bad habit of
labeling as nativist any kind of unfriendliness toward immigrants
or Catholic values had to be resisted. If nativism is not a mere term
of derogation, it can embrace only antagonisms that belong within
the ideologies of a passionate national consciousness.

As I studied the main nativist traditions, I discovered that over a
long span of time they had not changed conceptually as much as an

historian of ideas might suppose. Except on the subject of race (and in related forms of anti-Semitism), the kind of accusations which nativists leveled against foreign elements remained relatively constant. Anti-radical and anti-Catholic complaints in the twentieth century sounded much like those bruited in the eighteenth. The big changes were not so much intellectual as emotional. The same idea might be mildly innocuous at one time and charged with potent feelings at another. For the history of nativism, therefore, emotional intensity provided the significant measurement of change. If nativism was an ideological disease, perhaps, one might best diagnose it by observing when the fever raged and when it slackened.

The outlines of an over-all interpretation now became visible. During scattered intervals in American history (only two of which I studied in detail) nativism erupted powerfully enough to have an immediate impact on national development. In the late 1790's it produced the notorious Alien Acts. In the 1850's it contributed to the breakup of the party system. In the decade from 1886 to 1896 it magnified a host of social problems associated with unrestricted immigration. And in the period of World War I nativism unleashed repressive orthodoxies on a grand scale. In each of these four periods the United States was undergoing a major national crisis. In the 1790's international conflict intensified the cleavage between political parties. Sectional cleavage came to a head in the 1850's, class cleavage in the 1890's. World War I confronted an unprepared nation with the shock of total war. In each of these crises, confidence in the homogeneity of American culture broke down. In desperate efforts to rebuild national unity men rallied against the symbols of foreignness that were appropriate to their predicament.

My appraisal was more complex than this sketchy outline suggests, of course. And I have no doubt that nativist ideas deserve still further study, particularly to elucidate their relation to our traditions of individualism and Puritanism. What bothers me most, however, is that the concept of nativism has proved serviceable only for understanding the extreme and fanatical manifestations of ethnic discord. It illuminates the frenzies of the mob, the nightmares of the propagandist, the repressive statute, and the moments of national frustration. Nativism owes its significance to this intensity of feeling: and historians, fascinated by the men of passion and the moods of alarm, have neglected the less spectacular but more steadily sustained contentions imbedded in the fabric of our social organization.

In order to have a short-hand designation for such underlying stresses, we may call them status rivalries. By this I mean all of the activities—political, religious, economic, and associational—through which men of different ethnic backgrounds have competed for prestige and for favorable positions in community life. Status rivalries have not arisen from irrational myths but rather from objective conditions; they have not usually reached the point of hatred and hysteria; they have not depended upon ideological expression; they have not risen and fallen in cyclical fashion. Instead, they are part of the slow processes of ethnic integration, and they have shaped profoundly the course of our social development.

For a generation historians and even most social scientists interested in the jostling of Protestant and Catholic, of Christian and Jew, of old and new Americans, have not wanted to understand these tensions as basic structural realities. To do so is to recognize that our divergent and unequal backgrounds are causes—not just results—of our difficulties. It is more comforting to think that everyone is pretty much alike[2] and that our differences are foisted upon us by myths and stereotypes. Attributing ethnic cleavage to nativism or racism takes the curse off the fact of inequality.

By the same token, the nativist approach validates our sympathy with the out-group. Nativism is primarily a one-way street, along which the native American moves aggressively against the outsider. Thus, the history of nativism inevitably portrays minorities as victims rather than participants. It permits us to assume their relative innocence. We need not ask too closely why the Irish were the shock troops of the anti-Chinese movement in California,[3] how the American Protective Association could attract a following among Negroes,[4] or why the Scots in America brought so much wrath upon themselves during the Revolution.[5]

At this point you may concede that many peripheral frictions do occur outside the orbit of nativism; but you may still insist that it explains the more persistent difficulties, such as those which Catholics and Jews have met. At times, of course, irrational myths have played the decisive part in these encounters, but not as commonly

[2] Boyd C. Shafer, "Men Are More Alike," *American Historical Review*, LVII (1952), 593–612, exhibits the prevalent point of view.

[3] Joint Special Committee to Investigate Chinese Immigration, *Report* (Senate Report No. 689, 44 Cong., 2 Sess., 1877), 55–56; New York *Tribune*, February 19, 1879.

[4] New York *Tribune*, June 14, 1895; Ruth Knox Stough, "The American Protective Association" (unpublished master's thesis, University of Nebraska, 1931), pp. 6, 63.

[5] Ian Charles Cargill Graham, *Colonists from Scotland: Emigration to North America, 1707–1783* (Ithaca, 1956), pp. 128–180.

or exclusively as historians have suggested. The real issues of faith which set religious groups apart can not fairly be reduced to nativist terms. Moreover, struggles for status underlie much that we attribute too easily to irrational prejudice, and I suspect that the question of status has touched the daily life of most Americans more intimately than any ideological warfare.

Consider for a moment the situation of the Irish Catholic in the late nineteenth or early twentieth century. Did he suffer much from nativist visions of popish conspiracies? It seems unlikely. He worshipped freely and had no legal disabilities; the most extravagant propaganda against him circulated in completely Protestant rural areas remote from his own urban habitations. The great handicap he faced was his social and economic subordination to the older Americans, who treated him partly as a joke, partly as an underling, and partly as a ruffian.[6] And when he compensated in politics for his inferiority in other spheres, all the forces of Yankee respectability mobilized in Republican ranks against him. In scores of communities throughout the North both political parties were essentially ethnic coalitions.[7] Even the American Protective Association was, perhaps, chiefly effective as an instrument for ousting the Irish from the municipal jobs which they held to the disadvantage of their ethnic rivals. In the western cities where the A.P.A.'s greatest strength lay, Yankees, Scandinavians, and British used it to get control of school boards, police forces, and fire departments.[8]

[6] In spite of the vast integration that has taken place since that time, status rivalry still plays a key role in our religious divisions. A priest from Virginia recently indicated to me how much less important ideological conflict may be when he remarked that the real anti-Catholics in the South are Episcopalians. When I inquired about the Fundamentalist churches, he admitted indifferently that some rural preachers might still be thundering against the pope far from any Catholic ears; but what pained him was to be told by well-to-do Episcopalians that they could not become Catholics, although Catholic doctrines attracted them, because they would lose their standing in the community if they did so.

[7] "When he went to the Church Seminary, it was a matter of course that every member of the faculty was a Republican, and that every one of his classmates had come from a Republican household. . . . Indeed, even among the laity, Theron could not feel sure that he had ever known a Democrat; that is, at all closely. He understood very little about politics, it is true. If he had been driven into a corner, and forced to attempt an explanation of this tremendous partisan unanimity in which he had a share, he would probably have first mentioned the War, the last shots of which were fired while he was still in petticoats. Certainly his second reason, however, would have been that the Irish were on the other side." Harold Frederic, *The Damnation of Theron Ware* (New York, 1896), pp. 75–76. Cf. also Frederic C. Howe, *The Confessions of a Reformer* (New York, 1925), pp. 3, 64.

[8] The fullest evidence is in Donald Kinzer, "The American Protective Association: A Study of Anti-Catholicism" (Ph.D. thesis, University of Washington, 1954).

Similarly, the Jews came up against actual conflict situations which affected them at least as seriously as did the slanders of anti-Semitic ideology. The evidence seems clear that the social discriminations which began to limit the opportunities of American Jews in the late nineteenth century owed little to nativist sources, in the sense in which I have used the term. Discrimination developed where and when Jews participated heavily in a general middle class scramble for prestige; it developed where and when a hectic pace of social climbing made the guardians of distinction afraid of being "invaded." It grew in eastern summer resorts, fraternities, and urban real estate offices, not in the South and the West where farmers were beginning to murmur about the shadowy power of the International Jew.[9]

The decisive significance of reality situations as opposed to anti-foreign propaganda may also be gauged from the very favorable reception which English immigrants have always enjoyed. If nationalist ideas dominated American ethnic relations as much as we sometimes suppose, English immigrants should have been among the most unpopular minorities at least until the 1870's. When Britain was our historic adversary, when Anglophobia was an editorial habit and twisting the lion's tail a political pastime, the English in America escaped opprobrium. In spite of their identifiable accent, their disinterest in naturalization, and their proud retention of British loyalties, the English did not differ enough from native Americans, socially and culturally, to seem outsiders.[10] Since they had no status as ethnic rivals, the nativist crusade passed them by.

How, then, are we to explain those ethnic relations which are not simply nativist, and which rest on broader or deeper foundations? We must assume, I think, that in a competitive society everything which differentiates one group from another involves a potential conflict of interest, and we must proceed to analyze the historical composition of American society in ethnic terms. The little work so far done along these lines is not only fragmentary. It is also inadequate because the historians of immigration have focused too narrowly on the problem of cultural assimilation. Treating each

[9] John Higham, "Social Discrimination Against Jews in America, 1830–1930," *Publications of the American Jewish Historical Society*, XLVII (1957), 1–33.

[10] The English indifference to American citizenship was, paradoxically, one reason for the absence of conflict with native Americans, since it meant that ordinarily there was no "English vote." The English emerged as a group in American politics only on the few occasions when a goodly number of them were mobilized to counteract the more "foreign" vote of the Irish. On this whole subject cf. Rowland Tappan Berthoff, *British Immigrants in Industrial America, 1790–1950* (Cambridge, 1953), pp. 130–142.

group separately, they have weighed the effects of its old world culture against its Americanization. *Cultural* assimilation, however, does not necessarily involve *social* assimilation,[11] as the history of the Negro clearly demonstrates. Ethnic identity affects men's position in the social structure long after their ancestral culture has largely disappeared.

Since we know very little about the stratification of our society in any period, particularly in its ethnic aspects, I can offer only a few suggestions for inquiry. Probably one of the crucial determinants of ethnic status has simply been the order of arrival. In the founding of communities, in the settlement of new areas, and in the development of new industries, the first-comers secured a preferential position. Groups arriving later have usually had to enter on terms acceptable to their predecessors, who owned the land, offered the jobs, provided the credit, and controlled the sources of power and prestige. In these circumstances the new group had to accept or to struggle for a long time against a subordinate status.[12]

Immigrants have generally had such a disadvantage in America, since most of them were not pioneers. Sometimes, however, foreign groups did arrive at a sector of American society during its formative stage, thereby establishing a local respect that was not easily upset, particularly if they filled a vital need in the community. In many western communities the Irish met far less resistance than they did in New England, where the social system had congealed long before their arrival.[13] Although the Protestant Irish on the eighteenth-century frontier are the most striking example of the prestige to be derived from an early arrival, the Catholic Irish did not wholly miss comparable benefits in the new West of the first half of the nineteenth century. Their religion, far from carrying a uni-

[11] This distinction is perceptively elaborated and applied in Peter A. Munch, "Segregation and Assimilation of Norwegian Settlements in Wisconsin," *Norwegian-American Studies and Records*, XVIII (1954), 102–140.

[12] For an illuminating example involving Norwegians cf. Evon Z. Vogt, Jr., "Social Stratification in the Rural Middlewest: A Structural Analysis," *Rural Sociology*, XII (1947), 364–375.

[13] T. C. Grattan, *Civilized America* (London, 1859), II, 28; John Richard Beste, *The Wabash: or Adventures of an English Gentleman's Family in the Interior of America*, 2 vols. (London, 1855), II, 300. On a crude regional basis, census data strengthen the impression that the Irish succeeded more easily in new western communities than they did in the older parts of the country. In 1890 only 1.8 per cent of the Irish stock (first and second generation males) employed in the North Atlantic states had high status occupations classified as professional. In the North Central states and in the Far West, however, three per cent of the Irish were in the professions. *United States Census, 1890: Population*, Part II, pp. 490, 494.

versal stigma, might even prove a social asset in the fairly numerous localities where the Catholic Church established the first and (for quite a while) the best academies and colleges. High status Protestants in Cincinnati, Terre Haute, and elsewhere not only welcomed the schools created by Jesuits, Sisters of Mercy, and other religious orders; they also enrolled their children to mingle on equal terms with Catholic students.[14]

Similarly, the Jews have found a relatively secure niche in places where they contributed significantly to the establishment of the community. In San Francisco Jews acquired an especially favorable status from their large share in molding the basic institutions of the city. On the other hand, they have endured a particularly bad situation in Minneapolis where they arrived late in the city's development.[15] The same relationship applied to the Japanese in two adjacent California towns in the early twentieth century. In one the Japanese settled first and were accepted in the civic life of the American society that grew up around them; in the other they came later and met bitter persecution as their numbers grew.[16]

How swiftly a group advances after its arrival also affects very strongly the reception it meets. Americans have expected immigrants to move toward cultural homogeneity but not to crowd the social ladder in doing so. When a new group, relatively depressed at the outset, pushes upward rapidly in the status system, conflict almost surely ensues. This happened in the late nineteenth century in the cases of the Irish and the Jews. Both came up against cruel social discriminations designed to retard the large proportion of each group who were getting ahead quickly.[17]

Contrarily, a group that stayed put might escape opprobrium, once the older Americans had become accustomed to its presence, even if it retained a good deal of its cultural distinctiveness. The Germans, who did not bear the stigma attached to the more rapidly Americanized Irish, are a case in point. Although measuring rela-

[14] One Catholic parent reported that three-quarters of the boarders in many convent schools were Protestants, and that in Terre Haute the Protestant townspeople built the teaching and living quarters for the nuns whom the local priest procured. Beste, *The Wabash*, I, 222; II, 147. Cf. also on Cincinnati, the newspaper comment quoted in John G. Shea, *History of the Catholic Church in the United States*, 4 vols. (New York, 1892), III, 340; and, for a general view, John Tracy Ellis (Ed.), *Documents of American Catholic History* (Milwaukee, 1956), pp. 267–269.

[15] Higham, "Social Discrimination," *loc. cit.*, pp. 24–26.

[16] Emory Bogardus, *Immigration and Race Attitudes* (New York, 1928), p. 164.

[17] On the Irish cf. Thomas Beer, *The Mauve Decade* (New York, 1926), pp. 150, 156–165; John White, *Sketches from America* (London, 1870), p. 371.

tive rates of social mobility is obviously difficult, the census of 1890 offers an illuminating comparison between the Irish and the Germans. By comparing, for each nationality, the proportion of the first generation in various occupations with the proportion of the second generation in the same occupations, it becomes evident that the Irish were climbing the social ladder rapidly while the Germans were remaining relatively static, the sons being more content to occupy the stations of their fathers. The proportion of Irish in professional occupations almost doubled between the first and the second generations; the proportion of Germans did not change. The Irish entered other white collar jobs and fled from common labor at twice the rate of the Germans.[18] Here is an important reason why the ambitious Irish provoked a resistance which the more phlegmatic Germans did not face.[19]

	Irish		*German*	
		Second		*Second*
	Irish-born	*Generation*	*German-born*	*Generation*
Professional	1.7	3	2	2
Other White Collar	7	14	10	15
Common Labor	25	11	11	7

Compiled from *U. S. Census, 1890: Population*, Part 11, pp. 484–489, 502–507. As "other white collar" I have classified agents, auctioneers, bankers and brokers, bookkeepers and accountants, clerks, commercial travellers, merchants, company officials, salesmen, stenographers, telephone and telegraph operators, undertakers, manufacturers, and publishers. The figures for common labor include only "laborers, not specified." Consequently, this stratum is substantially under-represented, since the census counted many unskilled laborers under other occupational headings.

Although the Census does not offer occupational statistics on the second generation alone, it does tabulate the number of persons, in various occupations, having mothers born in Germany, Ireland, etc. I have derived second generation statistics by substracting the number of foreign born in these occupations from the larger number having foreign born mothers.

[18] Per cent of total employed males (ten years of age and older) of each ethnic category engaged in certain occupations:

[19] To account for the Irish-German difference in social mobility is not my present purpose, but one suggestion may be hazarded. The Irish began life in the United States with an advantage over the Germans in language and a disadvantage in status. Unlike the Germans, the Irish were concentrated chiefly in occupations and in areas where they were soon exposed to the competitive intrusion of newer nationalities—French Canadians, eastern Europeans, and Chinese. Thus the Irish were not only attracted by opportunity; they were *driven* upward by a burning desire to escape identification with these less American rivals. E.g., nowhere did an entire ethnic group improve itself more rapidly than did the Irish in the coal districts of Pennsylvania in the last quarter of the nineteenth century, when the Poles, Hungarians, and Italians poured in. The eastern Irish were a depressed and isolated class in the days of the Molly Maguires; by the end of the century they had become skilled, respectable, and indistinguishable from the older Americans. Charles B. Spahr, *America's Working People* (New York, 1900), p. 140.

To explain such differentials between ethnic groups, historians must not shrink, finally, from studying their respective national or social characters. Surely the boisterous, free-and-easy manners of the Irish, the humble patience of the Chinese, and many ethnic inclinations we have not learned properly to define have shaped the relations between our various peoples. Instead of washing all of the specific color out of our ethnic fabric in our fear of propagating stereotypes, let us look for the realities behind them.

What I miss, in the most general way, is any serious effort to study historically the structure of American society—to work out, in other words, the inter-relations between classes and ethnic groups, taking account of regional and local differences. This task transcends the dimensions of nativism. It transcends a preoccupation with conflict and discord, and urges us to confront our involvements with one another in comparative terms. But as this is done, the history of nativism itself should fall into a truer perspective.

17

IN THE history of Western thought few books have been recognized as influential as quickly as Charles Darwin's *Origin of Species,* first published in 1859. For half a century many intellectual currents had been preparing the world for Darwin's hypothesis that natural selection was the process whereby the thousands of different animal and plant species came into being. Among these precursors of Darwin was Herbert Spencer, a phenomenally learned Englishman with a prolific pen. His erudite, if pompous, writings had been proclaiming the doctrine of evolution for a decade before Darwin's treatise brought scientific rigor and a mountain of evidence to explain how it had come about. In one of the prefaces to his book, Darwin accepted Spencer's phrase "the survival of the fittest" as a shorthand description of the process of natural selection, that is, the competition among animals and plants for food and living space. The impact of Darwin's theory was felt far beyond the science of biology, for which it was intended, compelling men in a host of fields to rethink their preconceptions and assumptions.

In the 1940s, as historians reviewed the writings and utterances of late nineteenth-century public figures and businessmen in the United States, they concluded that a form of Darwinism had been used as a defense of big business. This Social Darwinism, as the historians named it, justified the wealth and power of the business magnates on the ground that in social and economic competition these men had proved themselves the fittest by virtue of their success. Hence their wealth and position were sanctioned by nature itself. The analogy with Darwin's doctrine of natural selection through unremitting competition was clear, if not entirely exact. Merle Curti's general intellectual history *The Growth of American Thought* (New

York, 1943) was among the earliest of historical works calling attention to Social Darwinism as a defense of the "robber barons." A
year later Richard Hofstadter in his *Social Darwinism in American
Thought, 1860–1915* (Philadelphia, 1944) devoted a whole book
to documenting and exploring the idea and its implications. Since
then, as Wyllie points out, Social Darwinism as a primary defense
of nineteenth-century business has become a staple ingredient in
several textbooks of American history.

Wyllie's article subjects this widespread acceptance to attack
from several angles. For one thing, the article is critical of the
representativeness of the evidence advanced—always a crucial point
in establishing a "climate of opinion." As Wyllie rightly points out,
more than a stray example or two has to be provided to show the
existence of a social attitude. If businessmen at the end of the nineteenth century employed Social Darwinism to justify their actions,
then there should be many examples to show it. The fact is, though,
that few businessmen expressed themselves in writing in such terms.
Moreover, those few businessmen who did write in Social Darwinist
language were clearly not the ordinary, run-of-the-mill variety;
generally they were unusually bookish men like Andrew Carnegie,
who moved in intellectual circles normally closed to or devoid of
interest for the average businessman of the day. Wyllie's *coup de
grâce* to the established view is to show that the most famous of the
formulations of Social Darwinism, allegedly uttered by John D.
Rockefeller, was actually made by his son at a considerably later
date.

But, it might be asked, is it not possible that Social Darwinism
was a widely used defense of big business, even if the businessmen
were too uninformed or inarticulate to use it themselves? Isn't it
enough to show that intellectuals, publicists, and others who were
sympathetic with business employed it? The answer must be no.
For as Wyllie shows, even when supplied with a social Darwinian
justification, businessmen rarely used it or incorporated it into their
own thought. When called upon to justify their actions in public or
in private, they fell back upon traditional Christian virtues and
simple moral platitudes that bore no relation to the Social Darwinist
formula. Furthermore, in practice, philanthropists like Carnegie
and Rockefeller clearly repudiated in their benefactions the Social
Darwinist tenet that deplored interference with a free, competitive
struggle among individual men.

Regarded more broadly, Wyllie's article is an important contribution to the general re-evaluation of the "age of the robber barons,"

which has already been referred to in the introduction to Alfred Chandler's article. Like Chandler, Wyllie approaches the business-men of that era without hostility, prepared to investigate their actions with the same absence of preconceptions and with the same critical tools that he brings to his examination of other social groups.

Wyllie also compels us to recognize that to the business leaders of the time the argument for *laissez faire* was not a reactionary or even a conservative doctrine. To them it seemed liberating; it freed the individual for the realization of his potentialities, thereby benefiting society as well as the individual. This conception has been set forth most persuasively by James Willard Hurst in his little book *Law and the Conditions of Freedom in the Nineteenth Century United States* (Madison, 1956). From an analysis of American law, Hurst illustrates the nineteenth-century view that freedom for enterprise was the key to economic development. It constituted, as he phrases it, "a release of energy," which an earlier regulated and controlled economy seemed to restrict and impede.

This article, therefore, is a critique of both the method and the substance of the argument of those who would see Social Darwinism as a primary defense of late nineteenth-century business activities. By showing that there is no clear connection between the utterances of businessmen and the principles of Darwinism he calls into serious question the methods of those who would find such a linkage. And by demonstrating that businessmen relied heavily upon Christian and other doctrines rather than Social Darwinist formulas, he forces us to abandon the view that Social Darwinism was the chief justifi-cation for the business practices of the day. As he remarks in the closing paragraphs of the article, recent historians like Thomas C. Cochran and Edward C. Kirkland have also begun to doubt the prevalence of Social Darwinism in the thoughts and assumptions of business leaders in the late nineteenth century. Indeed, Edward Kirkland in his recent study of the period, *Industry Comes of Age* (New York, 1961), has ignored the Social Darwinist argument completely, though he deliberately set out to ascertain "how the period actually looked to contemporaries who participated" in the building of the American economy. The names of Darwin, Herbert Spencer, and William Graham Sumner do not even appear in his index, while his chapter on the defenses of the age show that contem-poraries looked to "character" and other simple formulations of virtue to justify and explain the material success of American busi-ness.

Mr. Willie is Fox Professor of American Institutions at the Uni-versity of Wisconsin.

Social Darwinism and the Businessman

BY IRVIN G. WYLLIE

THE American humorist Mark Twain, when asked to explain why he wore a white suit, replied that clothes make the man, that naked people have little or no influence in society. Unlike Mark Twain, or his fellow countryman Alec Guinness, Charles Darwin was no man in a white suit. But he was a man who exerted a far-reaching influence in society. If Darwin had done no more than change the methods and assumptions of the biological sciences, and contribute to the general store of scientific knowledge, he would still be an important figure in world history. The impact of his ideas was by no means limited to the sciences, however. His theory of evolution touched off a general intellectual revolution that altered the course of religious thought, re-directed the social sciences, and contributed new insights and slogans to the popular and academic varieties of social theory.

The changes that flowed from the Darwinian revolution were so impressive as to suggest that it had unlimited transforming power. In the words of Bert J. Lowenberg, a pioneer student of this subject, "Evolution germinated ideas wherever it penetrated, and it penetrated everywhere." [1] Just as historians of the American and French and Russian revolutions sometimes overestimated the extent to which these upheavals transformed the societies in which they occurred, so historians of the Darwinian intellectual revolution have sometimes misjudged the outer limits of its influence and overestimated the completeness of its sway. The tendency to exaggerate the impact of Darwinism, especially on popular thought, is nowhere better illustrated than in the claim that American businessmen in the post-Civil War decades rationalized their personal careers and justified their business operations in terms of Herbert Spencer's competitive social version of Darwin's theory of evolution.

Even the most casual examination of American historical writing

SOURCE: Reprinted by permission from *Proceedings of the American Philosophical Society*, CIII (October 1959).

[1] Loewenberg, Bert J., Darwinism comes to America, 1865–1900, *Miss. Valley Hist. Rev.* 28: 339, 1941.

in the last twenty years reveals the prevalence of the assumption that entrepreneurs of the Gilded Age were not only practicing social Darwinists, but philosophical social Darwinists as well. Intellectual historians who treat ideas in their social contexts suggest that Darwinism served as an ideological shield and buckler for the Robber Baron generation of businessmen. In his Pulitzer prize-winning book, *The Growth of American Thought*, Merle Curti argued that defenders of rugged individualism, both inside and outside the business community, invoked Darwin to justify the struggles of the market place. Herbert Spencer became the oracle of the age, displacing Adam Smith and John Stuart Mill in the defense of *laissez faire*. In Curti's view social Darwinist doctrine "admirably suited the needs of the great captains of industry who were crushing the little fellows when these vainly tried to compete with them." [2] In his study of *The American Mind* Henry S. Commager not only conceded the usefulness of social Darwinism to dominant business interests, but also claimed for the Spencerian system an imperial sway over the minds of most middle-class people in the half-century after Appomattox. "Between them," wrote Commager, "Darwin and Spencer exercised such sovereignty over America as George III had never enjoyed." [3]

Richard Hofstadter's perceptive treatise on *Social Darwinism in American Thought* offered the most systematic statement by an intellectual historian of the case for the businessman as a Darwinist. "With its rapid expansion, its exploitative methods, its desperate competition, and its peremptory rejection of failure," Hofstadter wrote, "post-bellum America was like a vast human caricature of the Darwinian struggle for existence and survival of the fittest." In this circumstance businessmen accepted Darwinian terminology "almost by instinct," and discovered that the plausible analogies of social selection were most congenial to their ways of thinking. Hofstadter quoted leading entrepreneurs, among them John D. Rockefeller, Andrew Carnegie, James J. Hill, and Chauncey Depew, to establish the Darwinian cast of their minds. Depew testified that the guests at the great banquets in New York City in the Gilded Age represented the survival of the fittest, men who had come through the fierce competitions of the great city because of their superior ability, foresight, and adaptability. James J. Hill's career

[2] Curti, Merle E., *The growth of American thought*, 568, 571, 640, 641, New York, Harper & Brothers, 1943.
[3] Commager, Henry S., *The American mind*, 87, 89–90, New Haven, Yale University Press, 1950.

in the railroad industry led him to observe that the fortunes of railroad companies were determined by the law of the survival of the fittest, a conclusion that John D. Rockefeller also allegedly reached as a result of his operations in the oil industry. When Hofstadter cited Andrew Carnegie's assertion that competition is "best for the race, because it insures the survival of the fittest in every department," this bit of evidence seemed almost superfluous in light of the case that he had already built for the captain of industry as a disciple of Herbert Spencer.[4]

Business historians, economists, anthropologists and journalists have likewise portrayed Herbert Spencer as the patron saint of the late nineteenth-century entrepreneur. In the *Age of Enterprise* Thomas C. Cochran and William Miller argued that men of affairs in post-Civil War America found a much-needed philosophy for industrial progress in the Spencerian system. "To a generation singularly engrossed in the competitive pursuit of industrial wealth," they wrote,

> it gave cosmic sanction to free competition. In an age of science, it "scientifically" justified ceaseless exploitation. Precisely attuned to the aspirations of American businessmen, it afforded them a guide to faith and thought perfectly in keeping with the pattern of their workaday lives. . . . Their cupidity, it defended as part of the universal struggle for existence; their wealth, it hallowed as a sign of the "fittest." Business America in the Gilded Age had supreme faith in itself; no wonder it embraced Spencer's philosophy, which sanctified business activities.[5]

So well did this rationale serve the businessman's purposes, according to Cochran and Miller, that he was reluctant to abandon it even after business practices made Spencerianism obsolete. Joseph J. Spengler, an economist who examined the impact of Darwin's theory on economics, shared the Cochran-Miller view that social Darwinism exactly suited the business temper of the Gilded Age. "An outstandingly successful business man," Spengler observed, "was hard put to find a philosophical basis for his *apologia* . . . more satisfactory than this essentially perverted form of Darwinism." [6]

---

[4] Hofstadter, Richard, *Social Darwinism in American thought, 1860–1915*, 30–32, 34, Philadelphia, University of Pennsylvania Press, 1945 (hereafter cited as *Social Darwinism*).

[5] Cochran, Thomas C. and William Miller, *The age of enterprise*, 119, 120–123, New York, Macmillan, 1951.

[6] Spengler, Joseph J., Evolutionism in American economics, 1800–1946, in Stow Persons, ed., *Evolutionary thought in America*, 212, New Haven, Yale University Press, 1950.

Others who have looked upon competitive social Darwinism as a perversion, such as Ashley Montagu, the anthropologist, have insisted that it was a perversion freely indulged in by the business community. Even though in his little book on *Darwinism, Competition & Cooperation* Montagu attributed the Spencerian aberration to the impact of social thought and social conditions on Darwinian biology, rather than the other way around, he accepted the idea that Spencer and Darwin supplied nineteenth-century industrialists with a welcome pseudo-scientific sanction for free competition.[7] In *The Age of the Moguls* Stewart Holbrook, a journalist, suggested that business barons purged their consciences by accepting Darwinism. "It was welcome balm to their impaired consciences," Holbrook declared, "to be told they enjoyed their riches simply because of the working of natural laws over which neither they nor anyone else had control." In accounting for the decline of the moguls in the twentieth century Holbrook wrote,

> They became extinct because they were too stupid to comprehend the danger from the changes of the jungle environment which their business methods and their ways of living had helped to bring about. It was full circle. Darwin had explained their origin and prophesied their end. . . .[8]

The fact that the social Darwinist businessman has made his way into American history textbooks is but another indication of the consensus that scholars have reached on this question. The novice who discovers the Gilded Age through Henry Bamford Parkes, *The United States of America*, will learn that Spencer "provided the big businessmen of America with exactly the justification they needed," and that industrialists "learned from him to apply phrases like 'survival of the fittest' to the formation of trusts and monopolies and to regard the millionaire as the finest flower of evolution."[9] In *A history of the United States*, only recently off the press, three leading historians declare that Darwinism explained for many businessmen both their own success and the nature of the society in which they operated.

> The weak went down, the strong endured and became stronger, and society was benefited because the unfit were eliminated and the fit survived. Men who had risen to dominance by crushing their competitors were intrigued

[7] Montagu, Montague Francis Ashley, *Darwin, competition & cooperation*, 32–33, 46, New York, Henry Schuman, 1952.

[8] Holbrook, Stewart, *The age of the moguls*, 89, 320, Garden City, Doubleday, 1953.

[9] Parkes, Henry B., *The United States of America*, 488, New York, Alfred A. Knopf, 1953.

and comforted by a doctrine that justified any methold that succeeded and proclaimed that wealth was a reward of competence.[10]

The clear implication of the foregoing statements is that the captain of industry was a conscious, philosophical social Darwinist, and not just a tough competitor. The world has known many businessmen, before Darwin's time as well as after, who were sharp in tooth and claw. To put such men down as social Darwinists, in the absence of evidence that their thinking reflected the influence of Darwin or Spencer, would be to deprive the term of meaning. Those who represent the entrepreneur as a Darwinist portray a man who had a conscious Darwinian perspective on his personal success, his business activities, and his general social role. He was a man who not only recited Spencer's phrases, but understood their implications, and perhaps even their intellectual derivation. He was, in other words, a man of the type of Andrew Carnegie. An avid reader of Spencer, Carnegie was converted to social Darwinism at an early age. "Few men have wished to know another man more strongly than I to know Herbert Spencer," Carnegie testified in his *Autobiography*, "for seldom has one been more deeply indebted than I to him and to Darwin." [11] He came to know Spencer extremely well, and during Spencer's memorable visit to the United States in 1882 had the satisfaction of having Spencer single him out publicly as one of his two best American friends. Carnegie's addresses, essays, and books are so full of Spencerian allusions, of references to men like himself who came into the business world as "athletes trained for the contest, with sinews braced, indomitable wills, resolved to do or die," that it would be impossible to deny his Darwinist orientation. Because Carnegie supplied such clear evidence of his intellectual indebtedness he is invariably cited to prove the case for the entrepreneur as a social Darwinist.

What is puzzling, especially in light of the claim that businessmen generally took their cues from Spencer, is that so few others have testified so clearly on this point as Carnegie. If men of affairs explained their personal success and justified their business operations in terms of natural selection and the survival of the fittest we should have abundant evidence on this point. It would be

[10] Williams, T. Harry, Richard N. Current, and Frank Freidel, *A history of the United States* 2: 58, New York, Alfred A. Knopf, 1959. See also Thomas A. Bailey, *The American pageant*, 532, Boston, D. C. Heath and Company, 1956.

[11] Carnegie, Andrew, *Autobiography*, 338, Boston, Houghton, Mifflin, 1920. See also Hendrick, Burton J., *The life of Andrew Carnegie* 1: 239, Garden City, Doubleday, Doran, 1932; and Hofstadter, *Social Darwinism*, 35.

folly to deny that such evidence exists, but it is accurate to say that so far it has not been adduced. The men that historians have called to succeed Carnegie on the witness stand have not only been few in number, but on the whole incompetent as well. In support of their case Cochran and Miller cite only one businessman in addition to Carnegie, the publisher Henry Holt. Holt, like Carnegie, was as much an intellectual as a businessman. A graduate of Yale, he was an author and a scholar as well as a publisher, and therefore not truly representative of the business community in his intellectual sensitivity. Furthermore, he did not testify that he was a social Darwinist, but rather that Spencer had considerable vogue among informed people in England and America in the years between 1870 and 1900. What appears to be a case for the businessman as a disciple of Darwin is in *The Age of Enterprise* merely an elaboration of Holt's point, a demonstration that intellectually sophisticated men like Edward Livingston Youmans, John Fiske, Charles W. Eliot, Henry Cabot Lodge, and Nicholas Murray Butler did read Darwin and Spencer.[12]

Hofstadter's case, though it relies more directly on business testimony, also leaves room for doubt. Even if we were to accept all of his evidence without question, we would still be accepting a case based on the statements of only four businessmen. Part of the evidence must be questioned, however. The statement attributed to John D. Rockefeller is one he never made, namely that "The growth of a large business is merely a survival of the fittest. . . . The American beauty rose can be produced . . . only by sacrificing the early buds which grow up around it." [13] This sentiment, uttered by John D. Rockefeller, Jr. in 1902 in an address to the YMCA at his alma mater, Brown University, may prove that the university-trained son knew how to use Darwinian phraseology, but it does not prove that his Bible-reading father was a Spencerian in the Gilded Age.[14] Chauncey Depew's observation that the guests at the great banquets in New York represented the survival of the fittest is likewise open to objection. Since he recorded this observation in 1922, when, thanks to William Jennings Bryan, the air was filled with evolutionary discussion, we may ask how reliably this state-

[12] Cochran and Miller, *Age of enterprise*, 124–128.

[13] Hofstadter, *Social Darwinism*, 31. I call attention to this error with proper humility since it also appears in my own book, *The self-made man in America*, 84, New Brunswick, Rutgers University Press, 1954 (hereafter cited as Wyllie, *Self-made man*).

[14] Fosdick, Raymond B., *John D. Rockefeller, Jr., a portrait*, 130–131, New York, Harper & Brothers, 1956.

ment reflected Depew's thinking forty years before.[15] Even if it mirrored his early thought perfectly, the fact remains that in his intellectual awareness he was no more representative of the business community than Henry Holt. A bookish man, and a Yale graduate in 1856, he was a lifelong intimate of Andrew Dixon White, the historian-president of Cornell University. He also served as a regent of the University of the State of New York from 1877 to 1904. Unlike most post-Civil War men of affairs he moved in intellectual circles, and therefore had ample opportunity to master Spencerian clichés. James J. Hill's observation that the fortunes of railroads were determined by the law of the survival of the fittest is likewise open to the objection that a statement made in 1910 does not necessarily prove that its author took his cues from Spencer in the 1870's and 1880's.[16] To make the case for the post-Civil War businessman as a social Darwinist we need direct testimony out of the Gilded Age.

Such testimony may be available, but so far it seems to be in short supply. In 1888 Henry Clews resorted to Darwinian analysis to explain the displacement of Wall Street's conservative old guard by a young, imaginative group of financiers after the Panic of 1857. "The change was a fine exemplification of the survival of the fittest," Clews declared, "and proved that there was a law of natural selection in financial affairs that superseded old conservatism and sealed its doom." [17] In June of 1899 Henry O. Havemeyer, President of the American Sugar Refining Company, replied affirmatively when a member of the United States Industrial Commission asked him if he believed that a trust or combine represented the survival of the fittest in business. Havemeyer testified that he rested his whole political philosophy on this proposition.[18] Nathan A. Taylor, an independent tin-plate manufacturer, also explained failures in his industry in terms of the survival of the fittest.[19] If Gilded Age businessmen were social Darwinists, they could be expected to give evidence of this fact in their discussions

---

[15] Depew, Chauncey, M., *My memories of eighty years*, 384, New York, Charles Scribner's Sons, 1922.

[16] Hill, James J., *Highways of progress*, 126, New York, Doubleday, Page, 1910.

[17] Clews, Henry, *Twenty-eight years in Wall Street*, 6, New York, Irving, 1888.

[18] United States Industrial Commission, *Preliminary report on trusts and industrial combinations*, House Documents, vol. 1, no. 476, pt. 1, p. 135, Washington, Government Printing Office, 1900 (hereafter cited as Industrial Commission, *Preliminary report on trusts*).

[19] *Ibid.*, 941.

of industrial concentration. Yet in the mountain of testimony piled up by the Congressional investigations of 1889 and 1899, talk of the survival of the fittest is exceptional, not common. And sometimes this talk originated with merchants of ideas, rather than with captains of industry. It was a newspaperman, Patrick C. Boyle of the *Oil City Derrick,* and not an official of Standard Oil, who told the United States Industrial Commission in 1899 that "Darwin's theory of survival of the fittest was never better illustrated than in the organization of the Standard Oil Company; it represents the best element in all branches of the trade." [20]

Sometimes the direct testimony of businessmen revealed only that they were religious evolutionists, not social Darwinists. In the year 1900 the banker Roeliff Brinkerhoff reported that "I am an evolutionist of the Herbert Spencer type and have been so from the earliest announcement of that theory, and with me it has been a power for good, and not for evil." [21] In context Brinkerhoff's testimony indicated that evolution had influenced his religious thinking, but not his social views. In an autobiography published in the year 1885 Thomas Mellon, founder of the Mellon banking fortune, devoted fifteen pages to a discussion of evolution, all dealing with the impact of the theory on religion. He revealed himself to be a Christian and an evolutionist, but not a social Darwinist.[22] Though Mellon believed in competition and *laissez faire,* he found his sanction in classical economics, not in Spencer's *Social Statics.*

The testimony of other businessmen before Congressional committees also revealed the persistent influence of pre-Darwinian economic ideas in the late nineteenth century. When Benjamin Brewster, president of the National Transit Company, told the House Committee on Manufactures in 1889 that there were natural laws of commerce as well as of science, he did not refer to evolution, but rather to the law of gravitation and the law of supply and demand.[23] John E. Parsons, a trustee of the Sugar Refineries Company, invoked John Stuart Mill to defend his views in the same investigation.[24] It was Jeremy Bentham, not Spencer, who

[20] *Ibid.,* 489.

[21] Brinkerhoff, Roeliff, *Recollections of a lifetime,* 342, Cincinnati, Robert Clarke, 1900.

[22] Mellon, Thomas, *Thomas Mellon and his times,* 568–583, Pittsburgh, W. G. Johnson, 1885.

[23] Committee on Manufactures, House of Representatives, *Report in relation to the Sugar Trust and Standard Oil Trust,* 50th Congress, p. 372, Washington, Government Printing Office, 1889 (hereafter cited as Committee on Manufactures, *Sugar Trust and Standard Oil Trust*).

[24] *Ibid.,* 54.

was cited as authority for attorney John R. Dos Passos' observation to the United States Industrial Commission that "Society is so constituted that some must suffer. It is the sacrifice that the few are forced to make for the good of the whole." [25] Such usages require that we reconsider prevailing assumptions concerning the extent to which Herbert Spencer and William Graham Sumner displaced the classical economists as the high priests of *laissez faire*. Even more, they require that we exercise caution in attributing to Darwin and Spencer ultimate responsibility for the competitive social ideas of the businessman in the Gilded Age.

Too often, after an uncooperative captain of industry has refused to identify himself as a social Darwinist, he has been asked to step down from the witness stand, so that a sociologist or economist might take his place. Richard Hofstadter, convinced that businessmen "are not the most articulate social philosophers," called upon a reform-minded University of Chicago sociologist, Charles R. Henderson, to testify to the Darwinian cast of the entrepreneurial mind. [26] "It would be strange if the 'captain of industry' did not sometimes manifest a militant spirit," Henderson wrote in 1896, "for he has risen from the ranks largely because he was a better fighter than most of us. Competitive commercial life is not a flower bed of ease, but a battle field where the 'struggle for existence' is defining the industrially fittest to survive." [27] All this statement proved was that Henderson, an intellectual, had the ability to see Darwinian meaning in the struggles of the business world. He did not pretend that the businessman saw his activities in the same light. In fact he deplored the ideological gulf that separated the entrepreneur from the social theorist, and acknowledged that businessmen did not hold the intellectual in high esteem. "They say, with some touch of contemptuous sarcasm and cynicism," Henderson wrote, "that they can hire talkers and buy books." [28]

Gilded Age businessmen were not sufficiently bookish, or sufficiently well educated, to keep up with the changing world of ideas. As late as 1900, 84 per cent of the businessmen listed in *Who's Who in America* had not been educated beyond high school. [29] Though college men in business increased steadily in the last decades of the nineteenth century, they were always a minority.

[25] Industrial Commission, *Preliminary report on trusts*, 1156.
[26] Hofstadter, *Social Darwinism*, 30–31.
[27] Henderson, Charles R., Business men and social theorists, *Amer. Jour. Sociology* 1: 385, 1896.
[28] *Ibid.*, 386.
[29] Dexter, Edwin G., A study of 20th century success, *Popular Science Monthly* 61: 248, 1902.

The uneducated majority had little time for books. Cornelius Vanderbilt, who read only one book in his life, *Pilgrim's Progress,* after he was seventy years of age, once remarked that if he had taken time to learn education he would not have had time to learn anything else. Many an unlettered businessman undoubtedly shared this view, and also subscribed to Daniel Drew's opinion that "Book learning is something, but thirteen million dollars is also something, and a mighty sight more."[30] Since in the late nineteenth century Darwin's adherents were for the most part scientists, social scientists, philosophers, clergymen, editors, and other educationally advantaged persons, it would be surprising to find a really large contingent of businessmen in his camp. The minority of college graduates and devotees of self-culture may be found there, but the untutored majority probably will not.

Scholars whose work requires them to deal with ideas in a systematic way, and to keep abreast of changing modes of thought, are generally reluctant to concede that other men may be far behind the times, and philosophically disorganized and inconsistent as well. To them it is unthinkable that any influential body of men in the Gilded Age should have failed to embrace the most advanced idea of that age, and that businessmen in particular could have ignored a formulation like that of Spencer, which seemed to explain so many hard facts of business life. However, there is considerable wisdom in the observation that "It must not be thought that Social Darwinism made brutal misanthropists of the Great Entrepreneurs and the Finance Capitalists. They were, by and large, too simple-minded for that; it was only an intellectual like W. G. Sumner who became a misanthropist." [31] Though John D. Rockefeller might transact business according to the law of the jungle, he was a pious Christian who looked upon his wealth as a God-given reward for virtue. Railroad executives, who by certain reckonings were social Darwinists, sometimes violated Spencerian efficiency by decreeing that in slack times single men should be fired first, to be followed by men with the least seniority.[32] Andrew Carnegie, a secular-minded man and a tough-minded Darwinian, was also a generous philanthropist who gave a practical demonstration of the social utility of the old Christian doctrine of the stewardship of

[30] White, Bouck, *The book of Daniel Drew,* 309–310, Garden City, Doubleday, 1937.
[31] Baldwin, Leland D., *The stream of American history* 2: 248, New York, American Book, 1952.
[32] Cochran, Thomas C., *Railroad leaders, 1845–1890,* 174, Cambridge, Harvard University Press, 1953.

wealth. Robert Harris, whose job as president of the Chicago, Burlington, and Quincy Railroad might have been expected to put him on the side of the survival of the fittest, testified that "As a general proposition, it seems to me that the strong should help the weak, now by one course and now by another; and in exercising authority to do it as we would wish it done to ourselves." [33]

Anyone who examines the voluminous nineteenth-century literature of business success cannot fail to be impressed that businessmen who talked about success and failure took their texts from Christian moralists, not from Darwin and Spencer. In the race for wealth they attributed little influence to native intelligence, physical strength, or any other endowment of nature, and paramount influence to industry, frugality, and sobriety—simple moral virtues that any man could cultivate. They urged young men to seek the business way of life in the Bible, not in *The Descent of Man* or *The Principles of Sociology*. The problem of success was not that of grinding down one's competitors, but of elevating one's self—and the two were not equivalent. Business practice may have suggested a Darwinian struggle for existence, but self-help advisers of the Gilded Age suggested that the only struggle of consequence was the struggle for good character. Failure was likewise attributed to defective character rather than to deficiencies of endowment or opportunity. Opportunities for success, like opportunities for salvation, were limitless; heaven could receive as many as were worthy. Because American businessmen operated in a land blessed with an abundance of resources they rejected the Malthusian idea that chances were so limited that one man's rise meant the fall of many others. Theirs was a more optimistic view, that every triumph opened the way for more.[34] Advanced thinkers might explain both success and failure in terms of social Darwinism, but most businessmen were probably inclined to follow the lead of the *Commercial and Financial Chronicle* in permitting "this fashionable philosophy . . . to spin its shining web and to apply its specious theories where it can." [35]

In order to deprive the captain of industry of the public relations advantage he enjoyed when he passed himself off as a model of virtue, critics of business in the late nineteenth and early twentieth centuries represented that the great barons were robber barons who knew no moral law except that of the jungle. They inverted the

[33] *Ibid.*
[34] Wyllie, *Self-made man*, 83–87.
[35] *Commercial and Financial Chronicle* 19: 361–362, October 10, 1874.

businessman's moral pyramid and tried to demonstrate that he owed his success not to simple Christian virtues, but to brutality, rapacity, dishonesty, and cunning. Augustus Tack, a petroleum refiner who had been squeezed out by Standard Oil, gained a measure of revenge in 1889 when he described Rockefeller as a heartless Darwinist to the House Committee on Manufactures. Tack testified that he had gone to Rockefeller, hoping for a reprieve, but that he had been sent away with the brutal comment, "There is no hope. . . . The weakest must go first." [36] Henry Demarest Lloyd, that erstwhile critic of Rockefeller and student of Standard Oil, observed in *Wealth Against Commonwealth* that "The man who should apply in his family or his citizenship this 'survival of the fittest theory' as it is practically professed and operated in business would be a monster, and would be speedily made extinct, as we do with monsters." [37] When John D. Rockefeller, Jr. made his unfortunate remarks about the American Beauty rose in 1902 he discovered that he had played into the hands of his father's enemies as well as his own. Critics who denounced him as "a young scion of wealth and greed, possessed of more dollars than ideas," forgot that the title of his talk had been "Christianity in Business," and that he had entered a plea for more Christian virtue in the transaction of business.[38] In the spring of 1905, at the height of the "tainted money" controversy, his father's enemies depicted the senior Rockefeller, pruning shears in hand, cutting away the buds that had grown up around the finest flower of the oil industry.[39]

Rockefeller was not the only businessman to be tarred with the brush of social Darwinism in the era of the muckrakers. In his criticism of the men who organized the Beef Trust, Charles Edward Russell explained that "They have merely followed to its logical conclusion the idea of the survival of the fittest, the right of the strong to annihilate the weak, the theory that in business any advantage is fair—the accepted creed of inordinate gain." [40] All the leading muckrakers sensed that there was no better way to discredit a businessman than to portray him as a renegade of the jungle. In light of the eagerness of early twentieth-century critics to condemn the entrepreneur as a Spencerian, it is ironic that

[36] Committee on Manufactures, *Sugar Trust and Standard Oil Trust*, 215.

[37] Lloyd, Henry Demarest, *Wealth against commonwealth*, 495, New York, Harper & Brothers, 1899.

[38] Fosdick, *John D. Rockefeller, Jr.*, 130–131.

[39] Nevins, Allan, *John D. Rockefeller* 2: 545, New York, Charles Scribner's Sons, 1940.

[40] Russell, Charles Edward, The greatest trust in the world, *Everybody's Magazine* 12: 643, May, 1905.

sympathetic students of business in our own time have tried so hard to link the businessman to social Darwinism.

There is reason to believe that this mode of interpretation is changing. In his 1953 study of *Railroad Leaders, 1845–1890,* Thomas C. Cochran stated the case for social Darwinism more cautiously, and with greater awareness of exceptions and complexities than in his earlier *Age of Enterprise.* Though he still argued that railroad executives more or less consciously subscribed to Spencerian ideas, he conceded that few of them read Spencer, and indicated instances in which they violated Darwinist precepts in word and deed.[41] My own *Self-Made Man in America,* published in 1954, directly challenged prevailing assumptions on this question. In *Dream and Thought in the Business Community,* published three years ago, Edward C. Kirkland suggested that Darwinism may have done no more than furnish new terms for old ideas in the years after Appomattox, and that businessmen may have derived their ideas of competition and survival from experience and observation, rather than from Spencer.[42]

In the years ahead we can look forward to a more complete and discriminating appraisal of the businessman's acceptance of social Darwinism. Greater awareness of the weaknesses of the old assessment will contribute to the strengthening of the new. In the future historians will distinguish between representative and unrepresentative views, between the ideas of an intellectually unsophisticated majority and those of an educated, bookish minority. They will also discriminate between positive social Darwinists and mere biological or religious evolutionists. They will ask whether competitive social Darwinism did fit the businessman like a glove, whether it served all of his interests and satisfied his every aspiration. Was he a Spencerian when he cooperated with other businessmen in pools and trusts that throttled competition? What did he contribute to the survival of the fittest when he practiced philanthropy? From a public relations point of view, who profited more from the claim that he was a social Darwinist, the businessman or his critics? As historians undertake to explain what the businessman actually thought about social Darwinism they will recognize that their greatest single need is a need for more direct, reliable evidence on all the points at issue. This means evidence out of the Gilded Age, and evidence supplied by businessmen themselves, not by outside

---

[41] Cochran, *Railroad leaders,* 173–174.
[42] Kirkland, Edward C., *Dream and thought in the business community, 1860–1900,* 13–14, 18, Ithaca, Cornell University Press, 1956.

observers. It also means testimony that leaves little or nothing to interference, testimony that ties ideas to their actual and not their assumed sources. My prediction is that such evidence will force us to revise downward our estimate of the impact of social Darwinism on American business thought. The businessman drew his ideas and social values from many sources, not just one. He would not have been ideologically naked without the Spencerian formulation.

18

WHEN Frederick Jackson Turner began writing in the early 1890s about the influence of the frontier on American development, he naturally interpreted the contemporary Populist movement as a manifestation of that influence. The revolt of the West against the East was being re-enacted, as it had been many times before. Now he saw such radicalism, additionally, as a response to the ending of free land.

Turner himself made no detailed study of Populism and agrarian radicalism, but those who did saw a fruitful explanation in the Turnerian suggestion of a rapidly constricting western frontier. Solon J. Buck's two books, *The Granger Movement* (Cambridge, Mass., 1913) and *The Agrarian Crusade* (New Haven, 1921), reflected this approach of Turner to farmer radicalism. Other, more detailed studies like H. C. Nixon's "Populist Movement in Iowa," *Iowa Journal of History and Politics*, XXIV (January 1926), 3–107, also looked to the closing of the frontier in accounting for the Populist outburst. John D. Hicks in his pathbreaking and still very useful *The Populist Revolt* (Minneapolis, 1931) succinctly expressed this view in the first sentence of his book: "The role of the farmer in America has always been prominent, but it is only as the west wore out and cheap lands were no longer abundant that well-developed agrarian movements began to appear." Farm discontent, in short, was a phase in the history of the frontier.

There was another Turnerian conception that underlay much of the early writing about agrarian discontent, particularly Populism. That was the old Jeffersonian view that the farmer was by nature the democrat and radical in American society. Turner himself and many of those who followed him could hardly escape absorbing such a view, since throughout most of their lives criticisms of American society in one form or another had issued from the farming West. Not only was this true in the last quarter of the nineteenth century with the Grangers and Populists but also in the 1920s with the Non-Partisan League, the farm bloc in Congress, and the activities of western Progressives like Senators George W. Norris, Robert La Follette, and William A. Borah.

Since the 1930s, however, farmers have become the mainstay of conservative politics in the United States. During the 1930s and until the 1950s it was organized labor which seized the radical platform, leaving the farmers to defend rather than to attack the *status quo*. There are a number of reasons why the erstwhile radical farm tradition has died out, but Wilcox's article supplies at least one of the important ones. Essentially, his argument is that despite the radical rhetoric of their protest the farmers never really challenged the economic *status quo*, even when they seemed to be doing so most vociferously during the Populist period. Rather than being a product of ideology or principle, farmer radicalism derived from the peculiarities of certain kinds of agriculture, principally the growing of wheat. The cultivation, handling, and marketing of wheat were at once riskier and less profitable than corn-hog and dairy farming in the western states. Hence the protest movement that arose out of these conditions, for all its radical rhetoric, was basically a cry for higher profits and more stability in the industry —two very solid business goals. Instead of argicultural radicalism's being a function of the frontier experience, it was really a transient phase in the farmer's becoming a businessman.

To establish further his position, Wilcox extends his examination of farmer protests in the Northwest to include the Non-Partisan League's activities in the early 1920s. He is able to show that the areas of Populist strength, for many of the same reasons as obtained in the Populist days, constituted the heart of the Non-Partisan League's territory. Indeed, the striking thing is that in the 1920s, as in the 1890s, the political radicalism of certain farmers received little support outside of the wheat-growing localities. This observation brings us to Wilcox's method, which is an additional merit of his important article.

If one describes Populism and farmer protest movements in these years as a western movement in general, then Turner's conception of the role of the closing frontier easily recommends itself. (Populism was an important movement in the South, too, but there the causes and circumstances were quite different; hence no analysis of southern Populism appears in the article, and accordingly it is ignored in this introduction.) Any analysis of Populism as a political force quickly reveals that farmer discontent and radicalism did not move into politics uniformly throughout the West. Consider, for example, the following table, which shows for eight western states the percentage of the vote won by James Weaver, the Populist candidate for president in 1892:

STATE	PER CENT OF POPULAR VOTE	STATE	PER CENT OF POPULAR VOTE
Illinois	2.5	South Dakota	37.6
Wisconsin	2.7	Nebraska	41.0
Iowa	4.7	Kansas	48.4
Minnesota	11.4	North Dakota	49.0

All eight of these states were agricultural, but the striking fact is Weaver's lack of appeal in the states in the first column as compared with those in the second. It was this disparity that obviously led Wilcox to his conclusion that the differences between wheat culture on the one hand and hog-corn production and dairying on the other account for the political radicalism of some farmers in the 1890s. Wheat growing is characteristic of agriculture in the group of states that strongly supported Weaver, while hog-corn raising or dairying is typical in those that did not. As we have observed in connection with other articles, it is sometimes as fruitful in historical analysis to pay heed to differences in social and political behavior as it is to look for similarities. Through analysis of differences of response the historian may find his way to causes. It is the closest the historian can come to the testing of various causal explanations, a procedure that the physical scientist employs as a matter of course in his laboratory.

Another technique is illustrated by this article. One of the most valuable, if tricky, tools of historians is the correlating of two factors, on the assumption that if there is a correspondence between them, then one may well be the cause of the other. Actually when two factors do vary together, there is always the possibility that the correlation is the result of a third factor which lies behind them. Wilcox's article illustrates this possibility in regard to the voting for the Non-Partisan League in North Dakota. He notices that the towns and farming regions of the Red River Valley in the eastern portion of the state did not support the League to the same degree as the western part of the state. The obvious explanation, as he points out, is that the Red River Valley region was the wealthier of the two and therefore "less radical." As he shows, though, the difference in wealth between the two regions is itself susceptible of explanation by noting the difference in the character of the two sections. Wealth, in short, is only a superficial explanation.

Since Wilcox's article appeared, the study of the causes of agricultural discontent and Populism in particular has largely accepted his conclusions. He showed that farmer radicalism was derived from the farmer's problems as a producer for a world market rather than from the frontier influence or from the ending of free land. In this way he brings Populism into line with the contemporary conservative political posture of farmers. As Theodore Saloutos, in "The Agricultural Problem and Nineteenth Century Industrialism," *Agricultural History*, XXII (July 1948), 156–174, observed, farmers at the end of the nineteenth century were businessmen dealing with economic difficulties, not socialists challenging the capitalist order. Richard Hofstadter in his *The Age of Reform* (New York, 1955) made the same point when he noted that once farmers received some government aid in raising their standards of living, their radicalism faded. Allan G. Bogue's *From Prairie to Corn Belt* (Chicago, 1963), in a thorough and fascinating study in depth of two states, also can be said to follow the general conclusion of Wilcox's article. Bogue notes that in the 1880s and early 1890s the middle-western corn-hog states were more prosperous than the wheat-growing plains states.

Most recently the study of Populism has shifted to analysis of the movement's ideology, notably in Norman Pollack's *The Populist Response to Industrial America: Mid-Western Populist Thought* (Cambridge, Mass., 1962). But the article of Wilcox and the writings of those who have followed him, with their emphasis upon the essentially capitalist character of agriculture, casts serious doubt upon any analysis that finds, as Pollack asserts, a fundamentally anticapitalist ideology in the rhetoric of aroused farmer-businessmen in the 1890s.

At the time he wrote this article Mr. Wilcox was supervisor of the Wisconsin Historical Records Survey.

An Historical Definition of Northwestern Radicalism

BY BENTON H. WILCOX

FARMERS the world over and through all ages have been so notedly conservative that one might well be justified in asking about so-called northwestern radicalism:[1] Is it real? Or has it been a mere bogey, conjured up by wily politicians to scare into line a jittery eastern electorate? That it has often served this useful purpose, no one can doubt. But that there has been in the West a definite something, for the designation of which we have developed the stereotype of *radicalism*, cannot be denied. Grangers, Populists, Progressives, Nonpartisan Leaguers, and Farmer-Laborites have all been so vigorously aggressive and so vocal that they can be lightly dismissed no more by the historian than by the practical politician.

Nor have they been. Since the appearance of the first manifestations of this malady in the 1870's, each succeeding organization has had its contemporary apologists and chroniclers, while following years have witnessed a constantly growing body of more or less scholarly literature devoted to the explanation of this strange phenomenon. It was indeed unfortunate for the accuracy of the forming stereotype that these writers found themselves dealing with organizations and men—Sons of the Wild Jackass—who not only were so near as to distort the perspective, but who also furnished almost the only splash of crimson in an otherwise drab and dreary scene. Under the circumstances it was probably inevitable that in the painting the colors should be so heightened and the figures so distorted that the completed picture became almost if not entirely a caricature.

SOURCE: Reprinted by permission from *The Mississippi Valley Historical Review*, XXVI (December 1929). Copyright, 1939, by the Mississippi Valley Historical Association.
[1] While this article deals only with radicalism in the North Central states, and particularly the West North Central states, it is recognized that such radicalism, in keeping with the interpretation here advanced, was as broad as the new agriculture out of which it grew.

Without trying to trace in full the development of this mis-shapen idea, it may not be at all amiss to cite a few of the more widely accepted details which entered into its composition. The playup given by most writers to such picturesque figures as "Sockless" Jerry Simpson and Mrs. Mary K. Lease, with her advice to "raise less corn and more hell," are of course familiar to everyone. Illustrating the idea of frontier barbarism was the jocose but seriously taken phrase of the New York *Evening Post:* "We don't want any more states until we can civilize Kansas." A more brilliant hue was introduced in the days of the Nonpartisan League when, among others, Theodore Roosevelt and Kenesaw M. Landis declared that radicalism was a foreign importation of Euro-pean socialism, red and most decidedly un-American.[2] André Siegfried emphasized still another but by no means original angle when he found this strange farmer spirit to be the offspring of a union between the fierce, brooding Nordic spirit of the Scandi-navian immigrants and the wild, untamed spirit of the western plains.[3] Historians themselves at one time or another borrowed most of these ideas and under the spell of the Turnerian hypothesis wove them into a scholarly tapestry in which the frontier appeared as the *bête noire*, directly responsible for the birth of so hideous a spectre. The proof of this parentage has been found in the location of the radical movements, and the explanation has most commonly stressed either frontier psychology with its ignorant and explosive emotionalism, or the fact that with the end of cheap land the rest-less frontiersmen, who for generations had fled westward before their economic and social ills, were at last brought to bay and forced to turn and fight.

In more recent years this caricature has been undergoing a revision which when completed will give a picture that will be decidedly more rational and realistic, although more prosaic and much less likely to catch the eye of the sensation-loving, reading public. Increasingly it is being recognized that the real basis of this radicalism is not to be found in frontier conditions, nor in recurrent drouth, but in the economic revolution which transformed agriculture from a self-sufficing into a commercial, highly special-ized, capitalistic form of business enterprise.[4] It is being recognized

[2] Fargo (N. D.) *Nonpartisan Leader*, November 1, 1917; cartoon in *Satur-day Evening Post* (Philadelphia), October 12, 1918, p. 5; Minneapolis *Journal*, June 25, 1918.

[3] André Siegfried, *America Comes of Age, A French Analysis* (New York, 1927), 287–288.

[4] Charles A. and Mary R. Beard, *Rise of American Civilization* (New York, 1935), II, 271–284; Harold U. Faulkner, *American Political and Social His-tory* (New York, 1937), 433–440.

that the measures, political and economic, which constitute the content of this radicalism flowed from the struggle between the capitalistic farmers and those other capitalistic groups—bankers, carriers, middlemen, manufacturers—who were in competition with the farmer for a share of the consumer's dollar. In this revisionist movement, however, the factors which account for the lack of cohesion, the division of agrarian radicals into provincial groups, have not been adequately exploited. Little attention has been given to the relationship existing between the various farming systems and particular farmer organizations, nor to the effect upon the intensity of radicalism of such differences as farming system, distance from market, prevalence or absence of monopoly in the transportation and marketing system, and other similar conditions which affect directly the profits of the producer. A study of the influence of these practical factors may not only go far toward clearing up the difficulties that have been experienced in explaining differences in radicalism between state and state, between sections of a given state, or from decade to decade, but should also throw a clearer light upon the underlying character of this radicalism itself.

Take for example the well defined division in the Northwest of the 1870's between the Granger states—Illinois, Iowa, Wisconsin, and Minnesota—and the older states—Ohio, Indiana, and Michigan. That such a difference should exist in the reactions within a section so nearly homogeneous in climate, soil, and general type of agriculture suggests immediately that a satisfactory explanation would be very revealing of the nature of radicalism. For many years the frontier hypothesis has done yeoman service in this respect, but a mere glance at the Granger program is sufficient to show its inability to carry the load. This program, conveniently summarized, called for: governmental regulation of the railroads, regulation of the terminal marketing facilities, the breaking of the farm machinery monopolies, and the reduction of retail prices to the farmer through cooperation.[5] Certainly, these were issues which could only arise out of a highly organized, specialized economic system. Frontier psychology can not explain why such evidences of advanced economic organization and specialization were stronger in the new states than in the old. On the other hand, if it can be proved that there were significant differences in economic organization as between the two sections, differences which would make the problems of capitalistic farming press more heavily upon the farmers in the

[5] Solon J. Buck, *The Granger Movement, A Study of Agricultural Organization and Its Political Manifestations, 1870–1880* (Cambridge, 1913), 111–124.

new states of the West as compared with their adjacent but longer settled neighbors, this would at least create a strong presumption that the difference in radicalism was attributable to these economic factors.

Since the heart of capitalistic farming is the making of a profit upon the invested capital, just as in any manufacturing or business enterprise, differences between sections to have any significance for this problem must affect the farmers' profits. That is, they must bear directly upon either the cost of production or the farm price for the product. In this connection it is apparent that the western section enjoyed one distinct advantage, the possession of cheaper, virgin soil.[6] In every other respect the advantage lay with the farmers of the eastern states. Being much nearer the Atlantic seaboard as well as possessing a growing local market because of the rapid development of local, industrial cities, freight rates consumed a much smaller share of the value of the product, whether in the form of grain or livestock.[7] It was estimated, for instance, that when the farm price for wheat had fallen to approximately eighty-five cents per bushel in Ohio, it went down to around fifty cents in interior Illinois.[8] Secondly, the presence of local trading relations and channels of commerce which had been developed before the building of the railroads prevented the immediate centralization and accompanying monopoly control of broad areas within the older states. On the other hand, Chicago and the Chicago Board of Trade had secured control of the grain traffic in the western states, and by the system of warehouse and traders fees had added still another inflexible element to the list of charges which had to come out of the value of the grain.[9] Finally, although the western land was cheaper acre for acre, the eastern farmer was much more advantageously situated for weathering a depression. He had not at that

[6] *Ninth Census of the United States, 1870,* III, *Industry and Wealth,* 80–84.
[7] Benjamin H. Hibbard, "The Effect of Freight Rates on Agricultural Geography," *The Journal of Farm Economics* (Lancaster, Pa.), IV, 1922, p. 135; *United States Department of Agriculture, Yearbook, 1921* (Washington, 1922), 138, 208, 300.
[8] Ernest L. Bogart and Charles M. Thompson, *The Industrial State, 1870–1893* (Springfield, Illinois, 1920), Clarence W. Alvord, ed., *The Centennial History of Illinois,* IV, 82–88; Eugene H. Roseboom and Francis P. Weisenburger, *A History of Ohio* (New York, 1934), 342. See also *U. S. D. A., Yearbook, 1921,* 138, 208; "Geography of Wheat Prices," *U. S. D. A. Bulletin,* No. 594.
[9] Arthur C. Cole, *The Era of the Civil War, 1848–1870* (Springfield, Illinois, 1919), Clarence W. Alvord, ed., *The Centennial History of Illinois,* III, 75–76; Guy A. Lee, "The Historical Significance of the Chicago Grain Elevator System," *Agricultural History* (Washington), XI, 1937, 17–26.

time forsaken entirely the habits of self-sufficiency which were developed previous to the building of the railroads nor was he so dependent on the staple crops, wheat and corn.[10] Moreover, in the majority of cases the farm had been paid for prior to the introduction of the new agriculture. Although low farm prices might reduce or even wipe out the profit margin, the farm still produced a living and the operator could bide his time if necessary. As compared to this a large percentage of the new western farmers had launched their business on borrowed capital, had capitalized their future earnings in the form of a mortgage or loan.[11] Under such conditions, the cessation of profits for one year was calamitous, and if continued would bring ruin to many farmers. Interest and principle were fixed charges and would not wait for a return of prosperity. Thus the western farmer was spurred on, not simply by the lust for gain, but by the immediate danger of losing his entire investment and home as well. Little wonder that he sought avidly for every possible way to increase his income and attacked with vigor where evidences showed that middlemen, manufacturers, and carriers were holding their charges up to unjustified, monopoly levels! [12]

Here were differences between the two sections, but not a difference in kind. There is little if any evidence that the greater radicalism in the newly settled regions was due to a difference in culture, to the presence of the wide open spaces, or to innate radicalism among those who fled to the frontier. There is ample evidence that the farmers of the more western states were less able to endure a recession of profits, that they were more subject to monopolistic control by middlemen and carriers, and that lower prices were a greater threat to their economic life. In short, radicalism appears to have been simply an effort on the part of business farmers to protect their margin of profit and preserve their capitalistic enterprise.

Further opportunity to observe this relation of radical movements to the practical problems of capitalistic farming is afforded by the Populist movement of the succeeding generation. In this case the storm center of discontent seemed to hover over the newly settled states of Kansas, Nebraska, western Minnesota, and the Dakotas. Again the older states to the east—the Granger states in

---

[10] *Ninth Census of the United States, 1870,* III, 81–87; Buck, *Granger Movement,* 1–9; Roseboom and Weisenburger, *History of Ohio,* 306–315.

[11] Adequate statistics covering the distribution of farm mortgages are not available for the 1870's, but see: *Eleventh Census of the United States, 1890,* XIII, *Farms and Homes,* 26, 246; Buck, *Granger Movement,* 20.

[12] Buck, *Granger Movement,* 1–24.

this instance—proved relatively immune to the siren song, while the still older region of Indiana, Ohio, and Michigan was hardly affected at all. This superficial fact of the location of Populism, along with the frontier location of the earlier Grangerism, has seemed to many to demonstrate conclusively the influence of frontier conditions and psychology in producing frenzied political rebellion.

In large part this attitude is based upon the misapprehension that agrarian agitation during the period under consideration was limited to those who called themselves Populists. It loses sight of the fact that the revived Grange was at the same time rapidly organizing the farmers of the Northeast, from Ohio to Maine, and in its annual pronouncements calling for political and economic action little less radical than that of the hell-raising Populists of the West.[13] It loses sight also of the agrarian movement in the South which in its later phases became more or less identical with Populism.[14] But still more seriously, this viewpoint neglects consideration of the very real agitation in the Granger states which bordered directly on the Populist area.

Although there was no new party in Illinois, nor even a unified farm organization, the farmers of that state did succeed in the period under discussion in pressing their demands upon the state legislature in such fashion as to shape essential legislation.[15] In Iowa, William Larrabee, with the support of the Farmers' Alliance, was twice elected governor of the state as the champion of the agricultural interests.[16] William D. Hoard was chosen governor of Wisconsin in 1888 by an upsurging farmer sentiment which temporarily broke the hold of the machine politicians upon the state.[17] Through the 1880's there is nothing to distinguish between the movements in these states and those which agitated Kansas, Nebraska, Minnesota, and the Dakota territories. All were simply movements in which the farmers sought legislation in the interest of their fight for profits, primarily through railroad legislation and a redistribution of the tax load.

[13] Thomas C. Atkeson, *Semi-Centennial History of the Patrons of Husbandry* (New York, 1916), 158–163; *Proceedings of the National Grange, 1890–1899.*
[14] John D. Hicks, *The Populist Revolt* (Minneapolis, 1931), 104–112.
[15] Bogart and Thompson, *The Industrial State,* 178–182.
[16] Hicks, *Populist Revolt,* 148; Herman C. Nixon, "The Populist Movement in Iowa," *Iowa Journal of History and Politics* (Iowa City), XXIV, 1927, pp. 36–39.
[17] Louise P. Kellogg, "History of Wisconsin," *Wisconsin Blue Book, 1929,* 23; Robert M. LaFollette, *Autobiography* (Madison, 1913), 170.

But if there was no essential difference in the 1880's, the birth of local People's Parties at the end of the decade did reveal a deep division between the two sections. Such parties achieved a considerable notoriety and success in Kansas, Nebraska, and western Minnesota, but failed to make any serious headway in Iowa, Wisconsin, and Illinois. Were there practical economic differences which might account for this?

During the years intervening between the Granger movement and Populism, a new refinement of capitalistic agriculture had developed in the upper Mississippi basin. Here there was sectional specialization. By the time Populism appeared, there were three such sections, each dominated by a single type of farm system: corn-live stock farming in a wide belt stretching from Ohio westward through Iowa and gradually pushing into eastern Kansas and Nebraska; dairy farming, found principally in Wisconsin and southeastern Minnesota; and grain farming, predominantly wheat, which had been pushed out into a broad crescent sweeping from Kansas, through Nebraska, the Dakotas, and western Minnesota.[18]

Even if there were no agricultural economists to prove conclusively that corn-live stock farming was the superior system, and that dairying while inferior to the corn belt system is superior to wheat farming, the very fact that these two had ousted wheat from Illinois, Iowa, and Wisconsin would indicate that such was the situation. But not only did corn-live stock farming produce the greatest returns on the investment in those areas where it was feasible; there were other advantages which loom large in connection with radicalism. The corn belt system felt the pressure of transportation costs and trade monopolies to a far less degree than did the wheat farmers. It has been estimated, for instance, that at one time the corn-live stock farmer was securing better than forty per cent of the cost of his product to the consumer, whereas the wheat farmer received at the same time only seventeen per cent of the value of his product.[19] Freight rates on cattle and hogs were a relatively small percentage of their value. Marketing was much simpler and much less subject to suspicion of gouging the producer. The grading system was based upon visible qualities which bore a direct relation to the value of the carcass as dressed meat. The element of personal bar-

[18] The development of agriculture in the West is conveniently summarized and graphically presented in: *U. S. D. A., Yearbook, 1921*, 89–92, 171–175, 232–239; *Yearbook, 1922*, 186–190, 297–319.

[19] *The Prairie Farmer* (Chicago), March 25, 1937; *U. S. D. A., Yearbook, 1921*, 300; *Yearbook, 1923*, 127; Oliver E. Baker, "Agricultural Regions of North America," *Economic Geography* (Worcester, Mass.), III, 459.

gaining was in large measure preserved, and there was no gambling in cattle or hog futures.[20]

Although geographic conditions prevented the spread of the corn belt system into Wisconsin and Minnesota, dairying possessed many advantages over wheat. The share of the producer in the value of his product to the consumer usually exceeded fifty per cent. Freight rates on butter and cheese, the principal marketable forms of the western product, were negligible in comparison to their weight value. The machinery of exchange was even simpler than in the case of livestock and never fell into the hands of monopolistic processers or middlemen; in fact, cooperatives early became the most important element in the exchange procedure.[21]

The evils or disadvantages of the situation in which the wheat farmers were caught are all too apparent. Far from market and with no competition in transportation, the freight on grain practically ate up not only the profit but often the value of the grain as well. The extremely complex character of the machinery which controlled the grain trade, with local buyers, local elevator fees, commission merchant fees, terminal elevator charges, miller's profits, etc., all taking a toll from the passing stream of grain, ate still more deeply into any prospective margin of gain. The grading system, based upon external characteristics and arbitrary, all too often had the appearance of cheating. Trading in futures, in which huge fortunes were often made, was not conducive to creating trust in the hearts of farmers who often toiled for naught. Thus, the grain farmer, in comparison with corn and dairy farmers, not only found his margin of profit disappearing, but was able to put his finger on many practices which appeared unjust and which if remedied would leave to him a greater share of the value of his product.[22]

Beyond these factors of railroad rates and trade practices, there was also the question of credit. Here, too, the grain growing West was at a disadvantage. In the first place, being only recently settled, there had not been time to pay off the loans and mortgages by which the farmers had capitalized their anticipated earnings, this step usually being necessary to secure the farm plant. Secondly, be-

[20] U. S. D. A., Yearbook, 1921, 277–312; Yearbook, 1922, 227–246.

[21] Baker "Agricultural Regions of North America," loc. cit., IV, 44–74; U. S. D. A., Yearbook, 1922, 350–388.

[22] Hicks, Populist Revolt, 54–95; Hallie Farmer, "The Railroads and Frontier Populism," MISSISSIPPI VALLEY HISTORICAL REVIEW, XIII, 1926, pp. 387–397; Henrietta M. Larson, The Wheat Market and the Farmer in Minnesota, 1858–1900 (New York, 1926), Columbia University Studies in History, Economics, and Public Law, CXXII; U. S. D. A., Yearbook, 1921, 122–145.

cause of the less stable and profitable character of their farm system, they who were less able were forced to pay higher interest for their loans. Consequently, any diminution of normal profits, either through crop failure or because of falling prices, placed the wheat farmers of the plains in a much more precarious position than did similar occurrences in the corn and dairying states.[23]

If there is any need for additional evidence of the influence of the crop systems, with their attendant problems and advantages, it is supplied by the regional distribution of radicalism within the states affected by Populism. The northwestern counties in Iowa, where cattle and hog feeding had progressed least and the prevailing farm system was still that of growing grain for sale, were the counties where a comparatively large Populist vote showed greatest dissatisfaction with conditions in that state.[24] Within Minnesota there was throughout the farmer agitation of the period a distinct cleavage between that part of the state where dairying had developed and the western counties which were predominantly given over to wheat production.[25] If Kansas and Nebraska are divided into zones of Populist concentration, it is found that the western counties, which were still cattle country, and the eastern counties, where the corn-live stock farming system had gained a foothold, were least affected, while the center of Populist power was in the central part of the two states where grain farming was still the dominant system.[26] Thus, as in the case of Grangerism, the difference in radicalism as between sections of the West can be explained most clearly by practical economic factors rather than by references to frontier psychology or any innate radical tendencies to be found in those who forsook the settled abode of older communities for the wilder, freer West.

After the death of Populism, or its transmutation into Progressivism, the next distinctly farmer uprising of cyclonic proportions to catch the public eye was the Nonpartisan League. Formed in North Dakota in 1915 under the leadership of A. C. Townley, it quickly gained political control of that state, forced much of its program upon the dominant Republican machine in South Dakota,

[23] *Eleventh Census of the United States*, 1880, XIII, *Farms and Homes*, 103–122, 246, 542; Hicks, *Populist Revolt*, 20–25, 81–84.

[24] Herman C. Nixon, "The Populist Movement in Iowa," *Iowa Journal of History and Politics*, XXIV, 1927, pp. 15, 58, 75; *Iowa Official Register, 1893*, 119–193; *1895*, 107–183.

[25] *Legislative Manual of the State of Minnesota, 1895* (St. Paul), 462–463.

[26] *Nebraska Blue Book for 1901 and 1902*, 204–233; Raymond C. Miller, "The Economic Basis of Populism in Kansas," MISSISSIPPI VALLEY HISTORICAL REVIEW, XI, 1925, pp. 468–489.

and seriously threatened the position of the machine politicians in Minnesota and Montana. Efforts were made to carry the organization into all the other West North Central states, either by professional Nonpartisan League organizers or by local leaders who attempted to copy the league methods. But despite the use of trained organizers and the financial support of the parent organization, the league was never able to secure a real foothold, either as an organization or as a program, outside the hard spring wheat region tributary to the Twin Cities.

It is apparent that any satisfactory explanation of this inability of the league to spread beyond certain definitely marked limits would give a valuable insight into the real motivation of so-called western radicalism. This has led to many efforts at explanation: in terms of frontier conditions, in terms of Scandinavian cultural background, and in terms of drouth and indebtedness. But all such explanations break down under scrutiny; break down because they are not based upon a set of factors peculiar to the Nonpartisan League territory. In fact, radicalism was not limited to that territory; it was rampant at that time throughout the neighboring states as well. The Farmers' Union and Equity, both farmer organizations which were avowedly and admittedly radical, experienced a rapid growth paralleling that of the Nonpartisan League, the Farmers' Union in the outlying parts of the western corn belt, Equity in Wisconsin.[27] During the same period such well known political radicals arose to importance as Capper of Kansas, Brookhart of Iowa, Blaine of Wisconsin, and Norris and Howell of Nebraska. Just as the league was passing its zenith, the Farm Bureau was born and swept into its membership the bulk of the hitherto unorganized corn belt, and while this latter organization may have been conservative in its origin, it was soon captured by western leaders and committed to a program little if any less radical than that of the Nonpartisan League.[28] The league, it is clear, represented only one wing of the radical front. Admittedly, it did differ in certain respects from other organizations and other movements. Mayhap, it was more rabid and socialistic. But that they all were similar in fundamental character and objectives is beyond dispute.

There were good reasons for the limitation of the league to the hard spring wheat area tributary to the Twin Cities. The program

[27] Edward Wiest, *Agricultural Organization in the United States* (Lexington, Ky., 1923), 483–502; *Nebraska Union Farmer* (Omaha), 1914–1923; *Wisconsin Equity News* (Milwaukee), 1909–1923.

[28] O. M. Kile, *The Farm Bureau Movement* (New York, 1921); Wiest, *Agricultural Organization*, 508–511.

or platform upon which the organization fought its battles contained two principal objectives, the first of which concerned reforms within the machinery and practices of the grain trade of that area.[29] In this the league was attacking a problem as old as the agriculture of the region; it was continuing a war in which there had been no truce since before the days of Populism. Concerned at first with securing through state legislation the right of scoop shovel loading and shipping through cooperatively owned local elevators, the securing of these rights had only served to acquaint the producers with more serious problems related to the handling of the grain at the terminal market in the Twin Cities. As a result of legislative investigations, studies emanating from the agricultural colleges, and the revelations of individuals connected at one time with the trade, a series of serious charges were brought against the traders and their organization, the Minneapolis Chamber of Commerce. It was charged that the grading of the grain was unscientific and capricious: that often different cars of wheat from the same field and of identical quality were placed in different grades. It was charged that although No. 2 Northern often sold at a discount of eight to twelve cents per bushel as compared with No. 1, and No. 3 at a discount of twelve to twenty cents, there was actually little appreciable difference in the milling quality of the different grades, so that the lower price represented in large part additional profits to the traders or millers and a loss to the farmers. Furthermore, it was charged, and proved by statistics, that grain shipped into the terminal elevators by the farmers at one grade was often shipped out at a higher grade. It was charged that while a dockage was deducted from the farmer's price for his grain to cover weed seeds and other grain present with the wheat, this dockage was actually sold out by the traders at a good profit. Finally, it was charged that the Twin Cities market was monopolistic, that by combination all competition in the buying of grain had been eliminated and the prices were set in such a way as to assure monopoly profits to the traders. And, as if to prove this charge, the Minneapolis Chamber of Commerce steadfastly refused to allow any farmer-owned cooperative organization to trade directly on the floor of the grain exchange.[30]

[29] Fargo *Nonpartisan Leader*, September 6, 1920.

[30] Paul R. Fossum, *The Agrarian Movement in North Dakota* (Baltimore, 1925), *Johns Hopkins University Studies in Historical and Political Science*, XLIII, 1–87; Charles E. Russell, *The Story of the Nonpartisan League, A Chapter in American Evolution* (New York, 1920), 25–130; *North Dakota Experiment Station Bulletins.* No. 114, 119; *Senate Documents*, 50 Cong., 2 Sess., No. 278; *ibid.*, 60 Cong., 1 Sess., No. 116.

These were charges which could not be duplicated against the middlemen handling either the hogs and cattle of the corn belt or the dairy products of the dairying region. Even in the winter wheat area marketing practices were almost entirely free from such suspicions of injustice and fraud. Although the Chicago Board of Trade played a large part in its marketing, much if not most of the winter wheat passed directly to local mills or through local grain exchanges, as at Omaha, Kansas City, Wichita, or St. Louis. According to the United States Department of Agriculture, competition in buying was much more in evidence on these local exchanges of the winter wheat belt than at the Twin Cities. Proof of this is found in the fact that No. 2 winter wheat often sold as high as No. 1, and the discount for No. 3 seldom exceeded four or five cents per bushel.[31] Also there was in this region no such close tie-up between the grain exchanges and the local elevators as prevailed in the hard spring wheat area, and farmer cooperatives were early admitted to trading privileges in all of them. Under these comparative circumstances it is hardly strange that when Nonpartisan League organizers entered these other regions to preach the gospel of state owned terminal elevators and mills and a closer governmental supervision of grain exchanges as a remedy for trade malpractices, they were met with rather cold indifference. Without a devil from whom to be saved, there was no pressing need or desire for league salvation.

Like the first, the second part of the league program, state socialism, grew directly out of peculiar local conditions. North Dakota was a helot state, without industries or financial institutions of its own, a producer of raw materials and a consumer of manufactured goods to the profit of corporations located beyond the state borders. While the ultimate ownership of these corporations might be in the East, so far as Dakota was concerned they were located in the Twin Cities. All the railroads led thither and were controlled from that center. Banking, insurance, and wholesale corporations all had their headquarters there. Under the stress of milling in transit rates, all the flour mills and packing plants of any consequence which served North Dakota were located either in the Twin Cities or nearby. Consequently, not only was the state being bled white, but there was no possible way by which the local legislature could attack the monopolies beyond its borders.[32]

[31] Baker, "Agricultural Regions of North America," loc. cit., III, 309–339; U. S. D. A., Yearbook, 1921, 143.
[32] Mildred L. Hartsough, The Twin Cities as a Metropolitan Market (Minneapolis, 1925) ; Fossum, Agrarian Movement, 1–27.

Those who had the welfare of the state at heart, such as Dr. E. F. Ladd of the Agricultural College, pointed out the unwise and unprofitable character of such an economic position. They cited the loss to the state in the form of freight rates paid for shipping wheat and live stock to the Twin Cities and then shipping flour, feed, and meat back to North Dakota. They pointed to the loss in the form of interest and insurance premiums paid to eastern investors and corporations. They aroused state pride and drove home to the consciousness of the citizens of the state the necessity of establishing home industries, home banks, and home insurance companies.[33] But the private capital for such undertakings was not to be found within the state. How then could the vicious hold of the outside corporations be broken? By cooperation, or by the use of the credit of the state. So the Nonpartisan League championed state hail insurance, state rural credits, state owned flour mills and packing plants. It appeared to be the only practical way of freeing the state from subserviency to foreign masters, the way to keep the wealth of North Dakota in that state.[34]

For the purposes of this study the really significant phase of this socialistic movement came when Townley tried to carry, not only the organization but this specific program, into the surrounding states. South Dakota, which was similarly situated as to domestic industry and finance, welcomed the program. Peter Norbeck, a good Republican, refused to join the league but appropriated its program almost *in toto*, thus consolidating his control of the state for many years. True, he did not build a flour mill or a packing house, but he did set up a state rural credits system, a state owned coal mine, and a state cement plant. Furthermore, he promised that if the North Dakota mill and packing house proved successful, South Dakota would follow suit in those fields also.[35]

As compared with the ready acceptance of state socialism by South Dakota, Minnesota offered a sharp contrast. The grain farmers of that state had been fighting for years for state regulation of the terminal markets and welcomed the plan of political organization offered by the league for making that fight effective. They were even willing to try a small state owned mill as a sort

[33] *Bismarck Daily Tribune*, December 17, 1912; *Nonpartisan Leader*, September 23, 1915, January 13, 20, 1916; *North Dakota Experimental Station Bulletins*, No. 114.
[34] *Nonpartisan Leader*, January 20, 1916; September 6, 1920.
[35] Ralph E. Duncan, *The State in Business, What It Has Meant to South Dakota* (New York, 1926); *Aberdeen* (S. D.) *Morning American*, November 5, 1916; *Aberdeen* (S. D.) *Daily News*, January 2, March 3, March 5, 1917.

of laboratory to test out the ideas held with reference to the milling values of different grades of grain. But on the whole, the program of state ownership aroused no enthusiasm. With adequate state industries, they held that regulation should be the goal; with the ousting of Townley from control of their state organization, they quickly subordinated and soon dropped the demand for state owned enterprise.[36] A program, to be successful in these western states, had to grow out of and be based upon the peculiar economic organization of the particular state.

This practical character of the influences producing any organized radical movement in the West is still further emphasized by the distribution of league support within the states where it showed considerable strength. South Dakota, for instance, had a northeastern section that was almost wholly within the hard spring wheat region and almost as subservient to the Twin Cities as was North Dakota and a southeastern section which lay within the corn belt and found its outlet in Omaha, Sioux City, and Chicago. While recognizing the difficulty in interpreting election returns, particularly in view of the fact that the Republican party had borrowed much of the league program, the returns in the election of 1920 show a significant sectional distribution. In keeping with the thesis here offered, the league candidate for governor polled over forty per cent of the vote in the five northeastern counties which were wholly within the wheat belt, thirty-three per cent in the counties in which wheat was the principal crop, but less than fifteen per cent in those counties which lay within the clear bounds of the corn belt.[37] In like manner Minnesota was divided into a western wheat section and a southeastern dairying region. Here, in the election of 1920, in spite of efforts of the Minnesota League to reshape its purely wheat farmer program so as to include interests of the dairy industry as well, it was able to poll only twenty-four per cent of the votes for governor in the nineteen southern counties as compared with over forty-four per cent of the vote in those counties in which wheat was the staple crop.[38]

Still another illustration of this principle is supplied by the distribution of league support within North Dakota. Statistics show that on the whole the rural areas of the central and western parts

[36] C. J. Buell, *The Minnesota Legislature of 1919* (Minneapolis), 13; *Minneapolis Journal*, May 10, 1920, May 1, 1922; *Minnesota Leader*, April 10, August 28, 1920.

[37] Stuart A. Rice, *Quantitative Methods in Politics* (New York, 1928), 129, 130.

[38] *Ibid.*, 126–128.

of the state gave greater support to the league than did the Red River Valley and the towns.[39] This fact has usually been explained by saying the towns and the valley were less radical, less radical because they were more wealthy. It would be futile to argue with the census returns which show that farm for farm this difference in wealth actually did exist. To stop with that explanation, however, is to leave a distorted and incomplete picture of the situation, for back of that difference in wealth lay real, practical problems affecting the pursuit of profits.

First, with reference to the towns, it appears from a study of the election of 1916 that so long as the league program remained a matter of theory, there was no appreciable difference between the rural and town support of that program.[40] The difference appeared after the league, in power, had enacted various measures, not included in the original program, which were directly detrimental to the interests of the town population. By legislation it required all public funds to be deposited in the bank of North Dakota, which alienated all the local bankers. In every county it set up league newspapers which received all official printing, thus robbing the local editors of a major source of income. Also the league sponsored a system of cooperative stores which were designed eventually to cover the state, and which if successful would have destroyed the local, independent merchants.[41] These measures would seem to be sufficient to account for the swing of the urban vote into the opposition column, and that without resorting to fine-spun psychological differences of doubtful validity.

As for the Red River Valley, the farmers of that region enjoyed several advantages over their more western neighbors in the struggle for profits. Being nearer the Twin Cities, freight rates took a correspondingly smaller share out of the value of their grain. Since hail storms were almost unkown in the valley, the farmers there did not have to pay high premiums for insurance or run the risk of a complete loss of the entire crop. Because of better soil and a higher average rainfall the yield was greater and more stable from year to year. Interest rates within the region were lower, in keeping with the better ability to pay.[42] Thus, the urge to radicalism, a dis-

[39] *Ibid.*
[40] *North Dakota Blue Book, 1919*, 256–265; *Grand Forks Herald* (Grand Forks, N. D.), November 9, 1918.
[41] *Bismarck Daily Tribune*, February 22, 27, March 1, 3, 1919; *Nonpartisan Leader*, December 13, 1920.
[42] *Manual for the State of North Dakota, 1930*, 50; *U. S. D. A., Bulletin*, No. 384; *U. S. D. A., Yearbook, 1924*, 211.

appearing margin of profits, lacked the driving power in the Red River Valley which it had in the less favorably situated areas. Under the circumstances it would have been surprising indeed had not the farmers of the valley region shown a distinctly less enthusiastic welcome for the measures sponsored by the Nonpartisan League.

It is quite obvious, of course, that the few examples chosen here to illustrate the factors accounting for differences in radicalism as between state and state, or section and section, by no means exhaust the field. One could present the case of the division of Brookhart support in Iowa, a division between the rich, corn belt counties of the central and western part of the state on the one hand and the marginal corn belt counties, north and south, on the other. A similar situation existed in the distribution of the support given the radicals, Charles W. Bryan and R. B. Howell, in the Nebraska election of 1922. But while these and many other examples might offer variations in the details of the situation involved, they would only reiterate the practical character of the issues which gave rise to the programs and movements.

The examples herein discussed are enough to reveal the essential character of radicalism. They are sufficient to depict the western radicals, not as simply ignorant frontiersmen or innate radicals finally brought to bay by the disappearance of free land; nor as debt crazed farmers quixotically tilting at windmills; but as ordinary businessmen, slightly over-individualistic perhaps, seeking to correct injustices in the marketing and credit systems, trying to cut down fixed charges which threatened to devour their margin of profit, and endeavoring to build up the wealth of the community of which they were citizens. Such a definition of radicalism may lack something in the way of verve; it certainly is not picturesque. But, in view of the actualities of the situation, it does seem to be much nearer the truth than the older picture of sockless, hell-raising frontiersmen, grasping frantically at every crack-pot panacea offered them by self-styled messiahs who promised to lead the mortgage-ridden farmer out of bondage into a freer, happier land.

19

THE entrances of the United States into the great European wars in the twentieth century were traumatic experiences for the American people. In a sense, the tone of and the issues discussed in Birdsall's article are measures of that shock, both in what they reveal about America's entrance into war in 1917 and what they imply about the state of the public debate on the eve of war in 1939. For that reason the article is more than a scholarly article of importance; it is also a primary source reflecting the public anxieties and agonies of the late 1930s.

The United States did not enter the First World War completely united, but it was sufficiently so for the Wilson Administration to enjoy great popular enthusiasm and support for the prosecution of the conflict. But the idealism of a war to make "the world safe for democracy," as Wilson once called it, was soon lost in the bitter fight over the League of Nations and in the depressed economy and bickering power politics of postwar Europe. During the twenties the disillusionment of Americans with "the great crusade" hardened into a public resolve to avoid future repetitions of such foreign involvements. Americans refused not only to join the League of Nations but even to undertake a mild and limited international commitment like the World Court.

This reversion to isolation from European affairs (there was no comparable reaction against involvement in Asian or Latin American affairs) was reflected in writings about American entrance into war in 1917. Perhaps the most widely read book on the subject can also be taken as the announcement of the view that was to dominate thinking on the subject throughout the 1930s. C. Hartley Grattan's *Why We Fought* (New York, 1929) was a semischolarly study of the forces that seemed to lie behind the decision to declare war on Germany in April 1917. In reviewing the evidence Grattan emphasized, along with other factors, American economic ties with the Allies as a potent force in bringing the United States into the war. The general impression left by the book was that the American government had never been neutral—indeed, that it never realistically tried to stay out of the war. Scholars, to be sure, did not pay much attention to Grattan's appraisal, but the general public did.

Meanwhile, the principal scholarly study of American entrance took a quite different approach. Charles Seymour's *American Diplomacy During the World War* (Baltimore, 1934) concentrated on the narrow subject of its title, largely ignoring public opinion in the United States and Germany and the question of economic commitments to the Allies. But Walter Millis's *Road to War: America, 1914–1917* (New York, 1935), which followed closely on Seymour's book, continued the same kind of debunking of the official explanations of the war that Grattan had begun six years earlier. Once again the economic connections with the Allies received much attention, accompanied by sarcastic references to the handling of diplomacy by President Wilson and American Ambassador Walter Hines Page in London.

It was in 1935 that the economic explanation for American entrance into the war received its greatest push. Soon after Millis's book appeared, the newspapers began to feature the hearings of a Senate committee investigating the profits of munitions makers and bankers dealing with the Allies prior to April 1917. The findings of Senator Gerald Nye's committee were not new, but they provided an aura of governmental authority for the view that economic ties constituted the principal reason for entrance into the war. This extremely limited view of a complicated event so captured the American public mind, already oppressed and bewildered by a massive depression, that a series of laws was soon enacted based upon its conclusions. The Neutrality Act of 1935 and other laws that followed frankly assumed that if Americans did not lend money to belligerents or permit trade with them, the United States would not become involved in another war. Probably never before in American history had the foreign policy of the United States been so affected by a single Congressional investigation and a single idea. As Birdsall's article maker evident, even as late as 1939 American foreign policy was still being discussed in terms of cutting economic ties as a way of staying out of the impending European war. Charles C. Tansill's *America Goes to War* (Boston, 1938) also emphasized the role of the bankers and munitions makers in bringing America into the war in 1917, though Tansill's work was more thoroughly documented than Grattan's or Millis's.

Today most historians severely minimize the economic explanations for American entrance into the First World War. Ernest R. May's *The World War and American Isolation, 1914–1917* (Cambridge, Mass., 1959), the most recent and detailed account of American entrance into the war, barely discusses economic forces at all. Yet in Birdsall's article, for all its obvious concern with economic forces, the turn in the direction that May's book has taken can be seen. While accepting the importance of the economic forces, Birdsall puts them into a realistic perspective. He shows that the simple correspondence between economic ties and a declaration of war, which the Nye committee asserted and Grattan and Millis implied, hardly accords with the facts or with the subtle and myriad considerations affecting policy formulation. Moreover, Birdsall's documentation of the effect of the American economic support of the Allies upon the decisions of German leaders has been continued and elaborated upon by recent investigators like Ernest May in his 1959 volume.

Today Birdsall's article is most especially noteworthy for its realistic questioning of the traditional doctrine of neutrality. In effect he points out that for a great power, which the United States undoubtedly was by the 1930s, the concept of neutrality does not have the same content that it does for a Holland or a Peru. Since the Second World War this view has become commonplace in discussions of American foreign relations. As May's book makes evident, it has also colored historians' examinations of the diplomacy that led up to American entrance into the First World War. Few historians today, for example, would accept the narrow, legalistic approach to neutrality in 1914–1917 that Charles Seymour defended in his book in 1934.

In one further respect Birdsall's article marks a shift in historical writing about the First World War. Whereas in books like Millis's and Grattan's, sarcasm and a debunking tone were common, Birdsall carefully emphasizes the difficulties of the decisions facing the principal actors. Of the alternatives available, none was perfect, yet one had to be taken. This awareness of the pressures under which decisions of diplomacy are made is today the general approach in writing about international affairs.

Despite the mass of writing that has appeared since Birdsall's article was published, his essay is still highly regarded. Historians

like Ernest May would probably not be as charitable as Birdsall
toward the German civilian leaders' inability to resist the specious
arguments of the admirals and generals in behalf of unrestricted
submarine warfare. Nor would May subscribe to Birdsall's statement that "the fundamental cause of the failure of American neutrality was economic. . . ." But as diplomatic historian Richard
Leopold has written in "The Problems of American Intervention,
1917: An Historical Retrospect," *World Politics*, II (April 1950),
405–425: "Paul Birdsall's stimulating essay on economic pressures is still the best short discussion on the subject."

Mr. Birdsall was professor of history at Williams College until the
United States' entrance into the Second World War. After the war
he served in the American Foreign Service until his retirement in
1961. He now lives in the Virgin Islands. He is best known for his
penetrating evaluation of the Versailles Treaty, *Versailles Twenty
Years After* (New York, 1941).

Neutrality and
Economic Pressures,
1914–1917

BY PAUL BIRDSALL

TWENTY years of debate have not yet produced a satisfactory or
even a coherent neutrality policy for the United States, nor have
they yet offered any real understanding of the problem of neutrality in the modern world to serve as a basis for policy making. Until
we have some adequate analysis of the forces which destroyed President Wilson's neutrality policy between 1914 and 1917 no government is likely to be more successful than his in future efforts to
master such forces. Nor will the neutrality legislation of the past
years help very much if it simply ignores these forces.

The trouble with much of the writing on the World War period is
that it deals with separate aspects of the problem in watertight
compartments with complete disregard of the complex interrelations
between economic and political phenomena. Thus Charles Seymour

SOURCE: Reprinted by permission from *Science and Society*, III (Spring
1939). Copyright 1953, by Science and Society, Incorporated.

deals almost exclusively with the diplomatic record of our relations with Imperial Germany and from that record draws the only possible conclusion, that "It was the German submarine warfare and nothing else that forced him [Wilson] to lead America into war."[1] The late Newton D. Baker arrives by the same route at the same conclusion: "Certainly the occasion of the United States entering the World War was the resumption of submarine warfare." That Baker had a glimpse of more remote and subtle causation is indicated by his choice of the word "occasion" and by his admission that critics may with some justification charge him with oversimplification by confusing "occasion" with "cause." "This," he says, "I may to some extent have done."[2] Each of these authors is content with a surface record of diplomacy and politics without reference to the fundamental context of economic and social phenomena which alone can give it significance for analysis of the large problem of neutrality.

Nor does it advance the investigation to turn one's back completely on the diplomatic record and resort to a narrow economic determinism, as does Senator Nye. Ignoring the inescapable evidence that German submarine warfare was the immediate "occasion" for American entry into the war, he argues the simple thesis that American bankers first forced the American Government to authorize large loans to France and Great Britain, and when those countries were faced with defeat, then forced the American Government into the war to protect the bankers' investments. I have heard Senator Nye publicly express embarrassment at the lack of any direct evidence to support the second, and for his purposes the essential, part of his thesis, but what he lacks in evidence he makes up in faith.[3]

What is most needed is careful synthesis of the accurate and valid parts of the diplomatic and economic theses. Senator Nye's committee has given us invaluable data on the development of close economic ties with the Entente Powers in the face of a government policy of neutrality designed to prevent just that development, even if the committee failed to analyze the precise forces at work.[4] We

[1] *American Diplomacy during the World War* (Baltimore, The Johns Hopkins Press, 1934), p. 210. See also *American Neutrality, 1914–1917* (New Haven, Yale University Press, 1935).
[2] *Foreign Affairs*, XV (Oct., 1936), p. 85.
[3] C. C. Tansill, *America Goes to War* (Boston, 1938), p. 133.
[4] *Hearings before the Special Senate Committee on the Investigation of the Munitions Industry*. United States Senate. 74th Cong., 2nd sess. (Washington, 1937). Many of the same documents were published in the New York *Times* (Jan. 8–12, 1936). Many are to be found in R. S. Baker, *Woodrow Wilson* (Garden City, 1935), V.

have accurate and scholarly studies explaining the *immediate* cause
of American intervention as due to the German decision to wage unrestricted submarine warfare. But no one has yet demonstrated the
connection between American economic ties with Germany's enemies
and Germany's submarine campaign which provoked American
intervention. It is precisely this connection which reveals the true
significance of the economic relationship, namely that it makes
neutrality in modern war impossible—unless the economic relationships with belligerents can somehow be prevented. And that must
be the first subject of investigation.

II

If Senator Nye is right in contending that it was primarily the in-
trigues of the banking interests which prevented a genuine neutrality
policy, then the present legislation to curb such activity in the
future should prove adequate. But careful study of the evidence he
has himself unearthed does not bear him out.

The Wilson administration attempted to enforce a neutrality
policy identical with that now prescribed by statute in respect to
loans to belligerents. To be sure there was no effort to prevent the
sale of munitions to belligerents, and Secretary of State Bryan
explained why in a letter of January 20, 1915 to Senator Stone of
the Senate Committee on Foreign Relations. He said that "the duty
of a neutral to restrict trade in munitions of war has never been
imposed by international law or municipal statute. . . . [It] has
never been the policy of this government to prevent the shipment
of arms or ammunition into belligerent territory, except in the case
of the American Republics, and then only when civil strife prevailed." [5] Moreover the German government admitted the legality
of the munitions traffic as late as December 15, 1914 even while
they complained of its disadvantage to their cause.

Very different was the official attitude toward loans to belligerent
governments. The State Department recognized no greater legal
obligation to prevent them than the sale of munitions. Lansing,
Bryan's subordinate and successor, said he knew of no legal objection but agreed with Bryan in urging that the United States
government refuse to approve loans to belligerents. Bryan said that
"money is the worst of all contrabands," and on August 15, 1914,
wrote J. P. Morgan, who wished to finance a French loan, "There is
no reason why loans should not be made to the governments of

[5] Baker, *Wilson*, V, p. 179–184 and 189.

neutral nations, but in the judgment of this government, *loans by American bankers to any foreign nation which is at war are inconsistent with the spirit of true neutrality.*" [6] Our State Department has never received the credit it deserves for its realistic appraisal of the issues of neutrality and its refusal to take refuge in the technicalities of international law. It is scarcely the fault of the State Department that powerful economic forces almost at once began to undermine its policy and within the year forced its abandonment. Nor can it be denied that the German government itself helped destroy the policy by sinking the *Lusitania*.

The first efforts to modify the State Department's policy came from the bankers, specifically the house of J. P. Morgan. Lamont testifies that Morgan's firm accepted the State Department ruling but asked permission at least to extend credits to foreign governments to facilitate purchases in the United States, on the theory that this was purely a bookkeeping arrangement very different from the sale of belligerent bonds on the open market. On October 23, 1914 Lansing recorded a conversation he had with President Wilson dealing with this request, in which Wilson accepted the distinction as valid. "There is a decided difference between an issue of government bonds, sold in the open market to investors, and an arrangement for easy exchange in meeting debts incurred between the government and American merchants." The latter was merely a means of facilitating trade. Accordingly Straight of the firm of Morgan was authorized to open credits of this character for belligerent governments, particularly the French. On March 31, 1915 the State Department issued a public statement of its policy in the following press release. "While loans to belligerents have been disapproved, this government has not felt that it was justified in interposing objections to the credit arrangements which have been brought to its attention. It has neither approved these nor disapproved—it has simply taken no action and expressed no opinion." [7]

The destruction of the *Lusitania* by a German submarine undermined the State Department's neutrality policy in two ways, by causing the resignation of Bryan (who refused to take responsibility for Wilson's stiff notes of protest to Germany), and by establishing in the post of Secretary of State his former subordinate Lansing. Lansing says in his memoirs that after the *Lusitania* there was always in his mind the "conviction that we would ultimately

---

[6] New York *Times*, Jan. 8, 1936; Baker, *Wilson*, V, p. 175f.
[7] New York *Times*, Jan. 8, 1936. Also Baker, *op. cit.*, p. 186f.

become the ally of Britain." [8] He was therefore less disposed to maintain the rigid standards of neutrality set by Bryan. Yet in the event it was economic pressures that overwhelmed the policy.

In August of 1915 the British pound sterling began to sag in the exchange market under the pressure of war finance, and the first note of warning of threat to American export business appears in a letter of August 14 from Governor Strong of the New York Federal Reserve Bank to Col. House. Strong said that the drop of sterling to below $4.71 had already led to cancellation of many foreign contracts for the purchase of American grain. He predicted more to follow and feared for the drastic curtailment of all American exports. On August 21 Secretary of the Treasury McAdoo wrote to President Wilson, "Great Britain is and always has been our best customer. . . . The high prices for food products have brought great prosperity to the farmers, while the purchasers of war munitions have stimulated industry and have set factories going to full capacity. . . . Great prosperity is coming. It is, in large measure, already here. It will be tremendously increased if we can extend reasonable credits to our customers." It was therefore imperative, he said, that Great Britain be permitted to float a loan of $500,000,000 at once. "To maintain our prosperity we must finance it." Unfortunately, according to him, the way was barred by the State Department ban on foreign loans, and by the pro-German attitude of two members of the Federal Reserve Board, Miller and Warburg. [9]

Wilson's reply was an evasion. On August 26, he wrote Lansing, "My opinion is that we should say that 'parties would take no action either for or against such a transaction,' but that this should be orally conveyed, and not put in writing. Yrs. W. W." But Lansing wanted something more definite and wrote a long letter rehearsing all McAdoo's arguments. "Doubtless Sec'y McAdoo has discussed with you the necessity of floating government loans for the belligerent nations, which are purchasing such great quantities of goods in this country, in order to avoid a serious financial situation which will not only affect them but this country as well." He estimated excess of American exports over imports for the entire year at $2,500,000,000 and alleged that the figure from December 1, 1914 to June 30, 1915 was only slightly less than $1,000,000,000. "If the European countries cannot find the means to pay for the excess of goods sold them over those purchased

[8] *War Memoirs of Robert Lansing* (Indianapolis, 1935), p. 128.
[9] New York *Times*, Jan. 10, 1936. *Cf.* Baker, *op. cit.*, p. 380f.

from them, they will have to stop buying and our present export trade will shrink proportionately. The result would be restriction of output, industrial depression, idle capital, idle labor, numerous failures, financial demoralization, and general unrest and suffering among the laboring classes. . . . Can we afford to let a declaration as to our conception of the 'true spirit of neutrality,' made in the early days of the war, stand in the way of our national interests which seem to be seriously threatened?" McAdoo had stressed the opportunity for national prosperity; Lansing threatened the horrors of national depression. Wilson replied two days later, on September 8, "I have no doubt that our oral discussion of this letter suffices. If it does not, will you let me know that you would like a written reply? W. W." Shortly after this the house of Morgan floated a loan of $500,000,000 on behalf of the British and French governments.[10]

What of Senator Nye's contention that the bankers got us into the war by exerting direct pressure on Washington to protect their "investment"? It remains to be proved that the investment did get us into the war, and it is perfectly clear that direct pressure on Washington ceased when their desire to float loans for belligerent governments was granted. It is likewise clear that the government did not relinquish its ban on such loans out of any tender concern for the bankers as a group. What McAdoo, Lansing, and Wilson feared was a national economic depression. The bankers were in the happy position of being able to serve both God and Mammon. The situation is summarized in a single paragraph of Lansing's letter of September 6: "I believe that Secretary McAdoo is convinced, and I agree with him, that there is only one means of avoiding this situation which would so seriously affect economic conditions in this country, and that is the flotation of large bond issues by the belligerent governments. Our financial institutions have the money to loan and wish to do so." [11]

At this point the conclusions of Seymour and Baker seem irresistible. They conclusively demonstrate from the diplomatic record that German resort to unrestricted submarine warfare was the immediate cause of American participation in the war. Yet they are strangely incurious about the reasons for the German decision, which have a very direct connection with the American departure from its own deliberately adopted policy of forbidding loans to belligerents. The fact that the German decision was made with

[10] New York *Times*, Jan. 10 and 11, 1936. Baker, *op. cit.*, p. 381-383.
[11] *Ibid.*

full realization that it would force the United States into the war is certainly something that needs to be explained and the search for an explanation is revealing.

III

There were two forces struggling for control within Germany, the civilian government of Chancellor Bethmann-Hollweg, and the naval-military element. The latter favored extreme military policies without regard to diplomatic consequences, while Bethmann waged a losing fight on behalf of elementary political common-sense. In regard to the specific issue of submarine warfare the military group were uncompromising advocates of its unrestricted use as against Bethmann's warnings that such a policy was certain to bring the United States into the war in the ranks of Germany's enemies. After the sinking of the *Sussex* in March 1916 Bethmann was able to dominate the situation for the rest of the year. On May 4, 1916 the German Government gave to the United States a pledge to abide by the rules of cruiser warfare, abandoning the attacks on passenger ships, and promising to obey the rules of visit and search as they applied to merchant vessels. That the pledge was conditional on American enforcement of international law on Great Britain was a clear indication that Bethmann's victory was not decisive. The military element opposed the pledge from the beginning and fought for its abrogation from May throughout the rest of the year, with ultimate success.[12]

They did not in the least contest the civilian thesis that unrestricted submarine warfare would force the United States into the war. They blithely admitted it—and said it did not matter! Here is the reasoning. On May 4, the very day of the *Sussex* pledge, General Falkenhayn wrote Bethmann: "I consider unrestricted U-boat warfare not only one, but the *only* effective instrument of war at our disposal capable of bringing England to consider peace negotiations. . . . So far as this situation is concerned [the probable entry of the United States into the war] *America's step from secret war in which it has long been engaged against us, to an openly declared hostility can effect no real change.*"[13] Hindenburg and Ludendorff grew more and more impatient of the civilians' incurable timidity about war with the United States. They renewed their attack at the end of August, and Holtzendorff of the Admiralty Staff carried their complaints to Bethmann. "The objections

[12] Carnegie Endowment, *Official German Documents Relating to the World War* (New York, Oxford University Press, 1923), II, p. 1151, no. 155.
[13] *Ibid.*, p. 1151f., no. 156.

to this mode of warfare are not considered mainly from the stand-point of the effect upon England, but from that of the reaction upon the United States. . . . *The United States can scarcely engage in more hostile activities than she has already done up to this time.*" [14] On August 31 at Pless, the civilian and military elements fought it out, with Jagow, Helferrich, and Bethmann standing firmly together against the generals. All three warned that war with the United States must inevitably follow resumption of sub-marine warfare, and that active American participation would be fatal to Germany. For the time being they again won their point, and it was agreed that final decision might await the outcome of the Rumanian campaign.[15] Even after that Bethmann was permitted to try his hand at peace negotiations in December, but their com-plete failure, coupled with Wilson's inability to mediate, inevitably brought renewed pressure from the military. Ludendorff on De-cember 22 told the Foreign Office again that formal American participation in the war would alter nothing, and on the same day Holtzendorff brought in an Admiralty report to much the same effect. It dismissed the danger of American troops by show-ing how much time was needed for their training and transport; it calculated that the American supply of munitions—already at capacity—would be less rather than more available to Germany's enemies because they would be reserved for American use. Positive advantage would accrue to Germany from restored freedom of action in sinking even passenger ships which carried munitions. The only disadvantage conceded by the report was the possible increase in American loans to the belligerents, but the amount of these was already so tremendous a factor in the economic strength of the hostile coalition that little additional danger from that source was to be anticipated.[16] Bethmann had for some time been yielding to the arguments and the importunities of the military, and the conference at Pless on January 9, 1917 sealed his defeat by the decision to renew unrestricted submarine warfare. Hinden-burg's final words were, "It simply must be. We are counting on the possibility of war with the United States, and have made all preparations to meet it. *Things cannot be worse than they now are. The war must be brought to an end by the use of all means as soon as possible.*" [17] The United States declared war on April 6, 1917.

[14] *Ibid.*, p. 1153, no. 157.
[15] *Ibid.*, pp. 1154–1163, no. 158.
[16] *Ibid.*, 1200f., no. 177, and p. 1218f., no. 190.
[17] *Ibid.*, pp. 1317–1319, no. 212.

The civilians were right and the military were wrong in their calculations as to the ultimate importance of a formal declaration of war by the United States. But the arguments of the military were plausible and they carried the day. Their promise to reduce England speedily to prostration was tempting, but it was essentially a gamble, and it is hard to see how they could have overborne civilian opposition if they had not had so plausible an answer to the one serious argument that the civilians presented. The answer was always that formal participation of the United States in the war would bring no change in the fundamental situation of American economic support to the Allies. The major influence in shaping the decision which brought the United States into the war is to be found in American policy in the economic sphere, specifically the decision of the Wilson administration in August, 1915 to abandon a policy deliberately adopted in the interest of neutrality early in the war. It was government permission to bankers to float loans for belligerent governments in order to finance American export trade that provided the Allies with resources which Germany could not obtain. That in turn weighted the scales in favor of the extremists and against the moderates in Germany, and provoked the decision which forced the United States into the war.

It is equally clear that the administration yielded to pressures which no administration is likely to withstand. The alternative policy of strict adherence to its earlier standards of neutrality meant economic depression on a national scale. It is scarcely drawing the long bow to say that the fundamental cause of the failure of American neutrality policy was economic, nor is it unreasonable to suppose that the same economic factors will again in the future make a genuine and strict policy of neutrality unworkable, no matter what laws may be written on the statute books to enforce it. The only sensible course is to renounce our illusions and to face the world of reality where there is no longer any such thing as neutrality. In the face of a possible collapse of the collective security system as an alternative to ostrich isolationism and "neutrality" the area of choice is tragically narrowed. It would seem to involve a choice between deciding whether we should now affirm our decision publicly that we will align ourselves with the democracies of the world in the event of war on the long chance of preventing the war, or follow that policy of drift which will sooner or later involve us in inevitable war without our having any very clear cut program of war aims to achieve.

IV

Is such realism conceivable in the present state of confusion of
mind? Probably not, because of the tendency of outworn but
hallowed concepts and policies. Neutrality has a long history and
its own particular folklore. Two of its high priests, Borchard and
Lage, treat it as an all-sufficient decalogue when rightly interpreted
and strictly adhered to. ". . . Neutral rights were as clear in 1914 as
was any other branch of public law, and while the law was grossly
violated during the war, it has not thereby been ended or modified." [18] The real difficulty they discover in Wilson's repudiation
of "the very basis of American tradition in foreign policy." The
submarine controversy with Germany is made to turn on Wilson's
"insistence as a matter of National Honor that American citizens
were privileged to travel unmolested on belligerent vessels."[19] It
follows that there was no adequate excuse for the United States
to break "with its fundamental principles by the unprecedented
decision to participate in a European war. . . ." [20] Consequently
there is no need to explore the economic background against which
the drama of neutrality was played out, unless indeed there was no
such drama at all, but only a skillful bit of play acting. Borchard
and Lage devote exactly one page out of a total of three hundred
and fifty to the administration's retreat from its original prohibition of loans to belligerent governments, with the remark that "No
more than casual reference needs to be made to one of the more
egregious lurches into unneutrality, whereby the United States
and its people were led into financing the munitions supply of one
set of the belligerents, the Allies." [21] In their account this appears
as but a minor detail in a general policy of partisanship of the
Allies' cause. And so at the end they reject the argument that the
conditions of the modern world make American neutrality impossible as "humiliating to American independence." [22] Denying the
efficacy of any improvised formula, they recommend "an honest
intention to remain aloof from foreign conflict, a refusal to be
stampeded by unneutral propaganda, *a knowledge of the law and
capacity to stand upon it*, meeting emergencies and problems not

[18] *Neutrality for the United States* (New Haven, Yale University Press,
1937), p. 345.
[19] *Ibid.*, p. 346.
[20] *Ibid.*, p. 344.
[21] *Ibid.*, p. 40. The authors say, p. 41, that ". . . only public lending could
meet the need, and that meant war." They do not explain why.
[22] *Ibid.*, p. 345.

romantically but wisely." [23] It can be argued plausibly that President Wilson fought against overwhelming odds to realize exactly that program.

At least historians should not become victims of the legal exegesis that obscures the unreality of the neutrality concept. But the latest and most comprehensive account of American intervention in the World War, Tansill's *America Goes to War*, is almost totally lacking in interpretative treatment and completely lacking in synthesis. His very full chapters on the events leading to abandonment of the administration's loan policy are written largely in terms of "War Profits Beckon to 'Big Business,'" [24] with very little reference to the administration's concern with the economic condition of the country as a whole. Moreover he fails completely to show the political and diplomatic implications of the economic ties in his concluding paragraph that deals with them. "The real reasons why America went to war cannot be found in any single set of circumstances. There was no clear-cut road to war that the President followed with certain steps that knew no hesitation. There were many dim trails of doubtful promise, and one along which he travelled with early misgivings and reluctant tread was that which led to American economic solidarity with the Allies." [25] Tansill leaves it at that without any attempt to pursue the profound effect of this economic solidarity on the equilibrium of political forces in Germany which I have been at pains to trace in the central portion of this essay. This is all the more remarkable because Tansill is the only writer on the subject who has conscientiously studied that unstable equilibrium extensively in the German official documents. He has used most if not all of the documents I have cited to prove the decisive effect of the economic argument on the submarine decision—and many more—without ever apparently noting the presence of that argument at all. In his quotations from the documents he simply does not quote the passages where the argument appears. Despite his failure to see relationships, and his avoidance of interpretation, his account is still the fullest treatment available of all the complex phenomena, economic, political, psychological, inherent in the neutrality problem. But it is a compendium devoid of significance for an intelligent understanding of the neutrality problem.

---

[23] *Ibid.*, p. 350. (The italics are mine.)
[24] Title of chapter 3, 67–89.
[25] C. C. Tansill, *America Goes to War*, p. 134.

The definitive study at once analytical and interpretative as well as comprehensive has yet to appear, and until it does appear there is small hope of enlightenment.[26]

[26] I have deliberately omitted from consideration in these pages one of the most colorful of the historical accounts, Walter Millis's *Road to War* (Cambridge, 1935). It is journalistic and dramatic with little pretense at analysis. There is recognition that economic relations with the Allies were dangerous to neutrality, but no attempt to show precisely how. For example, p. 336. ". . . the United States was enmeshed more deeply than ever in the cause of Allied victory." But there is no effort to explain the submarine decision in these terms (p. 372f.).

20

$\mathbf{A}$S the continuing predominance of the Democratic party in the United States demonstrates, we still live under the influence of the Great Depression of the 1930s. The longest of depressions spawned the New Deal, shaped our modern conceptions of the role of government in the economy, and largely rewrote the American prescription for the good society. Even the two Republican administrations that interrupted the Democratic predominance accepted most of the social goals born of the Great Depression and the New Deal. A different sort of sign of the continuing influence of the Great Depression is the persistence of the conception of the decade of the twenties that was formed in the 1930s. As Professor William Leuchtenberg has written: "Each age seems to the next an era of matchless innocence and simplicity." So, under the impact of the stock market crash and the prolonged disaster of mass unemployment, the twenties quickly became the age of the flapper, Freud, the big money, and the hip flask.

Perhaps the best-known book on the twenties is Frederick Lewis Allen's *Only Yesterday* (New York, 1931), which still sells widely in paperback. The book does a masterful job of evoking an era as it was remembered in the early years of the Great Depression—but not necessarily as it actually was. Indeed, by emphasizing the sensational aspects of the twenties, such as the Hall-Mills murder case or the absurdities of prohibition, Allen's book neatly and sharply contrasts the decade's materialism, excessive individualism, and tawdry prosperity with the seriousness, the sense of community, and the poverty of the 1930s.

Only in the 1950s, as Americans enjoyed another great period of prosperity, has Allen's sharply etched stereotype begun to be compared with the sources and subjected to serious modification. Indeed, so recent and tentative has this re-evaluation been, that no single article can be truly designated as marking a shift, though perhaps May's article comes closest to being one. (Nor, it should be added, has the shift been completed. Despite the recency of *The Crisis of the Old Order 1919–1933* by Arthur M. Schlesinger, Jr. [Boston, 1957], it portrays the twenties in the lines and colors of Frederick Lewis Allen.)

Of all the articles included in this collection, this one by May probably least fits the stated requirements, for it is essentially a survey of writings on the twenties rather than a substantive reinterpretation of the period. At best, it is suggestive rather than definitive. Its inclusion is well justified, though, as a good introduction to the history of an era that is undergoing active and needed reinterpretation.

The decade of the twenties, as May makes clear, was much more complex than either those who lived through it or those of the depression years recognized. Indeed, it is the many diverse and often contradictory elements of the twenties that make the decade so difficult to characterize and that therefore cause it to present such a formidable challenge to the historian. If it was an era when quantity and size were equated with the good and the true, it was also an age when inexpensive automobiles, cheap food, and a new industrial revolution provided the highest standard of living ever enjoyed by the ordinary man. If on the one hand it was the period of the conservative politics of Harding and Coolidge, it was on the other also the era of La Follette, the revived Progressive party, Fiorello La Guardia, and Al Smith. The diversity and innovations of the decade are not exhausted by May's discussion. He might, for example, have gone on to discuss the changes in the status of women, which went far beyond the achievement of the suffrage, or the revolution in sexual morals, which also still continues, or the compulsive nationalism which manifested itself in the revived Ku Klux Klan and in the quasi-racist restrictions on immigration.

In bringing together a wide range of literature on the twenties May performs a difficult task with great competence. In perhaps only two places does he seem to misread or misinterpret the literature. Richard Hofstadter's *Age of Reform*, which May cites as relevant to the twenties, is actually not about that decade at all, either directly or by any generous interpretation. The "status revolution" that Hofstadter writes about took place in the two preceding decades, when he refers to it as one of the social sources of the Progressive movement. It is misleading, if not simply wrong, to introduce the concept into a discussion of writings on the 1920s. It is likewise misleading to cite, as May does, David Riesman's *The Lonely Crowd* as a contribution to new thought on the twenties. As a close reading of that book soon makes evident, the dominance of "other-direction" began much earlier, in Riesman's view, than the 1920s. Insofar as his book deals with specific time periods at all, it is essentially contrasting the ethos of the nineteenth century with that of the twentieth. For an elaboration of this interpretation of Riesman's book see Carl N. Degler's "The Sociologist as Historian: Riesman's *The Lonely Crowd*," *American Quarterly*, XV (Winter 1963), 483–497; for a criticism see Cushing Strout's "A Note on Degler, Riesman and Toqueville," *American Quarterly*, XVI (Spring 1964), 100–102.

Re-evaluations of the twenties have been so recent that few of them are direct and full-scaled reappraisals. As May points out, one of the few is Frederick Hoffman's *The Twenties* (New York, 1955), which frankly abandoned the prevalent view of the period as one of materialism, cynicism, and cultural superficiality. Hoffman's point of view, however, is that of the literary historian and critic. Since May's article appeared, a few political and social historians have joined him in sounding the tocsin of revisionism.

Notable in this regard is Arthur S. Link's "What Happened to the Progressive Movement in the 1920's?," *American Historical Review*, LXIV (July 1959), 883–851. Despite the unfortunately narrow title, Link's article is a review of several dozen recent political and economic studies of a revisionist nature. More substantively, he also reminds us that many historians have seen as antiprogressive measures enacted during the twenties were really implementations of old Progressive principles. Seen from that point of view the twenties, instead of being a negation of Progressive principles, becomes a fulfillment of them. Prohibition, which, though not enacted in the twenties, occupied the thoughts and actions of many Americans in those years, was, for example, an old Progressive goal. Similarly, the restriction of immigration had been an important social aim of Progressives. Link even includes the movement to ban the teaching of evolution in the public schools, which culminated in the famous "monkey trial" at Dayton, Tennessee, in 1925, as drawing upon Progressive principles. By using the state to inculcate proper values, such legislation was carrying out the Progressive tenet that the public power should be employed to support the people's beliefs. More convincing than this last example is his reminder that the 1920s witnessed a long and ultimately successful fight for the government operation of the hydroelectrical plant at Muscle Shoals, Alabama, and the farm bloc's fight for government assistance to agriculture.

Of the two full-length books about the twenties that have appeared since May's articles, one follows the path along which it pointed and the other ignores it. John D. Hicks's *The Republican Ascendancy* (New York, 1960), as the title suggests, walks the traditional road, emphasizing the conservative politics. William E. Leuchteberg's *The Perils of Prosperity, 1914–32* (Chicago, 1958), while less scholarly and more sprightly, leaves no doubt of its revisionist persuasion. Though never glossing over the unsavory aspects of the decade, of which the depression-influenced historians made so much, Leuchtenberg concludes that the twenties marked a turning point in the history of the United States. As he points out, even the politics of the decade, despite its dreary conservativism on the presidential level, marks the beginning of a new era with the political awakening of the big-city masses, whose arousal made possible the astonishing victories of Franklin Roosevelt in the 1930s. Leuchtenberg's recognition of the enormous economic gains of the decade also illustrates May's point that revisionism is reflecting a new appreciation of the twenties' commitment to abundance.

Two examples of more detailed, recent revisionism appeared in the summer issue in 1961 of the *American Quarterly*. They are "Education, Americanization and the Supreme Court: the 1920's" by Kenneth B. O'Brien, Jr., and "Business Thought in the Twenties: Social Responsibility" by Morrell Heald. Both articles call into question the prevailing view of the conservative and laissez-faire outlook of the Supreme Court and the business community during the 1920s.

May is professor of history at the University of California, Berkeley, where he specializes in intellectual history. His most recent book, *The End of American Innocence* (New York, 1960), is clearly relevant to his conclusions in this article. It is a study of the sharp change in values evident in the decade immediately preceding the 1920s.

Shifting Perspectives on the 1920's

BY HENRY F. MAY

To COMMENT on the 1920's today is to put oneself in the position of a Civil War historian writing in the 1890's. The period is over and major changes have taken place. The younger historian himself belongs to a generation which barely remembers the great days. From the point of view of the veterans, still full of heroic memories, such a historian obviously has no right to talk—he was not there. Yet historians are led by their training to hope that one kind of truth—not the only kind and perhaps not always the most important kind—emerges from the calm study of the records.

Calm study of this decade is not easy. Like the Civil War itself, the cultural battles of the twenties have been fought again and again. Successive writers have found it necessary either to condemn or to praise the decade, though what they have seen in it to condemn or praise has differed. Perhaps this fact offers us our best starting point. If we can trace the shifting and changing picture of the decade through the last thirty years, and still better, if we can understand the emotions that have attached themselves to one version or another, we may be closer to knowing what the decade really meant. In the process, we can hardly help learning something of the intellectual history of the intervening period.

It is immediately apparent, as one turns through the literature about the twenties, that most of the striking contributions have not come from men we usually think of as historians, but rather from journalists, literary critics, and social scientists. This is perhaps not surprising, since most of the excitement has centered in areas outside the historian's traditional domain. Historians today, of course, claim a territory stretching far beyond past politics; but this is a recent expansion, and all of us enter such fields as liter-

SOURCE: Reprinted by permission from *The Mississippi Valley Historical Review*, XLIII (December 1956). Copyright, 1956, by the Mississippi Valley Historical Association.

ature and science only with caution. Caution is necessary, but it must not prevent exploration. If the best insights into a period come from economists, or anthropologists, or literary critics, we must try to understand and even to assess them, hoping that our inevitable mistakes will be made in a good cause.

At least three pictures of the twenties had formed before the decade was over. For different reasons, spokesmen of business, social science, and literary revolt all wanted to get clear away from the past, to discard history. For this reason, all three groups were constantly discussing their own historical role. Perhaps the dominant current version was that proclaimed by the businessmen, the picture of the period usually conveyed by the phrase New Era itself. Out of the postwar upheaval was emerging, in this view, a new civilization. Its origin was technology, its efficient causes high wages and diffusion of ownership, its leadership enlightened private management. This picture of the period was far more than a matter of political speeches and *Saturday Evening Post* editorials. It was buttressed by academic argument and attested by foreign observers. To its believers, we must remember, it was not a picture of conservatism but of innovation, even, as Thomas Nixon Carver strikingly asserted, of revolution.[1]

It is not surprising that this interpretation of the period gained the allegiance of many of its first historians. Preston W. Slosson, surveying his own time for the *History of American Life* series, came to a typical New Era conclusion on the basis of a typical New Era criterion: "Often in history the acid test of wealth has been applied to a favored class; alone in all nations and all ages the United States of the 1920's was beginning to apply that test to a whole people." [2] James C. Malin found, with no apparent anguish, that political democracy was being replaced by self-government in industry.[3] No serious dissent was expressed in Charles A. Beard's great synthesis, published in 1927. Beard deplored the politics and other obsolete folkways surviving in the postwar era. But he found the center of current development, and the climax of his whole vast story, in the achievements of the machine age. Contin-

---

[1] Thomas N. Carver, *The Present Economic Revolution in the United States* (Boston, 1926), is perhaps the most effective single presentation of this common version of the period.

[2] Preston W. Slosson, *The Great Crusade and After* (New York, 1930), 729.

[3] James C. Malin, *The United States after the World War* (Boston, 1930), 530–43. Like some of the social scientists discussed below, Malin thought that "It is possible that in the long run the changes even extended effective governmental regulative powers, although critics of the new policies held the opposite view" (p. 540).

uous invention was the hope of the future. Standardization had made possible not only better living for all but a more generous support for the life of the mind. Those who feared the machine were lumped together by Beard as "artists of a classical bent and . . . spectators of a soulful temper."[4] Lesser and more conventional historians usually struck the same note; and the textbooks of the period, if they ventured beyond Versailles, emerged into a few pages of peace and prosperity.[5]

Sociologists of the period, full of the élan of their new subject, exultant over the apparent defeat of religious obscurantism, were as optimistic as the businessmen and the historians, though for different reasons. Their New Era lay in the future rather than the present; its motivating force was not technology alone but the guiding social intelligence. This picture of the decade as a transitional age emerges most clearly from the sociological periodicals of the early twenties, where one finds at least four important assumptions. First, the scientific study of society is just coming into its own. Second, social scientists are now able to abandon sentiment, impressionism, and introspection and seek accurate information, especially quantitative information. Third, this new knowledge should be, and increasingly will be, the guide for practical statesmanship, replacing custom and tradition. Fourth, Utopia is consequently just around the corner. The present may look chaotic, but the new élite will be able to lead us fairly quickly out of the fog of dissolving tradition and toward the end of controversy and the reign of universal efficiency.[6]

To condense is always unfair, and it would be incorrect to assume that all social scientists in the twenties saw their role or

[4] Charles A. and Mary R. Beard, *The Rise of American Civilization* (2 vols., New York, 1927), II, 729.

[5] Paul L. Haworth, *The United States in Our Own Times, 1865–1920* (New York, 1920), called his last chapter "A Golden Age in History," and left both title and contents nearly unchanged in his editions of 1924, 1925, and 1931. More temperately, Samuel E. Forman, *Our Republic* (Rev. ed., New York, 1929), 881, balanced "stupendous productivity" against such blemishes as technological unemployment and concluded that the country was "sound at the core."

[6] For optimism about the prospects of social science, see for instance Emory S. Bogardus' preface to Elmer S. Nelson, Charles E. Martin, and William H. George, *Outlines of the Social Sciences* (Los Angeles, 1923), xvii–xx. For a strong statement about the role of social scientists in correcting all existing abuses, see John Candler Cobb, "The Social Sciences," *American Journal of Sociology* (Chicago), XXXI (May, 1926), 721. An unusually strong statement of the necessity for the well-informed to control society is that by the historian of the social sciences, Harry Elmer Barnes, "History and Social Intelligence," *Journal of Social Forces* (Chapel Hill), II (November, 1923), 151–64.

their period this simply. Yet it is easy enough to find all these beliefs stated very positively in textbooks and even learned articles, with both the behaviorist dogmatism and the authoritarian implications full-blown. Part of the confidence of these prophets rested on real and important achievement by social scientists in the period, but those who had actually contributed the most new knowledge were sometimes less dogmatic than their colleagues. In *Middletown*, for instance, the social science interpretation of the twenties is buried in a mass of scrupulously collected facts, but it is there. At certain points in describing the decline of labor unionism or the standardization of leisure the authors seem to be deploring changes that have taken place since 1890. Yet in their conclusion they trace the tensions of Middletown to the lag of habits and institutions behind technological progress. Individual child-training, religion, and the use of patriotic symbols represent the past, while the future is represented by whatever is thoroughly secular and collective, particularly in the community's work life. The town has tended to meet its crises by invoking tradition in defense of established institutions. Their whole investigation, the Lynds conclude, suggests instead "the possible utility of a deeper-cutting procedure that would involve a re-examination of the institutions themselves." [7]

The typical economic thought of the twenties, while it avoided Utopian extremes, shared with the other social sciences an unlimited confidence in the present possibilities of fact-finding and saw in the collection and use of statistics much of the promise and meaning of the era. In his brilliant concluding summary of *Recent Economic Trends*, Professor Wesley C. Mitchell, for instance, found the main explanation for the progress of 1922–1928 in the new application of intelligence to business, government, and trade-union administration.[8]

The third contemporary interpretation of that period, that offered by its literary intellectuals, differed sharply from the other two. Completely repudiating the optimism of the businessmen, it agreed with the social scientists only in its occasional praise of the liberated intelligence. For the most part, as we are all continually reminded, the writers and artists of the twenties saw their age as one of decline.

The most publicized group of pessimists was that typified by

[7] Robert S. and Helen M. Lynd, *Middletown* (New York, 1929), 502.
[8] President's Conference on Unemployment, *Recent Economic Changes* (New York, 1929), 862.

Harold Stearns and his colleagues of 1922, who, with their many successors, left an enduring picture of a barren, neurotic, Babbitt-ridden society. These critics have drawn a lot of patriotic fire, and indeed some of them are sitting ducks. They were often, though not always, facile, unoriginal, and ignorant. They seldom made clear the standards by which they found American society so lacking. Yet their lament is never altogether absurd or capricious. If one studies the civilization they saw around them through its press, one hardly finds it a model of ripeness or serenity. The fact remains, for historians to deal with, that American civilization in the twenties presented to many of its most sensitive and some of its gifted members only an ugly and hostile face.

A more thoughtful and sadder group of writers than most of the young Babbitt-beaters traced their own real malaise not to the inadequacies of America but to the breakdown of the entire Western civilization. The New Humanists had long been deploring the decline of literary and moral discipline. At the opposite extreme in taste the up-to-date followers of Spengler agreed that decay impended. Joseph Wood Krutch in 1929 described the failure first of religion and then of the religion of science to give life meaning: "Both our practical morality and our emotional lives are adjusted to a world which no longer exists. . . . There impends for the human spirit either extinction or a readjustment more stupendous than any made before." [9]

Many accepted this statement of the alternatives, and chose according to their natures. Walter Lippmann, who had played some part in the confident prewar attack on tradition and custom, chose the duty of reconstruction and published, in 1929, his earnest attempt to find a naturalist basis for traditional moral standards.[10] On the other hand, T. S. Eliot painted a savage and devastating picture of present civilization and left it to live in the world which Krutch thought no longer existent. As Eliot assumed the stature of a contemporary classic, his description of the Waste Land, the world of Sweeney and Prufrock, and also his path away from it, seriously influenced later conceptions of the period.

With the depression, the twenties shot into the past with extraordinary suddenness. The conflicting pictures of the decade, rosy and deep black, changed sharply, though none disappeared. Of them all, it was the New Era point of view, the interpretation of the decade as the birth of a new and humane capitalism, that

[9] Joseph W. Krutch, *The Modern Temper* (New York, 1929), 26.
[10] Walter Lippmann, *A Preface to Morals* (New York, 1929).

understandably suffered most. Ironically, the most plausible and heavily documented version of this description, and one of the most influential later, appeared only in 1932 when Adolph A. Berle, Jr., and Gardiner C. Means described the separation of management from ownership.[11] At the time, however, the economic order of the twenties was collapsing, and its harassed defenders retreated temporarily into the Republican last ditch.

The other optimistic vision of the decade, that of the social scientists, depended less directly on prosperity and in the thirties survived somewhat better, though it became difficult to see the preceding period as the triumphant application of social intelligence. It is a startling example of the prestige of the social science point of view in 1929 that a president should commission a group of social scientists to make a complete and semi-official portrait of a whole civilization. The fact that *Recent Social Trends* was not completed and published until 1932 probably accounts in part for its excellence; it is the most informative document of the twenties which we have and also a monument of the chastened social science of the thirties. The committee that wrote this survey still believed, as its chairman, Wesley Mitchell, had earlier, that much of the meaning of the twenties lay in the harnessing of social intelligence to collective tasks. Consciously and subtly, the various authors documented the contradiction between the period's individualistic slogans and its actual movement toward social and even governmental control.[12] Yet they were conscious throughout that all this had ended in depression.

Like the authors of *Middletown*, the committee found its synthetic principle in the doctrine that change proceeds at different rates in different areas. Again like the Lynds, it assumed that society's principal objective should be "the attainment of a situation in which economic, governmental, moral and cultural arrangements should not lag too far behind the advance of basic changes," and basic here means primarily technological.[13] Occasionally *Recent Social Trends* displays, as for instance in its chapters on the child and on education, a surviving trace of the easy authoritarianism of the preceding decade's social theorists, and occasional chapters refer in the early optimistic manner to the hope of solving

[11] Adolf A. Berle, Jr., and Gardiner C. Means, *The Modern Corporation and Private Property* (New York, 1932).

[12] President's Research Committee on Social Trends, *Recent Social Trends* (2 vols. New York, 1933). This is a main theme of Chapters 23 to 29, II, 1168-1541.

[13] *Ibid.*, I, lxxiv.

all social problems through the new psychological knowledge.[14] But in most of this great work, and particularly in its brilliant introduction, the authors left behind the social-science utopianism of the early twenties. It would take an increasingly powerful effort of social intelligence to bring us into equilibrium. Moreover, this effort must be a subtle one; the committee took pains to state that it was "not unmindful of the fact that there are important elements in human life not easily stated in terms of efficiency, mechanization, institutions, rates of change or adaptations to change." [15] Therefore, what was called for was not a ruthless rejection of tradition but a re-examination leading to a restatement in terms of modern life. *Recent Social Trends* is in places a work of art as well as of social science, and it is one of the few books about the twenties that point the way toward a comprehensive understanding of the period.

The view of the previous decade presented in the thirties by most historians was far less subtle and complete. Instead of either a New Era, a liberation, or a slow scientific adaptation, the twenties became a deplorable interlude of reaction. This view, stated sometimes with qualifications and sometimes very badly, has continued to dominate academic historical writing from the thirties almost until the present.

Most of the historians who were publishing in the thirties had received their training in the Progressive Era. Many had been deeply influenced by Frederick Jackson Turner, and had tended to look for their synthesis not to the decline of Europe but to the expansion of America. Though the Turner doctrine can be turned to pessimistic uses, Turner himself in the twenties prophesied that social intelligence would find a substitute for the disappearing force of free land.[16] As this suggests, the outlook of John Dewey pervaded much of historical writing as it did the work of social scientists. Yet historians still tended to give most of their attention to politics. For these reasons, and because they shared the opinion of their readers, historians usually found the meaning of American history in the nineteenth-century growth of political and social democracy and the twentieth-century effort to adapt it to new conditions.

As we have seen, many of the historians actually writing in the

[14] *Ibid.*, II, 1185.
[15] *Ibid.*, I, lxxv.
[16] See his statement of 1924, quoted in Henry Nash Smith, *Virgin Land* (Cambridge, 1950), 258–59.

twenties had not found their own period an interruption of this beneficent adaptation. The interruption had come in 1929 and then, after an interval of confusion and paralysis, Franklin D. Roosevelt had appealed for support partly in terms of the progressive view of history. Roosevelt himself justified his program by pointing to the end of free land [17] and claimed the progressive succession from Theodore Roosevelt and Woodrow Wilson, his cousin and his former chief. Few historians were disposed to deny his claim, and accepting it made the twenties an unfortunate interregnum, sometimes covered by a chapter called "The Age of the Golden Calf," or "Political Decadence," or even "A Mad Decade." [18]

This does not mean that an emphasis on the political conservatism of the decade, or a hostile criticism of the Harding-Coolidge policies, is in itself a distortion. Yet stubborn standpattism was only one ingredient in a varied picture. It is not history to make the twenties, as some of the briefer historical treatments do, merely a contrasting background for the New Deal. Sometimes even prosperity—an important fact despite the exceptions—is belittled almost out of existence, the prophets of abundance are denied credit for good intentions, the approach of the depression becomes something that nearly anybody could have foreseen, and the decade's many advances in science, social science, medicine, and even government are left out.[19]

While they deplored the businessmen and politicians of the twenties, the progressive historians of the thirties and later tended

[17] See his famous Commonwealth Club Address, Samuel I. Rosenman (ed.), *The Public Papers and Addresses of Franklin D. Roosevelt* (13 vols., New York, 1938–1950), I, 742–56.

[18] The first two of these occur in Dwight L. Dumond, *Roosevelt to Roosevelt* (New York, 1937), the general title of which indicates its outspoken loyalties; the last in James Truslow Adams, *The March of Democracy* (2 vols., New York, 1933). Adams' best-selling *Epic of America* (Boston, 1931) contains one of the most complete indictments of all aspects of the culture of the twenties. The above generalizations about American historians do not, however, apply fully to Adams, whose ideas are somewhat atypical. His dislike of the decade's culture was expressed early in his *Our Business Civilization* (New York. 1929), which repeats many of the criticisms made by the literary anti-conformists.

[19] Fred A. Shannon, *America's Economic Growth* (Rev. ed., New York, 1940), describes the economic policies of the period thus: "It was in this atmosphere of rapacity and high-pressured seduction that governments reverted to *laissez faire* policy, contorted to mean government assistance to business" (p. 585), and refers to the "fools' paradise" and the "years of paper prosperity" of the period (pp. 701, 727). A later judgment is that of Henry B. Parkes, *Recent America* (New York, 1946), that "There was probably more materialism, more illiberality, and more cynicism than ever before in American history" (p. 464). One can think at least of close contenders to some of these titles.

also to belittle the period's literary achievement. This negative judgment was sustained by a powerful writer, Vernon L. Parrington, himself a thorough and fervent exponent of the progressive interpretation of American history. In Parrington's last, fragmentary volume, published in 1930, he read the younger authors of the twenties out of the American tradition as "a group of youthful poseurs at the mercy of undigested reactions to Nietzsche, Butler, Dadaism, Vorticism, Socialism; overbalanced by changes in American critical and creative standards, and in love with copious vocabularies and callow emotions." "With the cynicism that came with postwar days," said Professor Parrington, "the democratic liberalism of 1917 was thrown away like an empty whiskey-flask." [20]

Though Parrington did not live to explain this rejection or treat it at length, he obviously believed that the liberal whisky was still there and still potent, and so, in the thirties and often since, have many of his readers. Some historians, understandably impressed by Parrington's great architectural achievement, willingly and specifically took over his literary judgments; others doubtless arrived at similar opinions independently.[21] For whatever reason, by the thirties the most widespread historical picture of the twenties was that of a sudden and temporary repudiation of the progressive tradition by reactionary politicians and also by frivolous or decadent littérateurs.

Some of the historians writing in the thirties, and far more of the literary critics, found their historical principle not in American progressivism but in Marxism. John Chamberlain demonstrated to his own temporary satisfaction the futility of the preceding Progressive Era, and Lewis Corey and others depicted the resultant triumph of monopoly capitalism, characterized by a false prosperity and leading inevitably to the depression and (before 1935) the disguised fascism of the New Deal.[22] At their worst, and in most of their specifically historical writing, the Marxist writers seem now unbelievably crude and schematic. But the Marxist version

[20] Vernon L. Parrington, *Main Currents in American Thought* (3 vols., New York, 1927–1930), Vol. III, *The Beginning of Critical Realism in America,* 385–86, 412.

[21] An example is Louis M. Hacker, *American Problems of Today* (New York, 1938), which quotes and cites Parrington's judgments liberally (e.g., p. 165). A historian who states his admiration of Parrington very strongly in our own time is Henry Steele Commager, *The American Mind* (New Haven, 1950), 445.

[22] Lewis Corey, *The Decline of American Capitalism* (New York, 1934), and *The Crisis of the Middle Class* (New York, 1935). An example of Marxist interpretation at its simplest is Bruce Minton and John Stewart, *The Fat Years and the Lean* (New York, 1940).

of the twenties came not only from the pamphleteers but also from gifted literary artists. For many of the generation that grew up in the thirties the concept of the previous decade was strongly influenced by the work of John Dos Passos. His brilliant sketches of Woodrow Wilson, Henry Ford, Thorstein Veblen, and other giants, the post-war violence, the defeat of hopes, and the gradual inevitable corruption of the "big money" form a picture that is hard to forget—that Dos Passos himself in sackcloth and ashes is entirely unable to wipe out. Among the many critics and literary historians who were then Marxists, most of them dull and fashion-ridden, were a few writers of insight. It is still suggestive to see the literary rebellion of the twenties, through the 1935 eyes of Granville Hicks, as a reflection of the insecurity of the middle class.[23] Most of the rebellious writers *had* come from this class, and even from a particular segment of it that had lost prestige, and many of them had been self-conscious and worried about this origin.

Sometimes, despite their basic differences, the Marxist writers agreed in part in the thirties with the progressive historians. Often, however, the literary Marxists made a different combination. Starting in the twenties as rebels in the name of art, they had found their esthetic distaste for capitalism confirmed by prophecies of its inevitable doom. The resultant mixture of individualist rebellion and socialist revolution was unstable and short-lived, but in the thirties powerful. Edmund Wilson describes the representative mood, and the resultant attitude toward the twenties: "To the writers and artists of my generation who had grown up in the shadow of the Big Business era and had always resented its barbarism, its crowding-out of everything they cared about, these depression years were not depressing but stimulating. One couldn't help being exhilarated at the sudden unexpected collapse of that stupid gigantic fraud." [24]

One other and opposite group of writers in the thirties contributed to the previous decade's bad press. This was the varied group stemming from T. S. Eliot's neo-classical essays and I. A. Richards' effort at a scientific criticism that came to be known as "the New Critics." This school of writers could almost be defined as a counter revolution against the individualist rebellion of the twenties, in which some of them, not surprisingly, had themselves played a part. Some of the New Critics called for a

[23] Granville Hicks, *The Great Tradition* (New York, 1935), 215.
[24] Edmund Wilson, "The Literary Consequences of the Crash" (first published in 1932), in Wilson, *The Shores of Light* (New York, 1952), 409.

revival of the Catholic, or Anglo-Catholic, or humanist, or south-ern tradition; others hoped to find a new credo in literature itself. They agreed only in valuing such qualities as complexity, tension, and intellectual strictness. In the thirties, despite the noise made by opposite groups, it was the New Critics who were moving quietly toward a position of dominance in criticism and in the college teaching of literature; a position they clearly hold today.

Like their enemies, the Marxists and progressives, the New Critics found little to praise in the twenties. To begin with, they stoutly rejected any tendency to measure the progress of civiliza-tion in terms of technology or standard of living. Thus they saw both the business civilization of the New Era and the opposing humanitarian progressivism as two variants of the same shallow materialism.[25] To them the social science Utopias forecast in the twenties were merely a repulsive climax to current tendencies. Allen Tate, for instance, associated social science not only with innocent barbarism but with the current triumph of the total state: "What we thought was to be a conditioning process in favor of a state planned by Teachers College of Columbia University will be a conditioning equally useful for Plato's tyrant state. . . . The point of view that I am sketching here looks upon the rise of the social sciences and their influence in education, from Comtism to Dewey-ism, as a powerful aid to the coming of the slave society." Look-ing back at the previous period, Tate remembered sadly "How many young innocent men—myself among them—thought, in 1924, that laboratory jargon meant laboratory demonstration." [26]

Most of the New Critics rejected the rebellious literature of the twenties as completely as they did the business civilizations of the era. Exceptions had to be made, of course, for the more care-ful and rigorous poets—Marianne Moore, Eliot, sometimes Ezra Pound. The abler of the New Critics realized, as some moralists did not, that the writers of the twenties expressed, rather than caused, the disintegration of tradition which they deplored. Some of them were able to admire men like Ernest Hemingway and Hart Crane who bravely tried to give literary form to moral and intellectual

---

[25] This radical separation of material and spiritual values may be found in Eliot's essays in the early twenties and is strongly stated in John Crowe Ran-som, "Flux and Blur in Contemporary Art," *Sewanee Review* (Sewanee, Tenn.), XXXVII (July, 1929), 353–66. It was in the thirties, however, that the New Critic movement drew together as a school. As early as 1931, Max Eastman acutely pointed out that this radical dualism was a curious attitude in those who wanted to restore the unity of Western cultural tradition. East-man, *The Literary Mind* (New York, 1931).
[26] Allen Tate, *Reason in Madness* (New York, 1935), 7, 11.

disorder. But the general direction of the literature of the decade was, they agreed, disintegration.[27]

Progressives, Marxists, and neo-classicists all found the twenties deplorable, yet in writers from all these camps, and in others who wrote in the thirties, a note of nostalgia often broke through the sermon. Frivolous, antisocial, and decadent as the literature of the twenties seemed, it had to be conceded the somewhat contradictory qualities of freshness and excitement. And nostalgia, in the thirties, extended beyond the previous decade's literature to its manners and customs. In 1931 Frederick L. Allen performed a remarkable feat of impressionist recall of the period just over, and in 1935 Mark Sullivan brought back vividly its clothes and songs and sensations.[28] Already in the work of these two excellent reporters, and later in the versions of a number of minor and more sentimental merchants of nostalgia, the twenties appeared strange, fantastic, and appealing. They appealed with particular strength to those who did not remember them; it was the peculiar feat of these reporters to fill the new generation with nostalgia for scenes they had not seen. For the college student of the next decade, if the twenties was one half the betrayal of progress, the other half was the jazz age. Irresponsibility, to the solemn and uneasy thirties, was both deplorable and attractive.

This paradoxical attitude toward the twenties continued and the

[27] A good sample of the attitude of the New Critics toward the twenties, conveying both the acuteness and the dogmatism of the movement, is Richard P. Blackmur, "Notes on E. E. Cummings' Language," published in *Hound and Horn* (Portland, Me.), in 1931, and reprinted in Morton D. Zabel's very helpful anthology, *Literary Opinion in America* (New York, 1937; rev. ed., 1951), 296–314. A typical verdict from an atypical critic is that of Yvor Winters: "During the second and third decades of the twentieth century, the chief poetic talent of the United States took certain new directions, directions that appear to me in the main regrettable. The writers between Robinson and Frost, on the one hand, and Allen Tate and Howard Baker on the other, who remained relatively traditional in manner were with few exceptions minor or negligible; the more interesting writers . . . were misguided." Winters, *Primitivism and Decadence* (New York, 1937), 15. A little later Randall Jarrell acutely suggested, from a New Critic point of view, the similarity between the period's rebels and its dominant tendencies: "How much the modernist poets disliked their society, and how much they resembled it! How often they contradicted its letter and duplicated its spirit! They rushed, side by side with their society, to the limits of all tendencies." Jarrell, "The End of the Line" (first published in 1942), in Zabel, *Literary Opinion in America* (rev. ed.), 742–48.

[28] Frederick L. Allen, *Only Yesterday* (New York, 1931); Mark Sullivan, *Our Times: The United States, 1900–1925* (6 vols., New York, 1926–1935), Vol. VI, *The Twenties*. A later sensational and amusing treatment of some aspects of the decade is Laurence Greene, *The Era of Wonderful Nonsense* (Indianapolis, 1939).

paradox sharpened in the next period. In the dramatic and tragic days of World War II, few found much to admire in the age of Ford and Coolidge. James Burnham, combining Berle and Means's data on the separation of ownership and control with an apocalyptic vision of the rise of the total state, made the New Era into the beginning of the "Managerial Revolution." [29] To the F. D. R. liberals, who already blamed the twenties for abandoning progressivism, the period's major crime was now its rejection of the Wilsonian international program. Teachers worried whether the earlier postwar disillusion, which they had helped to propagate, would make it impossible to revive a fighting spirit—a worry which proved unnecessary and perhaps a little conceited. Editorial writers wondered whether the country would again fail in its responsibilities after the war. Above all, those who responded most generously to the call for the defense of Western culture feared that the literary rebels of the twenties had done great, even disastrous, damage to the nation's morale.

Even before the war broke out, Walter Lippmann was concerned about the lack of fighting convictions among civilized men and blamed, in part, the rejection of tradition in which he had long ago taken part. Archibald MacLeish blamed both the artist and the scholars of the previous period for their different kinds of detachment. Van Wyck Brooks, looking back at the writers who had answered his own summons for a new literature, found that they differed from all previous writers in one striking way: they had ceased to be "voices of the people." [30] "How could a world," he wondered, "that was sapped by these negative feelings resist the triumphant advance of evil." [31]

This high estimate of the power and responsibility of literature seemed to be shared by Bernard DeVoto, though he took writers to task for making literature the measure of life. Writers of the "Age of Ignominy" had condemned their period partly out of sheer ignorance. In his eagerness to demonstrate this DeVoto re-

---

[29] James Burnham, *The Managerial Revolution* (New York, 1941).

[30] Walter Lippmann, *The Good Society* (New York, 1937); Archibald MacLeish, *The Irresponsibles* (New York, 1940); Van Wyck Brooks, *The Opinions of Oliver Allston* (New York, 1941). "Allston" condemns the rebellious poets and novelists of the twenties and, even more vigorously, their opponents the New Critics (as "coterie writers," pp. 241 ff.). He rejects the "excuses" characteristic of the postwar authors and insists that the trouble is not relativity, mechanization, etc., but the emotional inadequacy of the writers themselves (pp. 249–50).

[31] Brooks, *Opinions of Allston*, 205. The opinions quoted are those of "Allston," Brooks's thinly disguised fictional counterpart.

vived, earlier than many, some of the New Era interpretation of the twenties. "What truly was bankrupt was not American civilization but the literary way of thinking about it." Actually, "The nation that came out of the war into the 1920's was ... the most cheerful and energetic society in the world." [32] A true picture of it would have emphasized its achievements in education, medicine, humanitarian improvement, and the writing of local history.

MacLeish, Brooks, DeVoto, and others condemned the writers of the twenties for damaging the nation's fighting morale, and strangely enough, Charles and Mary Beard, writing in 1942 of the American Spirit, made the same charges from an isolationist point of view. For the Beards, American cynicism had come from Europe: "In the tempers and moods fostered by foreign criticisms and by American weakness displayed in reactions to the impacts, multitudes of young men and women were brought to such a plight that they derided the whole American scene." [33]

All these works, including in part that of the Beards (which was not one of the major productions of these great historians), were wartime pamphlets rather than history. None of them offered a halfway satisfactory explanation of the alienation they discussed, which was certainly a more important phenomenon than the inadequacy of a few individuals. Yet one thing the wartime writers said was true and worth saying, that in the twenties a deep chasm had opened between the views of life of most writers and their fellow citizens. Perhaps the importance of this fact could not be emotionally grasped until the years when DeVoto heard Ezra Pound on the Italian radio.

Yet, even in wartime, and for some perhaps especially in wartime, the freedom and creativity and even the irresponsibility of the previous generation of writers had a paradoxical attraction. Alfred Kazin's admirable and by no means uncritical chapters on the period, which appeared in 1942, were called "The Great Liberation (1918–1929)." [34] And the paradox seemed to reach its most acute form in DeVoto himself. In the same short volume the literature of the twenties was "debilitated, capricious, querulous, and irrelevant" and yet the decade was "one of the great periods of American literature, and probably the most colorful, vigorous, and

[32] Bernard DeVoto, *The Literary Fallacy* (Boston, 1944), 123, 162.

[33] Charles A. and Mary R. Beard, *The American Spirit* (New York, 1942), 474. For the Beards, as for many other cultural historians, "The American Philosophy" is that of John Dewey (p. 665). This version of American intellectual history seems to need considerable qualification.

[34] Alfred Kazin, *On Native Grounds* (New York, 1942), 187.

exciting period." It was a literature that was "not . . . functional in American life," but "idle, dilettante, flippant, and intellectually sterile," and yet one which had "achieved something like a charter of liberties for American writers." [35]

In the nineteen-fifties, as in other periods, it is dangerous to equate the latest insights with truth. Yet it is hard not to conclude that now, in the second postwar period, some writers are converging from various directions toward a better understanding of the twenties. For one thing, the decade is longer past and it is no longer acutely necessary to break with its viewpoint. Fairly recently the twenties have come to be a fair field for the dissertation and the monograph, which bring at least a different kind of knowledge. One survivor of the period says that instead of being revived, it is being excavated like a ruin, and another complains that he and his friends are already being preserved in complete bibliographies while yet, as far as they can tell, alive.[36]

Disapproval and nostalgia, of course, remain. Editorials worry about the effect on Europe of the vogue there of the literature of the twenties. Professor Howard Mumford Jones has continued something like DeVoto's charges in more analytic tones, accusing the postwar writers both of brilliance and of detachment amounting to solipsism.[37] The choice of Scott Fitzgerald for revival and in some quarters canonization indicates the perverse attraction which self-destruction seems to hold for our period. Budd Schulberg's novel specifically contrasts a romantic and defeated alcoholic writer of the twenties with a crass, earnest young radical of the thirties to the latter's obvious disadvantage.[38]

In general, however, literary opinion seems to have gone beyond both nostalgia and reproof into a more mature and solidly based appreciation of the achievements of this era now so safely in the past. To many, the apparent sterility of the present literary scene furnishes a depressing contrast. Whatever else they rejected, writers of the twenties took their writing seriously, and, as Cowley has

[35] DeVoto, *Literary Fallacy*, 13, 15, 165–66, 169.

[36] Malcolm Cowley, *The Literary Situation* (New York, 1954), 3; Edmund Wilson, "Thoughts on Being Bibliographed," *Princeton University Library Chronicle* (Princeton), V (February, 1944), 51–61.

[37] Howard M. Jones, *The Bright Medusa* (Urbana, Ill., 1952). Jones analyzes with considerable success both the attraction of the twenties and what he sees as their characteristic fault.

[38] Budd Schulberg, *The Disenchanted* (New York, 1950). As some reviewers pointed out, Schulberg is not sure whether he more admires or pities his major character, clearly modeled on Fitzgerald. The Fitzgerald revival reached its greatest extent with the discussions arising out of Arthur Mizener's biography, *The Far Side of Paradise* (New York, 1950).

pointed out, publishers made it possible for them to do so.[39] Professor Frederick J. Hoffman in the most thorough of many recent accounts finds the period's literature full of daring, variety, and technical brilliance. This estimate by now represents more than a cult; it is an accepted consensus.[40]

One achievement of the twenties which has received only a little specific comment is nevertheless widely recognized today. The period of alienation and exile gave rise, curiously enough, to a thorough, rich, and continuing inquiry into the whole American past. The sources of this inward turn are as complicated as the decade itself. Many of the major historians who wrote then, including Parrington, Beard, Carl Becker, and Arthur M. Schlesinger, Sr., belong to the group that always found its major synthesis in the course of democratic progress. But others turned to the past with Van Wyck Brooks, partly in a spirit of cultural nationalism, to destroy the English and Anglophile genteel tradition and replace it with something native. Still others went first through a phase of violent rejection of American culture and then, finding Europe essentially unavailable as a substitute, returned to look desperately for roots at home. By the forties and fifties it was possible to see the lines converging in a cultural history which, at its best, could be critical, conscious of irony and failure, and yet, in a meaningful and necessary way, patriotic.[41]

With the literature and historical research of the twenties, its economic achievement, once overvalued and then rated too low, has

[39] Malcolm Cowley, "How Writers Lived," Robert E. Spiller *et al., Literary History of the United States* (Rev. ed., New York, 1953), 1263–72.

[40] Frederick J. Hoffman, *The Twenties: American Writing in the Postwar Decade* (New York, 1955). Another estimate that emphasizes the same qualities is John K. Hutchens in his preface to his anthology, *The Twenties* (Philadelphia, 1952), 11–34.

A critical but high estimate from the point of view of a present-day novelist is that of James A. Michener, "The Conscience of the Contemporary Novel," Lewis Mumford *et al., The Arts in Renewal* (Philadelphia, 1951), 107–40.

[41] For a helpful analysis of the development of American literary studies, see Howard M. Jones, *The Theory of American Literature* (Ithaca, 1948). A contemporary document which brings out the various approaches of the twenties to the American past is Norman Foerster (ed.), *The Reinterpretation of American Literature* (New York, 1928). An extreme example of the tendency today to credit the twenties with a major accomplishment in this respect is Malcolm Cowley's dictum that "Perhaps the greatest creative work of the last three decades in this country has not been any novel or poem or drama of our time . . . perhaps it has been the critical rediscovery and reinterpretation of Melville's *Moby Dick* and its promotion step by step to the position of national epic." Cowley, "The Literary Situation: 1953," *Perspectives USA* (New York), No. 5 (Fall, 1953), 5–13. This promotion began in the twenties and owes much to the outlook of that decade.

again turned the corner into a rising market. In the years of the Marshall Plan, when American capitalism was called on to shoulder an immense burden, it was hard to think of it as a failure and a mistake. And in the still rising prosperity of the Eisenhower period, far more widespread and soundly based than that under Coolidge but inevitably reminiscent, a reassessment of the earlier period was natural enough.

Part of the reassessment arose from the increasing complexity of economics and the development of a new economic history. Beginning about 1940, a number of economists and historians had demanded that American economic history separate itself from the political framework and give more attention to such matters as real wages and volume of production, and somewhat less to labor organization and the political struggles between farmers and merchants.[42] Even earlier, the business historians had been asking for a more analytic and less emotional approach to the history of management.[43] By the forties, it was impossible for an informed historian to duplicate the sweeping judgments about the boom and crash that had been easy ten years earlier. In 1947 George Soule, in his detailed economic history of the twenties, concluded perhaps rather to his own surprise that the rich grew richer without the poor growing poorer, that new amenities became available on a scale impossible to ignore, and that no measures then available would certainly have prevented the crash.[44] Most of the more recent economic history textbooks seem either to suggest a similar assessment or to avoid passing judgment altogether. Even the economic foreign policy of the twenties, long a favorite target of liberal historians, has been presented by Herbert Feis as a well-intentioned though ineffective forerunner of Point Four.[45] In 1955

[42] A most valuable account of the beginnings of this movement is Herbert Heaton, "Recent Developments in Economic History," *American Historical Review* (New York), XLVII (July, 1942), 727–46. But note that the results seem barely yet apparent to Mr. Heaton in a review of four economic histories in *Mississppi Valley Historical Review* (Cedar Rapids), XXXVIII (December, 1951), 556–61.

[43] Norman S. B. Gras, *Business and Capitalism* (New York, 1939), states the point of view of the business historians. The genesis and progress of the movement are excellently described in Henrietta M. Larson's introduction to her *Guide to Business History* (Cambridge, 1948), 3–37.

[44] George Soule, *Prosperity Decade* (New York, 1947), especially p. 335.

[45] Herbert Feis, *The Diplomacy of the Dollar: First Era, 1919–1932* (Baltimore, 1950). I have not mentioned among the recent optimistic historians of the twenties Professor Frederic L. Paxson, whose detailed volume on the period is, by the author's design, as lacking in interpretative comment as it is possible for a book to be. Paxson's occasional generalizations, however, indicate that he did not regard the twenties as an interruption in the read-

John K. Galbraith, even in a book on the "Great Crash," took historians mildly to task for underrating what was good in the Coolidge era, and unfairly blaming Coolidge himself for a failure of prophecy.[46]

Such opposite kinds of writers as Peter Drucker, Frederick L. Allen, and the editors of *Fortune* have argued, without special reference to the twenties, that American capitalism since about the turn of the century has been evolving into a new kind of democratic and humane economic order.[47] Most recently David M. Potter concludes that we have always been the "People of Plenty" and that this fact, more than the frontier or political freedom, has shaped our mores.[48] Professor Potter, more sophisticated than earlier prophets of abundance, has learned from the social scientists that a country has to pay for production in competitive strain, and perhaps later for security in loss of mobility. Yet his perspective, like that deriving from our whole political and economic climate, shifts the meaning of the earlier prosperity era. If productivity holds much of the meaning of American history, it is the depression and not the twenties that marks the interruption in a steady development. The New Era represents at worst a promising try at a new economy, a chapter in a book with a happy ending.

There is much in this reassessment that is invigorating, especially in a period when the leftist clichés are the tiredest of all. Yet several cautions are in order. Historians must remember, first, that the early 1880's and the 1920's and the 1950's are different and separated periods of prosperity, no matter how similar; second, that the depressions, even if in the long run temporary interruptions, did not look that way to their victims; and third, that even complete economic success does not, either now or for the twenties, refute all criticisms of American culture.

There is little danger that we will altogether forget this last caution. While some contemporary writers present a view of our

---

justment of the federal government to the facts of a changing life, "and even that a new pattern was developing in American society, a pattern which meant for many Americans a more open future." Frederic L. Paxson, *American Democracy and the World War* (3 vols., Boston and Berkeley, 1936–1948). Vol. III, *Postwar Years: Normalcy, 1918–1923*, introduction, 2.

[46] John K. Galbraith, *The Great Crash, 1929* (Boston, 1955) 608.

[47] Peter F. Drucker, *The New Society* (New York, 1949); The Editors of *Fortune, U. S. A.: The Permanent Revolution* (New York, 1951); Frederick L. Allen, *The Big Change* (New York, 1952). In the last two of these it is not altogether clear whether the twenties are a part of the fortunate development or a break in it.

[48] David M. Potter, *People of Plenty* (Chicago, 1954).

recent history that emphasizes economic success, to another group such success is not so much false as irrelevant. The anti-optimists today are not rebels but traditionalists, a group that can be lumped together as anti-materialist conservatives. Some of these derive from and continue the new criticism, others reflect the revival of theology, and still others rely partly on new scientific theory. All have been led or forced, during the recent era of world catastrophe, to place their trust not in secular progress but primarily in moral and religious tradition, and from this standpoint the twenties are difficult to rehabilitate.

Joseph Wood Krutch has devoted a volume to repudiating the mechanistic determinism he voiced so powerfully in 1930, and Walter Lippmann has even more specifically repudiated his early relativism. In 1955 Lippmann concluded that the whole debacle in international politics, starting in 1917 and continuing through and after Versailles, resulted primarily from "the growing incapacity of the large majority of the democratic peoples to believe in intangible realities," specifically in a transcendent, universally valid, natural law.[49]

Many powerful contemporary writers agree with Lippmann not only in his diagnosis of the trouble but in his fixing the responsibility for breakdown in the 1920's. Some of these, however, find in the decade enough just men to save it from complete condemnation. Russell Kirk, for instance, resurrects the New Humanists and marvels that "these years of vulgarity and presumption" produced the coming of an age of American conservatism in a group of thinkers who struggled against "the vertiginous social current of the Harding and Coolidge and Hoover years." [50] (It marks perhaps the high point in this reassessment to make Coolidge, rather than Freud or Einstein, a symbol of vertigo.) A more subtle conservative and anti-materialist finds in the literary rebels the saving remnant. In his curious, dogmatic, but occasionally suggestive *Yankees and God,* Chard Powers Smith suggests that the young iconoclasts of the twenties were really the last, or next-to-the-last, wave of Puritanism, despite their use of the term Puritan as the ultimate of abuse.[51] This apparently bizarre thesis is really neither absurd nor entirely original. Perry Miller in 1950 gave the rebels of the twenties a similarly respectable pedigree when he compared them to the transcendentalists. Both of these movements spoke for the

[49] Joseph W. Krutch, *The Measure of Man* (New York, 1953); Walter Lippmann, *The Public Philosophy* (Boston, 1955), 55.

[50] Russell Kirk, *The Conservative Mind* (Chicago, 1953), 362–63.

[51] Chard Powers Smith, *Yankees and God* (New York, 1954), 451–59.

spirit against the rule of things, and both, said Professor Miller, belonged in a series of "revolts by the youth of America against American philistinism." [52] One can go a very little further and agree with Mr. Smith that both are basically Protestant; it is not hard to recognize in the young intellectuals of the twenties together with their iconoclasm a tortured uneasiness, a conscious responsibility for the faults of the era that are suggestive of a long heritage.

In the 1950's, then, the familiar division continued. Spokesmen of the New Era rehabilitated the twenties by using one set of standards while anti-materialists blamed or praised them according to another. At the same time, however, a number of scholars of varying views were reaching toward an understanding of such paradoxes by treating the twenties as a period of profound social change. Most of these students derived their insights to some extent from the sociologists, and it is interesting that some of the gloomiest insights stem today from this once exuberant science. David Riesman's strikingly influential vision of the shift from inner-direction to other-direction is not strictly dated by its creator, but it often seems to be a description of the end of the genteel tradition and the birth of the New Era, the defeat of Wilsonian moralism and the victory of the Babbitts.[53] In different terms and with a more clearly stated value judgment, C. Wright Mills has documented the rise of a regimented, rootless, and docile new middle class to the arbitral position in American society.[54] The increase of the white-collar salariat and its implications extended before and after the twenties but went especially fast in that period, as the authors of *Recent Social Trends*, among others, pointed out. Samuel Lubell and others have seen another social change in the twenties, the beginning of the coming-of-age of the new immigration.[55] Drawing together Lubell's interpretation and Mills, Richard Hofstadter emphasizes the "Status Revolution" as a main event of the period about the turn of the century.[56] The Protestant upper middle class, long a semi-aristocracy with a monopoly on advanced education, had declined, and so had the independent farmers. In their places other groups had grown and gained some power—the new middle class, the ethnic minorities, and labor. All these proc-

[52] Perry Miller, *The Transcendentalists* (Cambridge, 1950), 8, 14–15.
[53] David Riesman, *The Lonely Crowd* (New Haven, 1950).
[54] C. Wright Mills, *White Collar* (New York, 1951).
[55] Samuel Lubell, *The Future of American Politics* (New York, 1953), 34–41.
[56] Richard Hofstadter, *The Age of Reform* (New York, 1955), 131–72.

esses of change had, by the twenties, proceeded a long way, and all were continuing and accelerating, with the partial exception of the rise of labor. Surely this social upheaval, impossible to see clearly until our own time, has considerable meaning for the intellectual history of the twenties as for its politics, for the collapse, that is, of a long-frayed moral and literary tradition.

The nearest we can come to summarizing or explaining the shifting opinions of the twenties may well be to see the period in some such terms as these, and to see it as a disintegration. There is certainly nothing original about such a conclusion, but perhaps we are now in a position to give disintegration a fuller and more various meaning. The twenties were a period in which common values and common beliefs were replaced by separate and conflicting loyalties. One or another of the standards arising from the age itself has been used by each of its historians ever since. This is what has made their judgments so conflicting, so emotional, so severally valid and collectively confusing. It is equally true and equally partial to talk about the rising standard of living and the falling standard of political morality, the freshness and individuality of literature and the menace of conformity, the exuberance of manufacturers or social scientists and the despair of traditional philosophers. Somehow, we must learn to write history that includes all these, and the first step is to understand the decade when the fragmentation first became deep and obvious.

At least two recent writers are useful to those who want to look at the twenties from this point of view. One is Lionel Trilling, who deplores and analyzes the split between liberalism and the imagination, between the values we take for granted as socially desirable and those that have now the power to move us in art, between collective welfare and individual dignity.[57] What is lacking, says Trilling, and what has been lacking specifically since the twenties, is a view of the world, in his word a faith though not necessarily a religion, that will give meaning both to society and to art, to progress and to tragedy. Professor Henry Nash Smith in a recent address has sketched, somewhat similarly, two diametrically opposite points of view which, he says, have divided our culture since 1910.[58] One he calls the realistic-progressive view and the other the counterenlightenment; one takes for its standards measurable welfare and

[57] Lionel Trilling, *The Liberal Imagination* (Pocket ed., New York, 1950 [first published, 1948]), especially pp. 97-106, 245-87.
[58] Henry Nash Smith, "The Reconstruction of Literary Values in the United States, 1900-1950" (unpublished manuscript, 1952).

humanitarian progress and equality; the other values only the individual imagination, nourished on tradition, holding out desperately against a mechanized culture, and accepting if necessary alienation and despair as the price of its survival.

The conflict of values that culminated, for it certainly did not begin, in the twenties was more than two-sided, and neither of these two critics has completely explored it. But they have indicated the right starting point. The way to understand our recent cultural history is to understand why and how its exponents fail to agree.

How can historians proceed further along this path? First, it hardly needs saying that to understand the twenties better we must make use of techniques drawn from various fields. The most important developments in the decade did not take place in the realms of politics, or economics, or literature, or science alone, but in all these areas and the relation, or lack of relation, among them. If one uses one kind of sources one will inevitably emerge with one point of view, which will be inadequate to understand the others.

Second, it seems clear that one cannot say much about the twenties as a disintegration or revolution without giving more attention to the old regime, the presumed prewar agreement. There seems to have been a greater degree of unity in American culture before 1917 or perhaps 1910, but a description of it is not easy and a casual reference to the genteel tradition or the cultural inheritance will not suffice. Immediately prewar America must be newly explored. We must look not so much at its articulate political or philosophical beliefs and more at its inarticulate assumptions—assumptions in such areas as morality, politics, class and race relations, popular art and literature, and family life. In short, we must concentrate on what Tocqueville would have called its manners. We are now, perhaps, in a position at least to undertake this recapture in an impartial mood. In 1956 we do not need to lament or rejoice at the destruction of the America of 1914; it is nearly as far off as Greece or Rome, and as inevitably a part of us.

Third, we must try to look at the succeeding disintegration, the revolution of the twenties, with a similar absence of passion. The literary scoffers who have been so thoroughly scolded were not, after all, the only rebels. The prophets of mechanization and welfare, the Fords and Edisons who scorned history and tradition, were equally revolutionary. Most revolutionary of all, perhaps, were the prophets of psychology and social science, with their brand new societies full of brand new human beings.

Finally, if we can really look back on this revolutionary decade from a perspective which has the advantage of thirty years of continuing revolution, we may be able to see which of the separate movements of the twenties has lasted best, and whether any of them are beginning to come together. Are there really in this decade of novelty beginnings as well as ends? Is it possible by now really to glimpse what so many have announced: the beginnings of a new period of American history and even of a new civilization?

21

THE election of John F. Kennedy in 1960 as the first Roman Catholic president not only shattered the "unwritten law" that no Catholic could be president but also provoked a renewed interest in the first election in which a Catholic ran for president. Indeed, the failure of Alfred E. Smith in 1928 so impressed itself on the calculations of later politicians that the supporters of Kennedy before his nomination deemed it essential to take action to counter the impression. They prepared elaborate statistical and analytical studies to present to Democratic party leaders, the purpose being to demonstrate that a Catholic candidate would gain more votes for the party than he would drive away. Interestingly enough, as Hofstadter's article points out, there is now a good bit of evidence to show that Al Smith's religion was in reality also a help to his party.

Certainly prior to the nomination and election of John F. Kennedy it was almost axiomatic, as Hofstadter notes, that though the defeat of Smith in 1928 was brought about in part by his being a "wet" on the liquor issue and in part by his urban background, his religion was generally viewed as his biggest handicap. At least one whole book has been devoted to the religious issue in the campaign. Edmund A. Moore's *A Catholic Runs for President: The Campaign of 1928* (New York, 1956) emphasizes the importance of religion despite its not receiving the space in the press devoted to other issues. (An exception to this general view is contained in William E. Leuchtenberg's *The Perils of Prosperity, 1914–1932* [Chicago, 1958], where it is concluded that probably not even a Protestant Democrat could have won in 1928.) Undoubtedly the primary reason for the priority generally given to the religious issue was the substantial losses that Smith sustained in the traditionally Democratic South. Before 1928 only one southern state, Tennessee, had ever defected from the party since the "solid South" was forged in the fires of the Reconstruction. Indeed, V. O. Key, Jr., in his *Southern Politics in State and Nation* (New York, 1950), concluded that only the presence of the Negro in great numbers kept the South as loyal to the Democratic party as it was in 1928.

What Hofstadter's article does is to put Smith's defeat in the perspective of other handicaps and to reduce it in the face of some substantial gains. Smith suffered not only from the disability of his religion but, perhaps as important, also from the attractiveness of his opponent. Hoover as a political personality and an alleged architect of Republican prosperity was simply a hard man to beat. In one place, however, Hofstadter overstates his argument. Where he says that since 1892 no incumbent party has been turned out of the presidency except when a war, depression, or party split occurred, he seems to be ignoring some pertinent examples. In 1920, 1952, and, of course, in 1960 parties changed in the White House without any of his three "jarring" events intervening.

Perhaps the most suggestive part of Hofstadter's little article is what it has to say about the catalytic effect of Smith's candidacy. Here his article marks an important reinterpretation of the election of 1928. There were at least two boons which Smith's candidacy brought to the Democratic party, thereby laying the foundation for the remarkable victories of Franklin Roosevelt in 1932 and 1936. One was Smith's gaining the support of more voters proportionately than any Democrat since William Jennings Bryan in 1896. The other was his setting in motion the shift of the big-city vote from the Republican to the Democratic column. In the presidential election of 1920 the Democrats did not capture a single big city (those of 250,000 or more in population) except the traditionally Democratic ones in the old Confederacy. In 1928, though, Smith won the support of seven of the big cities outside of the South. The source of his appeal to the cities was his religion and his immigrant background. (Actually Smith's parents were both born in New York City, but his urban upbringing and his Catholicism, which was still thought of as an "immigrant religion," marked him among immigrants as "one of our own.") The association between the increased vote for Smith and the urban immigrants is documented in Carl N. Degler's "American Political Parties and the Rise of the City: An Interpretation," *Journal of American History*, LI (June 1964), 41–59. There it is shown that cities with 50 per cent or more immigrant stock either supported Smith or increased their Democratic vote two- or three-fold over 1920. On the other hand, the big cities with fewer than 50 per cent immigrant stock all voted for Hoover and recorded only small increases in their Democratic votes. Irving Bernstein's *The Lean Years* (Boston, 1960) also points out the success of Smith in the cities.

Other studies since Hofstadter's article appeared have continued to play down the influence of Smith's religion in accounting for his defeat. Paul A. Carter's "The Campaign of 1928 Re-Examined: A Study in Political Folklore," *Wisconsin Magazine of History,* XLVI (Summer 1963), 263–272, is a case in point. Carter showed by an analysis of leaders and attitudes that religion was at best only one of several reasons for Smith's defeat. Senator Thomas J. Walsh of Montana, for example, was a Roman Catholic yet a prominent contender for the nomination in 1928. He, though, was a dry on the liquor question and a Westerner. It was Smith's association with New York City and his opposition to prohibition, Carter concludes, that really defeated him. The most recent full-length study of the election is Ruth C. Silva's *Rum, Religion, and Votes: 1928 Re-examined* (University Park, Pa., 1962). By the use of sophisticated statistical techniques, Silva demonstrates conclusively the great vote-getting power of Smith's candidacy, but she also concludes that no precise, statistical determination can be made as to which attribute of that candidacy—Smith's religion, his urban background, or his stand on Prohibition—was the principal reason for his defeat.

Hofstadter is DeWitt Professor of American History at Columbia University. His books *The American Political Tradition* (New York, 1948) and *The Age of Reform* (New York, 1955) are probably the two most influential and widely read interpretations of American political history in this generation.

Could a Protestant Have Beaten Hoover in 1928?

BY RICHARD HOFSTADTER

MY GENERATION was raised upon the cliché that no Catholic can be elected to the Presidency. This cliché is based upon one historical experience—Al Smith's losing campaign in 1928, during which the notion that a Catholic cannot be elected was often referred to as an "unwritten law."

Those who are still convinced that the unwritten law exists find the case of Al Smith conclusive. A few undeniable facts fit their argument. In a massive campaign, waged partly in the open and partly at the level of whispers and snickers, Smith's religion was used against him. This intolerance was repudiated by his opponent, but no one doubts that it affected many voters, and that hundreds of thousands, especially in the South and Middle West, voted against Smith partly or largely on this account. He lost the electoral votes of states in the Solid South that no Democratic candidate since the Civil War had ever come close to losing. He was overwhelmed by Hoover at the polls, receiving 40.8 per cent of the total popular vote as compared to Hoover's 58.1 per cent. He had only eighty-seven electoral votes to Hoover's 444, and in this respect no Democrat since the days of Jackson had fared so badly.

Although historians and political scientists have been careful in their generalizations about the role of religion in the outcome of the 1928 campaign, glib conclusions have been drawn in popular legend, and even among the educated public. Only recently William E. Bohn, writing in the *New Leader*, said of Smith: "He was defeated for the worst of reasons—because he was a Catholic." Absurd as it is, this notion has been too seldom challenged in public discussion. A little thoughtful attention to the history of the 1920's will convince almost any student that there was not a Democrat alive, Protestant or Catholic, who could have beaten Hoover in 1928.

The overwhelming character of Hoover's victory should itself suggest to us that the religious issue may not have been decisive.

SOURCE: Reprinted by permission from *The Reporter*, March 17, 1960. Copyright 1960 by The Reporter Magazine Company.

If the election had been very close in a number of decisive states, it might be easier to believe that the religious issue had tipped the balance and given the victory to Hoover. In fact, so far as the electoral vote is concerned, we know only that religious bias swung the votes of Florida and Texas and four normally or invariably Democratic states of the upper South into Hoover's column. But if Smith had won the electoral votes of all these states, he would still have been very far from winning. Even if he had then also added the few Northern states in which he ran reasonably well (that is, where he had forty-five per cent or more of the major-party vote), his electoral vote would still have been only half as large as Hoover's.

My contention is not that the religious issue was unimportant in the campaign, but that it worked both ways. The prime fallacy in the popular view of the 1928 election lies in noticing only what Smith lost from the religious issue and ignoring what he may have gained. Of course the number of voters who were decisively influenced by the religious issue is something that eludes exact measurement. But it is vital to remember that there are two such imponderables to be considered: not only the number of voters who voted *against* Smith but also the number who voted *for* him because of his religion. Smith's Catholicism, a grave liability in some areas, was a great asset in others. He made about as good a showing as could have been expected from any Democrat that year. Taken by itself, his religion proves nothing conclusively about the effect of Catholic adherence on a future Presidential candidacy.

Perhaps the most helpful way of isolating the significance of the religious issue in 1928 and chopping it down to size would be to imagine the difficulties the Democratic nominee would have had to face that year if he had been a Protestant.

HOOVER, "THE WONDER"

Above all, the Democrats were confronted with the overwhelming fact of prosperity. After seven years of Republican control, the golden glow was glowing more brightly than ever before, The business index was approaching its 1929 peak at the time the election took place, and the number of unemployed, though growing considerably, was only a little more than three per cent of the total labor force. In the history of the Presidency since 1892, no incumbent party has been turned out of power without the jarring effect of a depression, a war, or—as in 1912—a party split. Polls under Roosevelt, Truman, and Eisenhower have shown that the popularity of a President in peacetime tends to fluctuate along with the business cycle. In the autumn of 1928 the business cycle was voting Republican.

A second consideration working against the Democrats—one easily forgotten by Americans who have come to political maturity after 1930—was the immense prestige of Herbert Hoover. The dour, ultraconservative image of Mr. Hoover that is called up in the minds of his critics in both parties today was not the conventional image before the Great Depression. A successful relief administrator during the First World War, Hoover had won universal acclaim as an effective humanitarian. John Maynard Keynes had written of him that he was "the only man who emerged from the ordeal of Paris with an enhanced reputation." Both parties had hoped to have him in their ranks in 1920, much as both would have welcomed Eisenhower in 1948. It is one of the amusing ironies of our history that Franklin D. Roosevelt had hoped to promote him for the Presidency in 1920. "He is certainly a wonder," F.D.R. wrote in January of that year, "and I wish we could make him President of the United States. There could not be a better one."

As Secretary of Commerce, Hoover was one of the Cabinet members who survived the disaster of the Harding administration with a reputation largely untainted and undimmed. Even the liberals, though disappointed by his attitudes on several public questions, still kept an open mind about him, and some thought of him as one of the more progressive leaders of his party. Hoover's record inspired confidence that he would be an excellent custodian of prosperity. He took over the Republican standard from Coolidge with what appeared to be rosy prospects.

A third and strangely unremembered aspect of the 1928 candidacy was the hopeless condition of the Democratic Party when Smith took it over. Since the days of Bryan and McKinley the Democratic Party had been almost a permanent minority party. Between 1896 and 1908, no Democratic Presidential candidate had won more than 45.9 per cent of the total popular vote, and Woodrow Wilson's election in 1912 had been possible only because of the Republican split between Taft and Theodore Roosevelt. Elected as a minority President in 1912, with 41.8 per cent of the popular vote, Wilson was very narrowly re-elected in 1916, partly on the strength of his progressive achievements, and partly because of his success thus far in staying out of the war. Our entry into the war, the unpopularity of the peace, and the sweeping reaction against Wilson and all those associated with him left the postwar Democratic Party in ruins. As measured by the popular vote, the victory recorded by Harding over Cox in 1920 was the most decisive victory ever scored by a Presidential candidate.

Already deprived of the allegiance of almost two-thirds of the voting public in 1920, the Democrats themselves reduced their party to a shambles in 1924. Here the religious issue played a major part, but one that cannot be disentangled from related issues. The Democrats came to their 1924 convention sharply divided between the rural, dry, Protestant anti-Tammany contingent supporting Wilson's son-in-law William G. McAdoo and the urban, immigrant, Catholic, wet contingent supporting Smith. They wrangled furiously over a resolution condemning the Ku Klux Klan, and in the end narrowly failed to adopt it. The Smith and McAdoo forces fell into such an interminable Donnybrook that it became clear that the nomination would be worthless to the man who got it. John W. Davis, who was finally settled upon at the 103rd ballot by an exhausted mob of delegates, was unable in his campaign to exploit effectively even the ghastly scandals of the Harding administration. The support of most liberals that year went to Robert M. La Follette, who polled 4,892,000 votes on an independent ticket. Davis polled only 8,385,000, against Coolidge's 15,718,000.

Although the Democrats still held a respectable contingent in Congress, it seemed that for all practical purposes the two-party system had ceased to function at the level of Presidential politics. The outcome of the mid-term Congressional elections of 1926 confirmed the general impression that the country was overwhelmingly Republican. Normally, the party in power expects to lose a substantial number of seats in these off-year elections. In the five midterm elections from 1906 to 1922, for instance, the average loss had been sixty seats. In 1926 the Republicans lost only ten seats. In the summer of the following year F.D.R. confided to Josephus Daniels that he thought no Democrat could win in 1928 if "the present undoubted general prosperity continues."

Roosevelt's view was shared by most informed observers. Frank R. Kent, the veteran journalist and historian of the Democratic Party, pointing out that it was "without unity, intelligence, or courage . . . without leaders, without an issue or policy or program," had stated in 1926 that "no one capable of clear political judgment now believes it can be vitalized sufficiently to put up a formidable fight in the next Presidential campaign unless a political miracle occurs." Walter Lippmann observed that the Republicans could go into any campaign "knowing that normally there are enough Republicans to win. They do not have to convert anybody, but merely to prevent about ten per cent of their supporters from backsliding." In 1927 Lippmann thought (quite rightly) that Smith, though a losing candidate, would be the best the Democrats could find, and that "the best way for the Democrats to look at 1928 is to look beyond to 1932." After Smith's nomination, Lippmann remarked that the New Yorker had inherited nothing more than a party label, a small core of electoral votes, "two warring factions bound together by no common ideas," and a party "as nearly bankrupt intellectually as it is possible to be." Smith's task, he said, "is to re-create the Democratic party."

An anonymous "Democrat" writing in the *Century* magazine pointed out that practically every commentator who had written on the subject started from the premise that the Donkey was sick. The Democrats, he said, "know perfectly well that the Donkey can not win," and were thinking only of finding a Presidential candidate who could help their local tickets. He advised that the party give up altogether the goal of winning the Presidency and concentrate for the moment on capturing Congress, where it still had at least a chance. This was the situation that any Democratic nominee had to cope with in 1928.

BROWN DERBY

Finally, it should be remembered that in addition to their other handicaps the Democrats had no good issue. The tariff bores most voters, especially during prosperity. Prohibition did not bore them, and its failure was a usable issue in some areas, but a firm wet stand still seemed likely to lose more votes than it would gain. There were, of course, pockets of economic discontent. The most important of these was among farmers. Unfortunately, the most outspoken defenders of the farmers' interests outside the South were chiefly Republican insurgents in Congress who (with the exception of George W. Norris) were not bolting their party in a winning year.

A Midwestern Democrat might have done better than Smith in the farm areas, but it would have been difficult for any Eastern city Democrat to capitalize on the farm problem. F.D.R. had remarked in 1927 that he did not believe the Western farmers would vote Democratic "in sufficient numbers [for a Democratic victory] even if they are starving." Here his sectional and urban background was quite as much a handicap for Smith as his religion. It was difficult to persuade farmers that the man from the sidewalks of New York understood or felt deeply about their problems. Cartoons of Smith in his brown derby and gaudy tie peering over a farm fence were more formidable than anything the New Yorker could say on the farm problem. (This was a handicap which F.D.R. was able to overcome four years later, not merely because his up-state residence and his tree farm helped establish the image of a rural squire, but also because he had spent years traveling and cultivating political friendships in the agricultural states.)

If we suppose, then, that a Protestant had been nominated by the Democrats in 1928, what could his supporters realistically have expected? They might have hoped that, aside from helping some local candidacies, he could do three things: hold the minimal areas of Democratic strength, exploit residual areas of discontent to extend Democratic influence, and finally wage his campaign in such spirit and with such effectiveness as to restore the unity of the party and strengthen its morale for future compaigns. Smith did not, of course, succeed in the first of these, since he lost states in the Solid South. His failure here was what showed up on the electoral charts. Relatively unnoticed (though not unnoticed by Smith himself) was that he far exceeded what might have been expected on the second of these objectives, and that he did extremely well on the third.

THE WARRIOR'S FIGHT

Smith's showing is impressive when compared with that of his two postwar predecessors. The Democratic Presidential vote, which had been 9,128,000 for Cox and had sunk to 8,385,000 for Davis, was raised by Smith to 15,016,000. Cox had had only 34.1 per cent of the popular vote, Davis 28.8 per cent. After these two disastrous campaigns, the "Happy Warrior," in restoring his party's percentage to 40.8 per cent, had at least brought it to within hailing distance of the "normal" Democratic minority vote of the prewar years. The fact that he outdistanced his two predecessors by this much should arouse our curiosity about the sources of his gains.

Both 1928 candidates were immensely successful in overcoming voter apathy and bringing the public out to the polls. In 1924 only 51 per cent of the eligible voters had turned out; in 1928 it was 67.5 per cent—a striking show of interest for a year of prosperity. If we compare Smith with his Democratic predecessor and Hoover with his Republican predecessor, we find that the Democratic vote rose by 6,631,000 from Davis to Smith and the Republican vote rose by 5,673,000 from Coolidge to Hoover. Smith thus gained almost a million more votes for his party than Hoover did. He gained seventy-six per cent over Davis's vote and sixty-four per cent over Cox's. By comparison, Hoover gained thirty-six per cent on Coolidge and thirty-two per cent on Harding.

If Smith's religion had hurt him as badly on a nation-wide scale as we are expected to believe, it seems incredible that he should thus have outgained Hoover. In broad outline, what happened seems reasonably clear. There was a Catholic vote as well as a Protestant vote. (Neither, of course, can be isolated and measured with finality, because they were parts of a Catholic-wet-immigrant complex and a Protestant-dry-nativist complex.) Even though the country was two-thirds Protestant, Catholic voters were animated in equal or greater numbers to turn out and vote. Many of them were from the immigrant stocks that had poured into the country by the millions before the First World War, and among them were large numbers of new citizens who had never before been sufficiently excited by unfamiliar American domestic issues to bring them out to the polls. The number of previously unactivated Smith voters seems to have been much larger than the number of unactivated Hoover voters. But the distribution of the newly activated Protestant-dry voters and Catholic-wet voters was such that Smith lost some Southern votes in the electoral college. This, together with the overwhelming nature of the returns, obscured what he did achieve.

Not the least of Smith's achievements was to unify and remold his party. In the recent past the Democratic Party, under the leadership of men like Bryan, Wilson, and Cox, had been based mainly upon strength in the agrarian South and West. The Republican Party, as measured by the distribution of urban seats in Congress and popular votes in Presidential campaigns, had been the dominant metropolitan party. Even in his losing campaign, however, Smith turned the normally huge Republican pluralities in the twelve largest cities into a slender Democratic plurality. He brought into the voting stream of the Democratic Party ethnic groups that had never taken part in politics and others that had been mainly Republican. He extricated his party from its past dependence on agrarian interests and made it known to the great urban populations. He lost a campaign that had to be lost, but in such a way as to restore his party as an effective opposition and to pave the way for the victories of F.D.R. While he had to pay a political price for his religion, it must also be counted among the personal characteristics that made these achievements possible.

22

FOR Americans in the first half of the twentieth century one of the political facts of life has been the isolationism of the Middle West. At the time of the First World War the Middle West was the least enthusiastic region as the United States moved closer to and ultimately into a declaration of war against Germany. The attitudes established then became a habit by the 1930s, as war in Europe and Asia brought American diplomacy to a state of crisis and finally to a decision to oppose German and Japanese aggression. During those years probably a majority of Americans strongly resisted involvement in the European conflict that broke out in September 1939; the geographical heartland of that popular resistance was the Middle West. So familiar had the isolationism of the region become in American politics by the Second World War that the shift of Senator Arthur Vandenberg of Michigan from isolationism to active support of the new United Nations Organization was heralded as a watershed in the recent history of American foreign relations. As a Middle-Westerner and an erstwhile isolationist, Vandenberg has been credited with swinging his region to an acceptance of the new internationalism demanded by the world conditions of the 1940s and afterwards.

To Americans in the 1930s, the isolationism of the Middle West seemed as natural as it was tenacious. The very location of the region, comfortably distant from the two oceanic avenues of possible invasion and conflict, suggested a plausible explanation for its strong isolationist sentiment. But as Billington's article shows, the Middle West has not alway been hostile to foreign commitments on the part of the United States. And once one recognized that it was only in the twentieth century that the region assumed its isolationist stance, the geographical explanation could not carry much weight. The geography had been the same, after all, in the nineteenth century as it was in the twentieth.

Billington has suggested three explanations for the isolationism of the Middle West: (1) the region's deep allegiance to the Republican party, (2) the anti-eastern bias inculcated by the free-silver campaigns of the 1890s, and (3) the growing political power of the immigrants. Not all three of these explanations, however, deserve equal credence.

The allegiance of the Middle West to the Republican party is undoubted. Indeed, the party originated in the Middle West, and its strength had always been concentrated there, at least until the disastrous election of 1964. But in naming the region's party allegiance as a source of its isolationism, Billington overlooks the role of the Middle West in the formulation of the Republican party's policies. It is rather unrealistic to envision the region as blindly following party doctrine. The Republican party, in common with all political organizations, has no existence outside of the people who make it up; their opinions and judgments constitute the party's beliefs and principles or at least help to shape them. It is at least as logical and much more likely that the isolationism of the Republican party is to be accounted for by the large number of isolationistic Middle-Westerners within it, as it is to explain the region's isolationism by the party's policies. Party allegiance undoubtedly exercised some influence, but it is not the independent causal factor that Billington seems to make it.

Billington's second explanation is even less satisfactory than the first. There is no question that the free-silver campaigns of the 1890s were saturated with hostility toward England, eastern bankers, and the East in general. But it is misleading to suggest or imply that this prejudice became common among Middle Westerners as a result of that campaign. After all, it was the Democrats who were free silverites, while the Republicans—and the Middle West as a whole—opposed free silver in 1896. It is difficult to see how a region which was strongly Republican, according to Billington's own evidence, was made isolationistic by the campaign arguments of Democrats.

This leaves Billington's third argument. And it is his seeing the immigrants as the essential source of middle-western isolationism that makes his article a major contribution to American historical analysis. Much of the Middle West, as his figures show, was settled by immigrants from central and northern Europe. In the crises leading up to the two world wars in the twentieth century the powers with which the United States came into conflict were the homelands of many of these immigrants. Americans of German, Austrian, and Scandinavian descent are numerous in the Middle West. Those of German and Austrian descent had a natural predisposition to oppose American hostility toward the old country, while those of Scandinavian descent, coming from countries traditionally neutral in Europe's war, hoped that their adopted country would emulate that policy.

Attention should also be called to the three kinds of evidence Billington uses to ascertain public opinion. Obviously the attitudes of newspapers and periodicals afford some measure of public opinion. But are they as representative as votes in Congress, the second measure that Billington employs? Why would you accept a public opinion poll as the best of the three? Under what circumstances would the results of an election be superior to a public opinion poll? Under what circumstances would a poll be a more accurate measure of public opinion than an election?

In emphasizing the continuing influence of the old country on the attitudes and voting behavior of immigrants and the descendants of immigrants, Billington's article also epitomizes a recent and important development in historical writing. During the early twentieth century the idea of the "melting pot" enjoyed wide currency in American thought about immigration. Essentially that conception envisioned the immigrants' "melting" into a common pattern after an appropriate length of time in the United States. Certainly it was assumed that the children of immigrants would slough off the European concerns and attachments which their parents inevitably, if understandably, displayed. But this was not the way things worked out. For as Billington's article makes evident, the children and grandchildren of immigrants continued to have sentimental ties to and affections toward the old country which clearly affected their political behavior. Today realistic analyses of American public opinion on foreign and domestic affairs recognize this fact. Even after the Second World War, a full generation after the passage of the immigration restriction laws of the 1920s, the European background of various immigrant groups continued to be influential. Samuel Lubell in his *Future of American Politics* (New York, 1952) amply documented this fact in regard to voting during the Truman years. Analyses of presidential elections now customarily include studies of the ethnic background of voters in explaining the outcome. Lucy S. Dawidowicz and Leon J. Gold-

stein, in *Politics in a Pluralist Democracy* (New York, 1963), one
of the most recent and thorough of such studies, have documented
the ethnic and religious influences operating in the election of 1960.

Books dealing with isolationism that have appeared since Billington's article have generally accepted his immigrant explanation.
Samuel Lubell's *Future of American Politics* has already been mentioned. Two other such studies are Eric Goldman's *Rendezvous
with Destiny* (New York, 1952) and Selig Adler's *The Isolationist
Impulse* (London and New York, 1957).

Billington, prior to his becoming senior research associate at
the Huntington Library in San Marino, California, in 1963, was
for many years professor of history at Northwestern University.
His primary field of interest and writing has long been the history
of the American West.

The Origins of Middle
Western Isolationism

BY RAY ALLEN BILLINGTON

THROUGH the nineteenth century the Middle West shared with
the rest of the United States a lively interest in the world-wide
struggle against tyranny.[1] Its people, living in what they liked to
think was the cradle of democracy and invigorated by the influence
of the frontier, regarded themselves as the patrons of the liberal
uprisings that periodically rocked Europe; and they reacted accordingly. The Greek Revolt of the 1820's, the French Revolutions
of 1830 and 1848, the Hungarian struggle for independence in the
late 1840's, all aroused the westerners to violent demonstrations
of approval; fiery resolutions were adopted by mass meetings
and legislatures, funds were collected to aid the revolutionists, and

SOURCE: Reprinted with permission from *Political Science Quarterly*, Vol.
LX (March 1945), 44–64.

[1] The Middle West today comprises the areas defined by the Census Bureau
as the East North Central and West North Central States: Ohio, Indiana,
Illinois, Michigan, Wisconsin, Minnesota, Iowa, Missouri, North Dakota, South
Dakota, Nebraska and Kansas. Missouri has remained predominantly southern
in its social attitudes, but is included in the Middle West in this paper. See
Howard W. Odum and Harry E. Moore, *American Regionalism* (New York,
1939), pp. 462 *et seq.*

Congressmen were goaded into such violent speeches that they frequently embarrassed their neutral government.[2] Only a few of the more rabid midwesterners advocated American intervention in these European quarrels, but all paid enthusiastic lip service to each new blow struck at established authority.

In the first years of the twentieth century the western attitude shifted. The people of that section, above all others, insisted that Europe's fate was no concern of theirs; the United States, they said, should seek peace and security by isolating itself from the rest of the globe. This about-face was partly due to the changed relationships between the Old and New Worlds; for the shrinking Atlantic had brought the Americans uncomfortably close to an imperialistic, war-bound continent, and meddling now might mean actual involvement. Yet more than this was needed to explain the shift in midwestern ideology, for national security was not the only issue. The eastern and southern "militarists" of 1916, "internationalists" of 1919, and "interventionists" of 1940 were not concerned alone with preserving American nationalism through collective action; they believed that the eradication of Kaiserism, power politics and fascism was necessary to rid the world of anti-democratic institutions and ideals. The middle western "isolationists," although just as devoted to democracy, thought the rest of the world beyond redemption. These same people who in the nineteenth century had vigorously upheld universal self-government were in the twentieth content to protect their own treasures on their own soil.

This attitude became apparent during the chain of events leading to the Spanish-American War. The West's first reaction to the Cuban struggle for independence was true to the section's humanitarian traditions; westerners viewed the conflict as one between autocracy and self-rule which deserved their unwavering support. These sentiments were freely voiced in a number of mass meetings held during the fall of 1895 in middle western cities, where resolutions were passed favoring the immediate recognition of Cuban independence, government aid to Cuba, and even the American

[2] These activities are described in Myrtle A. Cline, *American Attitude toward the Greek War of Independence, 1221–1828* (Atlanta, 1930), pp. 62, 99–100; E. N. Curtis, "American Opinion of the Nineteenth Century French Revolutions," *American Historical Review, XXIX* (January 1924), 249–270; Arthur J. May, *Contemporary American Opinion of the Mid-Century Revolutions in Central Europe* (Philadelphia, 1927), pp. 49 *et seq.*; and in John W. Oliver, "Louis Kossuth's Appeal to the Middle West", *Mississippi Valley Historical Review*, XIV (March 1928), 481–495.

seizure of the island.[3] Those whose enthusiasm was not satisfied by these outspoken demands collected funds to aid the revolutionists, a cause sponsored by the Chicago *Tribune* and imitated by other midwestern papers.[4] Others joined the filibustering expeditions which were regularly launched against the Spanish rulers of Cuba. Chicago trade unions began contributing their men to this effort in the fall of 1895, and a year later a recruiting agent in Cincinnati reported that he had sent three hundred men from that city while a thousand had left from St. Louis and the entire Columbus, Ohio, contingent of the National Guard had offered its services.[5] No other section contributed so generously to the cause of Cuban independence.

Equally indicative of the region's humanitarianism was the attitude of its press, although here a significant division occurred which was of great importance in explaining the West's shift to isolationism. While editors stood in a solid phalanx to support the Cuban cause, their belligerency varied with their political beliefs. At first Republican editors were markedly more aggressive than their Democratic rivals. Most outspoken of all was the Chicago *Tribune*. As early as September 1895 it was saying: "Why do we wait longer? ... Is it not time to say to Spain, 'Take your flag out of Cuba and give the people their liberty.'" A year later this paper urged the use of American battleships against the Spanish fleet and referred to war as something inevitable and desirable. By November 1896, the *Tribune* favored immediate recognition of Cuban independence, "and if Spain wants to go to war about it, the war will be a welcome one and she will get all the fighting she wants." [6] This violent pro-war attitude was matched by other Republican papers, nine of which favored the recognition of Cuban belligerency during 1895 and 1896, while seven advocated forceful annexation of the island.[7]

[3] Chicago *Inter-Ocean*, October 1, 1895; Cincinnati *Tribune*, October 1, 1895; Marcus M. Wilkerson, *Public Opinion and the Spanish-American War* (Baton Rouge, 1932), pp. 56–60. At least eight of the twelve midwestern states participated in these meetings. Wilkerson, *op. cit.*, p. 57; Chicago *Tribune*, October 1, 1895; Cincinnati *Tribune*, October 8, 1895; *Congressional Record*, 54th Cong., 1st Sess., pp. 32, 140, 482, *ibid.*, 2nd Sess., p. 230.
[4] The campaign was started by the Chicago *Tribune*, April 14, 1896.
[5] Chicago *Inter-Ocean*, October 7, 1895; Cincinnati *Times-Star*, December 15, 1896; Wilkerson, *op. cit.*, pp. 59–60.
[6] Chicago *Tribune*, September 24, 1895, August 15, 1896, November 28, 1896. The quotations are from Wilkerson, *op cit.*, pp. 47–50.
[7] This is the conclusion of a careful student after a thorough study of the midwestern press during this period. George W. Auxier, *The Cuban Question as Reflected in the Editorial Columns of Middle Western Newspapers (1895–*

The election of McKinley in 1896 led to an immediate change of front. Although a few Republican papers, notably the Chicago *Tribune*, continued to demand war, the majority adopted a less belligerent tone. At the same time the Democratic press, although sympathetic to Cuba in the past, now grew more bellicose. Thus the Cincinnati *Enquirer* saw "no reason why Cuba should not be part of the United States within the next thirty days," the Cleveland *Plain Dealer* urged the use of the navy to protect our interests on the island, and the Omaha *World-Herald* branded as criminal McKinley's "dilly-dallying" attitude.[8] These editors were willing to advocate intervention partly to embarrass the governing faction. Yet there was no doubt that the Middle West favored the war; six of the eight important independent papers there constantly advocated intervention, while even the business leaders showed less fear of war than industrialists in other sections.[9]

This pro-war sentiment was made clear to western Congressmen by a flood of petitions from legislatures, boards of trade, mass meetings and organizations. Of seventy-nine received by midwestern Senators, seventy-four favored the Cuban cause. Ten of these merely expressed sympathy, but twenty-eight demanded the recognition of Cuban belligerency, thirty-two asked the recognition of the island's independence, and three urged the United States to enter the war at once.[10] Little wonder that the section's Congressmen played a leading rôle in the war party at Washington. Of the twenty-four Senators from the Middle West, all but four voted or spoke consistently for intervention.[11] Some of the most warlike demands were voiced by westerners, who urged everything from "sending the most powerful battleship of the United States to Cuban waters," to "giving Cuba what Lafayette gave to Washington at Valley Forge."[12] When the vote on war was taken,

---

1898) (Ann Arbor, University Microfilm, 1941), p. 244. This excellent work has been relied on for most of the material concerning the western press at this time.

[8] *Ibid.*, pp. 53, 57, 151–152, 233. Dr. Auxier examined more than a dozen Democratic papers and found the shift in policy clearly marked in all but two.

[9] *Ibid.*, p. 233; Julius W. Pratt, *Expansionists of 1898* (Baltimore, 1936), pp. 234–244.

[10] Compiled from petitions printed in the *Congressional Record* during this period.

[11] This figure has been arrived at by a study of the Senate speeches made during the first two sessions of the 55th Congress, and by an analysis of the vote on resolutions authorizing the recognition of Cuban belligerence, Cuban independence, and actual intervention. *Ibid.*, 55th Cong., 1st Sess., p. 1394, 2nd Sess., pp. 3993, 4040–4041, 4079–4090.

[12] *Ibid.*, 1st Sess., pp. 1132, 1170.

eighteen of these twenty-four Senators sided with the majority who favored military intervention. In the House of Representatives, where the war resolution was adopted by a vote of 173 to 121, only twenty-five westerners opposed the war.[13]

Western interest in expansion did not decline when the nation, with the war won, debated the disposition of the conquered Spanish territory. President McKinley sought an answer to this problem by sounding public opinion on a speaking tour through the Midwest. Wherever he went his oratorical question, "Who will haul down the flag?" in the Philippines, was answered with shouts of "It will stay there." "I know what this means", he told a cheering crowd at Terre Haute. "It means, my fellow citizens, that the people of the United States want the victories of the army and navy to be recognized in the treaty of peace." [14]

McKinley, in this judgment, failed to note two significant variations in the section's opinion. One followed economic lines, for, although the business interests solidly supported expansion, the workers and farmers were less sure that this was desirable. The farmer-labor point of view was expressed by the president of the Ohio Federation of Labor who argued that, as civilization could not be transplanted, low wages would continue in the Philippines and the United States be flooded with cheap tariff-free goods to the detriment of the American worker. Moreover, the $20,000,000 due Spain and the cost of developing colonial possessions promised higher taxes without immediate gain for the laborer or farmer.[15] Western business men, on the other hand, caught a vision of vast Oriental markets for their goods lying beyond the Philippine gateway. They stood solidly in support of McKinley's imperialistic inclinations and urged the retention of every inch of territory taken from Spain.[16]

[13] The war resolution passed the Senate by a vote of 67 to 21. *Ibid.*, 55th Cong., 2nd Sess., pp. 4063, 4079–4080.

[14] Columbus *Dispatch*, October 15 and 20, 1898. McKinley later declared that he based his decision to keep the Philippines partly on the enthusiastic response of western audiences to this suggestion. Quoted in Pratt, *op. cit.*, pp. 336–337.

[15] *United Mine Workers' Journal*, December 8, 1898; Ashland (Ohio) *Press*, November 9, 1898; Cleremont (Ohio) *Sun*, November 9, 1898; Harrison County (Ohio) *Democrat*, December 1, 1898; Chicago *Inter-Ocean*, quoted in *Literary Digest*, November 12, 1899. Western Congressmen received from farmers numerous petitions opposing expansion. *Congressional Record*, 55th Cong., 3rd Sess., pp. 1066–1067, 1157.

[16] Pratt, *op. cit.*, pp. 246–278, describes the conversion of this group. See also Bellaire (Ohio) *Herald*, August 11, 1898; Canton (Ohio) *Repository*, December 1, 1898; Cleremont (Ohio) *Sun*, November 30, 1898; Columbus *Dispatch*, January 23, 1899.

A second and more important division in middle western opinion followed political lines. In the debate over expansion Republicans were wholeheartedly in favor of colonial possessions, Democrats unalterably opposed. Only Republican domination of the West accounted for that section's imperialism.

This division was reflected in the editorial opinion which filled western newspapers between 1898 and 1902. Republican editors saw colonial possessions as the panacea for all the nation's ills; from them would stem eternal prosperity, the prestige fitting a great nation, and enlightenment for downtrodden natives of tyranny-ridden lands. They supported the Treaty of Paris with its provisions for annexation, and urged a vigorous war upon Aguinaldo and his rebellious followers.[17] The Democratic press, true to the section's established humanitarianism, saw expansion as a wicked conspiracy to steal possessions in the name of humanity, a sure prelude to participation in a world war, and the first step in the downfall of the Republic. Editors urged the defeat of the Treaty of Paris and looked upon Aguinaldo as a second Washington struggling for his people's liberty.[18]

These strict party lines influenced Congressmen more than did sectional attitudes. Democrats from the Middle West introduced resolutions against annexation, and heatedly declared that we should forsake McKinley imperialism and return to the principles of our Revolutionary forefathers who had fought to make a subject people free.[19] Their pleas went unheeded. Republicans controlled the Middle West and assured that section's support of expansion. When the final vote on the Philippine act was taken, sixty-four midwestern Representatives favored American control of the islands and only twenty-three were opposed; in the Senate the vote stood nineteen in favor and three against.[20] The Middle West remained true to expansionism, but now its loyalties to the Republican Party transcended any idealistic beliefs.

Behind this shift in opinion, which was to hold the key to later

[17] Columbus *Dispatch*, October 3 and 5, December 14, 1898; Bellefontaine (Ohio) *Republican*, November 1, 1898; Ashland (Ohio) *Times*, November 2, 1898; Dayton *Daily Journal*, February 7, 1899; *Literary Digest*, November 18, 1898, February 4, 1899.
[18] Bellaire (Ohio) *Herald*, July 28, 1898, August 25, 1898; Caldwell (Ohio) *Press*, November 10 1898, December 8 and 22, 1898; Ashland (Ohio) *Press*, December 7, 1898; Cleveland *Plain Dealer*, January 5, 1899; Delaware (Ohio) *Democratic Herald*, January 5, 1899; Coshocton (Ohio) *Democrat*, January 9, 1899; Hocking (Ohio) *Sentinel*, October 19, 1899; Milwaukee *Journal*, Chicago *Chronicle* and St. Louis *Republic*, quoted in *Literary Digest*, October 28, 1899.
[19] *Congressional Record*, 55th Cong., 3rd Sess., pp. 93, 1261, 1265, 1486, 1678.
[20] *Ibid.*, 57th Cong., 1st Sess., pp. 6231, 7487.

western isolationism, lay both changing economic and social conditions in the West and the turbulent domestic situation of the
1890's. The latter was particularly important, for the ramifications
of the free-silver crusade split the Middle West into two antago-
nistic camps and prepared both to adopt an insular attitude toward
their nation's foreign policy. One of these groups was composed of
the industrial-urban element which by 1900 was on the verge of
wresting economic supremacy from the traditional agrarian rulers
of the West. The other was made up of the farmers and workers
who had seized on free silver as a panacea for the depression in
which they had been bogged for a quarter-century.

The rabid enthusiasm of these agrarians profoundly shocked
the members of the first group, the western business men and city
dwellers. Bryan, to them, was the archetype of all that was bad;
his path led to inflation, destruction of private property, and an-
archy. McKinley, by contrast, was looked upon as the custodian of
all that was good; a vote for him in 1896 or 1900 was not only a
vote for sound business but also for civilization. The frantic efforts
of these conservatives prevented Bryan from carrying the Middle
West in either election, but the danger was too great to be forgotten. Any division within the party's ranks might open the door
to Bryan and chaos; blind adherence to Republicanism on every
issue would alone assure salvation. Hence when McKinley embraced the imperialistic cause, he swung a majority of midwestern
Republicans with him. From that time on they shaped their views
on foreign policy to that of their party's leaders. Any Democratic
president who favored interventionism was certain to meet determined resistance from middle western Republicans.

The free-silver crusade also moved the powerful agrarian groups
in the West along the path to isolationism. To them the defeat of
inflation, which doomed them to a continuing struggle with poverty and debt, could be laid at the door of eastern and British
capitalists. From this belief stemmed several prejudices which became entrenched in western thought. One was a dislike for England. Another was an intensified sectional antagonism which
inclined farmers there to look with disfavor on anything sanctioned
by easterners. Thus, if the East favored intervention in world
affairs, they would automatically swing in the opposite direction.
The third and most important prejudice was directed against
eastern bankers and industrialists. This "money power" had been
hated by the frontier since the days of Andrew Jackson, and now
these hatreds seemed confirmed. Its wealth not only had defeated

inflation but had engineered imperialism, after the Spanish-American War, for its own selfish ends. These antagonisms were strengthened by the violent anti-trust agitation of the Progressive era, and by the unfolding Caribbean policy which seemed to increase the poor man's taxes for the benefit of a few wealthy corporations. Thousands of westerners came to believe that intervention was only another tool of the trusts in their battle against the people.

The rapidly maturing industrial society of the Middle West also accounted for the section's changing opinion. Between 1880 and the turn of the century its manufactures increased threefold, until by 1900 the output of its 182,467 factories was valued at nearly four and a half billion dollars. Its agricultural products in the same year were worth nearly two and a half billion dollars.[21] This happy combination of farm and factory created an economic self-sufficiency unrivaled by any other section. Its farmers were no longer dependent on foreign or eastern markets, and its manufacturers were less concerned with international trade, for they could sell most of their produce in the rural regions at their door. The West, enjoying the prosperity of rapid expansion as it developed into a self-contained economic unit, could close its eyes to the rest of the world as could no other section.

As important as these material factors in explaining the growing isolationism of the Middle West was the rise to political power of the section's immigrant population. For a half a century its fertile lands had lured Europe's refugees until by 1900 more than half the male voters of every western state but Ohio, Kansas and Indiana were either foreign born or the children of parents born abroad; in Wisconsin, Minnesota and North Dakota they numbered almost eighty per cent of the population, in South Dakota nearly seventy per cent, and in Michigan and Illinois sixty per cent. The nationality of these immigrants helped shape their attitude toward world affairs. Of the four million foreign born living in the section at the turn of the century, half came from Germany or neighboring states in Central Europe, while another six hundred thousand were from the Scandinavian countries.[22]

The great mass of these first and second generation Americans favored isolation. Many retained a half-hearted loyalty to their

[21] *Abstract of the Twelfth Census of the United States, 1900* (Washington, 1904), pp. 250, 331.
[22] *Twelfth Census of the United States, Statistical Atlas* (Washington, 1903), Plate No. 46; *Abstract of the Twelfth Census*, pp. 58–63.

Central European homelands; for, although they were but lightly touched by the upper-class nationalism of that day, they still disapproved of American entry into wars directed against the Central Powers. Others feared that participation in world politics would reawaken Old World hatreds and retard the process of Americanization which was bringing them peace and prosperity. Still more, particularly among the foreign born, made the maintenance of their adopted country's democracy without essential change their principal political objective; and they shied with inherent conservatism from any deviation from the established courses. Finally, the second and third generations of newcomers developed an exaggerated Americanism as they hurried to slough off all Old World taints, and this too inclined them to look askance at entanglements which would revive influences they were anxious to leave behind. In general the immigrants were thoroughly conservative, particularly in the upper Mississippi Valley, and this fitted well with the pattern of isolationism.[23]

Less important than these economic and racial factors, but still of some influence, were the large number of evangelical religious sects that were rooted in the Middle West. Many of these were avowedly pacifistic; others were European in origin and spread their cynical Old World doctrines among their worshipers. Thus, many of the Lutheran pastors were immigrants who brought to the United States both a hatred of war and a belief that Europe's conflicts were imperialistic struggles engineered by a few greedy capitalists.[24] Listening to these messages from the pulpit, the Scandinavians and Americans who followed this faith were influenced against any participation in the quarrels of the Continent.

These prejudices of alarmed business men, discontented farmers, immigrant voters, and pacifistic churchgoers were openly expressed between 1914 and 1917 when the nation debated its rôle in the first World War. The West's first reaction was one of thankfulness for its geographic isolation from a war that was considered "wicked, unnecessary and altogether horrible", and a fervent prayer of thanks that "we have gone no farther than we have in becoming a world power." [25] This complacency was easily translated into an

[23] Marcus L. Hansen, *The Immigrant in American History* (Cambridge, 1940), pp. 77–96.

[24] George M. Stephenson, "The Attitude of Swedish Americans towards the World War," Mississippi Valley Historical Association, *Proceedings*, X (July 1920), 79–94; idem, *The Religious Aspects of Swedish Immigration* (Minneapolis, 1932), pp. 451–452.

[25] Dayton *Daily News*, August 8, 1914; Springfield (Ohio) *Daily News*, July 31, 1914.

indifference which was typified by the reply of a small-town policeman when asked, shortly after the *Sussex* sinking, what the people were saying about Germany: "Germany? Well, lessee. I reck'lect I *did* hear some of 'em talking about Germany along five or six months ago, maybe, but I don't think there's been no talk about Germans for a good while lately. No sir, not around *our* community." [26] That this attitude was common was shown by a poll of newspaper editors in the fall of 1914. In the Middle West 122 were either indifferent to the outcome of the war or pro-German, while only 13 favored the Allies. This contrasted with the East, where 44 were neutral or pro-German and 34 pro-Ally, and the South with 56 neutral and pro-German editors against 47 supporting the Allies. [27]

During the next two years this sectional attitude was clearly demonstrated in each issue that arose. Western opinion most violently opposed any increase in the army and navy, taking refuge in the belief that "preparedness brought on the war", and insisting that "our splendid isolation" made defense unnecessary. [28] This opposition was centered in the states west of the Mississippi where Populism had attracted most support [29] and was motivated partially by hatred of the eastern money trust. One Nebraska editor summed up the sentiment of his state when he charged the "pre-paredness-propagandists" with being in "the pay of the munitions-factory magnates and steel trust", and another insisted: "The terror which has seized Maxim and the manufacturers of war materials is not felt by the people of this section. There is no fear of invasion here." [30]

This sentiment helped shape western opinion on the sale of military supplies to the warring Powers. Petitions favoring an arms embargo were showered on Congress from the beginning of the

[26] Booth Tarkington, "Middle Western Apathy," *American Magazine*, LXXXIII (June 1917), 31–32. See also Cedric Cummins, "Indiana Looks at the War," *Indiana Magazine of History*, XXXVII (December 1941), 343.

[27] *Literary Digest*, November 14, 1914.

[28] *Ohio State Journal*, November 21, 1914, February 3, 1915.

[29] This was revealed by a poll of newspaper editors published in the *Literary Digest*, March 11, 1916, which showed that sixty-six living west of the Mississippi saw militarism as a real danger while sixty-four did not. This was in marked contrast with other sections, such as the East where eleven feared militarism while eight-five did not, or the middle western states east of the Mississippi whose editors voted twenty-three to sixty that such dangers were remote. This was also made clear by a large number of western petitions to Congress against increasing the size of the army and navy. *Congressional Record*, 64th Cong., 1st Sess., pp. 935, 1185, 1733, 2251, 2491.

[30] *Literary Digest*, March 11, 1916.

war, many of them from middle western communities with large German populations. "Better to have an embargo covering the entire coast," one editor wrote, "than to get into the war." [31] Senator Kenyon of Iowa expressed the views of many of his constituents when, in presenting Congress with an embargo petition bearing a million signatures, he declared: "The jingle of the dollar can not drown the cry of suffering from the battle fields of Europe. It may be all right to sell these things according to international law, but it is against the moral law." [32]

The western press did not react as violently to the German submarine campaign as did the editors of other sections. The only two papers to defend the sinking of the *Lusitania* were the Milwaukee *Free Press* and the St. Louis *Times*, both located in areas with a large German population. Others, unwilling to go this far, insisted that Americans should hold themselves aloof by refraining from travel on belligerent ships, and that U-boats had as much right in American waters as British warships.[33] When Congress in 1916 acted on a resolution forbidding citizens to travel in vessels of warring Powers, twelve of the fourteen favorable Senate votes came from middle westerners, while that section's Representatives alone cast a majority of votes in its favor.[34] Probably a Kansas farmer mirrored the views of many of his fellows when he told an interviewer:

> We will—every man of us—fight in a minute if the country is invaded, but we wont go a step farther. We'd keep every American off belligerent ships. We'd keep every American out of Mexico. We'd let the Japs take the Philippines and be damned, if they wanted 'em. We'd defend our homes, but when any American goes where he has no right to go, if he gets into trouble, it's his own fault. The honor of the country doesn't get outside our boundaries that we can see.[35]

By the spring of 1917 the Middle West was no longer isolationist, for the opening of unrestricted submarine warfare and the Zimmerman Note solidified national opinion in favor of war. Yet in that section, as in no other, there remained a group of die-hards who resisted the popular clamor. When President Wilson asked

---

[31] *Ohio State Journal*, February 7, 1915.

[32] *Literary Digest*, February 12, 1916.

[33] *Ibid.*, May 22, 1915. An excellent summary of western attitude concerning the submarine question is in H. J. Haskell, "The U-53 and the Middle West," *Outlook*, October 1916, pp. 414–415.

[34] In the House the delegations from Iowa, Nebraska, Minnesota and Wisconsin were unanimous in their approval. *Congressional Record*, 64th Cong., 1st Sess., p. 3720.

[35] *Literary Digest*, February 12, 1916.

Congress for authority to arm merchant vessels the resulting measure was talked to death by twelve Senators, eight of whom were from the West. Three of the five votes cast against the declaration of war in the Senate, and thirty-six of the fifty in the House, were from representatives of that section.[36] Hatred of the eastern money power, a large German population, and distrust of a Democratic president combined to center isolationism in the upper Mississippi Valley.

The important rôle of partisan politics in this attitude was again demonstrated when peace brought the League of Nations before the American public. The West's first reaction to Wilson's proposal was mildly favorable; even the Chicago *Tribune* admitted that "the scheme is not one which need be feared", and the equally isolationist Cincinnati *Times-Star* grudgingly conceded that the League "held promise to at least make wars less frequent." [37] A poll of newspaper editors in the spring of 1919 showed that 250 of the section's papers were favorable, 200 conditionally favorable, and only 70 absolutely opposed.[38] Yet only four months later these western editors were vying in heaping calumny on the League, and western Senators were preparing to cast a virtually solid vote against it. This abrupt change of front was caused by the decision of Henry Cabot Lodge and his Republican followers to fight the League as a means of discrediting Wilson and the Democrats.

The predominantly Republican West fell readily into line with this partisan campaign to obscure the Covenant by amendments and reservations, while delaying the final decision until popular interest waned. For two months the treaty languished in the hands of the Senate Foreign Relations Committee while its friends pleaded with Wilson to accept reservations and the President retaliated by carrying the case to the people. When debate began, the cause was already lost, but Republican obstructionists were still cautious. Their attack, mild at first, mounted in intensity as passing months lessened League support. By mid-September even such a vacillating politician as Warren G. Harding felt sure enough of his constituents' isolationism to take a firm anti-League stand, while other western Senators were warning that internationalism meant rule by the dark-skinned peoples of the world, or by the Pope.[39] By

[36] *Congressional Record*, 65th Cong., 1st Sess., pp. 412–413
[37] Chicago *Tribune*, February 17, 1919; Cincinnati *Times-Star*, April 29, 1919. See also *Literary Digest*, April 5, 1919.
[38] *Literary Digest*, April 5, 1919.
[39] *Congressional Record*, 66th Cong., 1st Sess., pp. 235–237, 1436, 4453–4455, 5219–5225.

this time, too, many moderate Republicans saw that Wilson would not compromise and reluctantly swung to complete opposition.

This increased bitterness in the Senate was reflected in the middle western press. As the summer progressed editors who had first favored the League turned gradually from cautious support to bitter attack. Some of the more outspoken, such as the Chicago *Tribune*, kept up a constant barrage of editorial invective and flagrant misrepresentation; others reflected a growing popular antipathy by refusing to print details of the wearisome Senate debate. Senator Lodge sensed this slump in public morale and in November agreed to a roll call on the fifteen reservations. In rapid succession they were taken up and passed, with the vote following rigid party lines.[40] With these reservations added, the treaty came before the Senate for final decision. Thirty-five Republicans and four Democrats recorded themselves as in favor, while forty-two Democrats and thirteen irreconcilable Republicans combined their votes to defeat the measure. Five of the thirteen irreconcilable votes were cast by midwestern Senators. A call for unconditional ratification of the treaty without reservations resulted in thirty-eight votes in favor and fifty-three opposed. Only one middle western Republican favored the League in this form, only one Democrat was opposed.[41] Partisan politics, centered in the Republican Middle West, had struck a death blow at Wilson's idealistic internationalism.

The President, however, was unwilling to admit defeat. In January 1920 he referred to the coming election as a "great and solemn referendum" on the League of Nations and appealed to the people to repudiate Republican opposition at the polls. This challenge the Republicans refused to accept openly but their candidate, Warren G. Harding, was known for his anti-League stand, and most people understood that a vote for him was a vote against internationalism. The result was decisive. Harding was carried into office by a landslide vote that was particularly pronounced in the Middle West. Republican Senators from that section now outnumbered their Democratic rivals by 21 to 3, while the Democrats could salvage only 5 seats in the House to 138 for their rivals. Domestic issues were more important than foreign in this one-sided victory, but most of Harding's Middle West applauded when he declared in his

[40] Only one western Republican, Senator Porter McCumber of North Dakota, voted against two of the reservations; only Senator James Reed of Missouri deserted his Democratic colleagues to vote for them.

[41] *Congressional Record*, 66th Cong., 1st Sess., pp. 8767, 8803. McCumber voted for the League without reservations; Reed was opposed.

victory speech: "You just didn't want a surrender of the United States of America; you wanted America to go under American ideals. That's why you didn't care for the League, which is now deceased." [42]

With this pronouncement friends of internationalism turned to the Permanent Court of International Justice in their attempt to salvage at least something from Wilson's peace program. In theory, at least, adherence to the World Court was not a partisan issue, for both Harding and Coolidge were favorable, so long as they could attach reservations divorcing the Court from any League connections. Thus safeguarded, the protocols were presented to the Senate in March 1924. A few midwestern papers, headed by the Chicago *Tribune* and the Kansas City *Star*, leaped to the attack with all the avidity that had marked their campaign against the League,[43] but the more usual reaction was one of indifference or ignorance. Most papers ignored the important Senate debate in both their news and editorial columns, for the average western editor shared with the average western citizen the belief that such impracticable matters deserved little attention amid the booming prosperity of the 1920's. When the amended protocol was accepted by the Senate in January 1926 by a vote of seventy-six to seventeen, ten of the small opposition group were from the Middle West, a disproportionate number which indicated the continued isolationism of the section.[44]

When the reservations insisted on by the Senate proved unacceptable to the League Council, western editors shed no tears. "The reds, pinks and yellows may rave and try to change the situation," one declared, "but they will find . . . that the color combination loved by the citizenship of America is red, white and blue." [45] Statesmen, however, refused to give up hope of a formula that would be acceptable to both the League Assembly and the United States; they helped develop the Root Plan which was accepted by the League and submitted to the American government in 1929. Traditionally isolationist papers in the West looked upon this compromise with jaundiced eye, but President Hoover was sufficiently impressed to sound the state of public opinion on the

[42] New York *Times*, November 5, 1920.

[43] Chicago *Tribune*, January 21, 23, 25, 27, 1926; Kansas City *Star*, April 29, 1925, January 9, 1926; Cincinnati *Enquirer*, January 2, 1926.

[44] In a proportional distribution these twelve states should have cast only five votes against the Court. *Congressional Record*, 69th Cong., 1st Sess., p. 2820.

[45] Cincinnati *Enquirer*, February 11, 1927. For similar comments see Chicago *Tribune*, February 11, 1927, and Kansas City *Star*, February 10, 1927.

thorny issue. A careful survey showed that sixty-six per cent of the people favored the World Court, while twenty-six per cent were opposed. Forty-one per cent of the opposition vote came from the Middle West—another indication of that section's isolationism. Yet two out of every three people favored adherence, and in December 1929 Hoover transmitted the protocols with the Root amendments to the Senate with a request for favorable action. They were referred to the Foreign Relations Committee where they remained until January 1935.

When at that time President Roosevelt urged their adoption a storm of protest arose from the Middle West. Congressmen and editorial writers hurled again the anti-Court barbs a decade old, and added others even more telling. Why, they asked, should the United States meddle in European affairs when so much economic reconstruction was needed at home? Why should the nation bother with a world drifting anew toward war when our reward for saving civilization in 1917 had been unpaid debts? Why should a depression-ridden country enmesh itself in the debased standards of the poverty-stricken Old World when millions of Americans were out of work? [46] As the time for a Senate vote neared, the isolationist fervor steadily mounted. Thousands listened to the Reverend Father Charles E. Coughlin, the rabble-rousing Michigan priest, whose pleas to radio listeners to wire their Congressmen swamped one Ohio newspaper with calls from persons asking the names of their Senators.[47]

The final vote showed fifty-two of the Senate in favor, thirty-six opposed. This was seven votes less than the necessary two-thirds, and the World Court was again, and finally, defeated. Thirteen of the thirty-six negative votes were cast by middle western Senators. Thus the resolution failed to secure even a majority vote from this section, while every other section was favorable by more than a two-thirds majority.[48] Partisan politics doubtless played some part in explaining the West's isolationism. for the Demo-

[46] A number of western editorials against the Court are in *Congressional Record*, 74th Cong., 1st Sess., pp. 686–687. The same point of view is expressed by a petition from the Wisconsin legislature in *ibid.*, pp. 1296–1297.

[47] Cleveland *Plain Dealer*, January 28, 1935.

[48] The sectional division was more important than the political. Twenty Democrats deserted the administration to vote with fourteen Republicans and two Independents against the Court; forty-four Democrats and eight Republicans voted for adherence. A bloc of four western states, North Dakota, South Dakota, Minnesota and Iowa, cast no votes in favor, while every other state in the section supplied at least one negative vote, excepting Michigan, Indiana and Missouri. *Congressional Record*, 74th Cong., 1st Sess., p. 1147.

cratic origins of the Court and its endorsement by Roosevelt rankled some western Republicans. Ignorance and indifference, combined with post-war disillusionment and preoccupation with depression problems, were more important in shaping the opinion of the Middle West.

It was in this state of mind that westerners listened approvingly to the findings of the Nye Committee, solidly supported by the so-called neutrality legislation of the mid-1930's, and then smugly watched Europe drift toward war, certain that this struggle was no concern of theirs. Nor did the Munich settlement jar their complacency; for, while most agreed that war was now inevitable, they clung to the belief that the United States would surely remain aloof. A majority firmly opposed the attempted repeal of the arms embargo during the summer of 1939,[49] and applauded their congressional representatives who urged the people to "refrain from making the job of halting the drifting border sands of Europe a W. P. A. project for the relief of the unemployed millions of our American homes."[50] Only in this section, according to an Institute of Public Opinion poll in the fall of 1939, did a majority favor retention of the embargo on the shipment of arms abroad.[51]

Hitler's invasion of Poland and the outbreak of war did not materially change western opinion. When President Roosevelt called a special session of Congress to repeal the neutrality legislation he was opposed by a solid bloc of isolationist Congressmen from the Midwest. Some maintained that England and France were the aggressors and did not deserve aid; others that we would certainly be drawn into the war, or that repeal was favored only by munitions makers and international bankers "to sell guns to make a profit even if those guns bathe the earth in mothers' tears." [52] When the final vote was taken in November 1939, the Middle West was the only section to cast a majority of its House votes against repeal. In only two western states, Illinois and Missouri, did a majority favor revision; in the four states of Wisconsin, Nebraska, North

[49] Chicago *Tribune*, August 24 and 25, 1939.

[50] *Congressional Record*, 76th Cong., 1st Sess., Appendix, p. 3377. For other expressions of this sentiment by western Congressmen see *ibid.*, pp. 1144, 1573, 2025, 2687. Western petitions against repeal of the arms embargo are in *ibid.*, pp. 1144, 1573, 4516.

[51] Repeal was favored by fifty-one per cent of the people of the East, sixty per cent of the southerners, fifty-one per cent of the Pacific coast residents, and only forty-seven per cent of the westerners. *Public Opinion Quarterly*, IV (March 1940).

[52] *Congressional Record*, 76th Cong., 2nd Sess., p. 1306. For a convenient summary of isolationist argument during this debate see *New Republic*, May 18, 1942.

Dakota and South Dakota the entire delegation voted for retention. While a slim majority of midwestern Senators opposed the embargo, in no other section was the vote so close. The important rôle of partisan politics was indicated by the fact that only two of the West's thirty-five Representatives who voted for repeal were Republicans.[53]

The next months witnessed a rapid shift of American opinion as the fall of Norway, the Low Countries and France brought home the dangerous position of the United States. Some westerners showed the futility of opposition and increased their demands for complete neutrality, but a larger number decided that American preservation depended on greater aid for the democracies and the increase of our own defenses.[54] Yet even now the West lagged significantly behind other sections. In June 1940 a poll of its people showed that, while fifty-seven per cent of them favored peacetime conscription, sixty-eight per cent of the rest of the nation thought this step necessary.[55] When this issue was presented to Congress in the Burke-Wadsworth Selective Service Act the middle westerners in both House and Senate cast a majority of their votes in opposition, while every other section was favorable. Michigan, Wisconsin, North Dakota and South Dakota gave the measure no support, and only one Representative each from Nebraska, Kansas, Iowa, Minnesota and Indiana voted in favor. Again the rôle played by partisan politics was shown when only one midwestern Republican in the House and one in the Senate backed the administration bill." [56]

These sectional lines did not waver during the critical spring of 1941 when Congress debated the Lend-Lease Bill. Although national opinion was now almost solidly behind the President, a few die-hards fought to the bitter end. In the vanguard were a number of western Congressmen and the Chicago *Tribune*—which hailed the passage of the act in March 1941 with banner headlines

[53] Only nine Democrats deserted their party to join the solid Republican bloc for the embargo. In the House the eastern states voted 53 to 37 for revision, the southern 102 to 5, the Pacific states 23 to 9, and the middle western 35 to 73. In the Senate the East voted 12 to 6 for revision, the South 27 to 4, and the Middle West 13 to 11. *Congressional Record*, 76th Cong., 2nd Sess., pp. 1024, 1389.

[54] For a convenient summary of western editorial opinion on this subject see *What America Thinks* (Chicago, 1941).

[55] *Public Opinion Quarterly*, IV (September 1940).

[56] The Middle West cast 84 votes against and 23 in favor. In the East conscription was favored by a vote of 70 to 21, in the South 103 to 3, and in the Far West 20 to 12. In the Senate the West voted against compulsory service 14 to 7, while the East was in favor 14 to 3 and the South 28 to 2. *Congressional Record*, 76th Cong., 3rd Sess., p. 11142.

proclaiming "Senate Passes Dictator Bill". "Sinister and suspicious demands for dictatorship powers", "the complete abdication of Congress", "a war bill, a dictatorship bill, a bankruptcy bill"— these were phrases used by midwesterners in their attack. Nor did the final vote show any change in sectional alignment. Again the West, alone among the sections, cast a majority of its votes against Lend-Lease in both House and Senate.[57] On this last important issue before the bombs that fell on Pearl Harbor substituted action for debate the Middle West remained true to its isolationist tradition.

From this survey certain conclusions seem obvious. The western swing to isolationism coincided with the free-silver excitement, which solidified political divisions and intensified sectional jealousies. From that date the Middle West viewed with suspicion the extension of American interests beyond the seas, partly because Democratic presidents were largely responsible and partly because interventionism was favored by eastern bankers and corporations. Important, too, in shaping that attitude were the large numbers of first and second generation Americans who lived in the upper Mississippi Valley: Germans who disliked to make war on the Fatherland and Scandinavians who brought from the Old World a strong tradition of isolationism. These national attitudes were bolstered by the religious concepts of the many evangelical sects which flourished in the West. Humanitarianism and missionary zeal enlisted their support for the Spanish-American War, but their pacifism inclined them against participation in the wars of Europe.

These prejudices and attitudes, bolstered by the sense of security which stemmed from the section's geographic position and economic self-sufficiency, help to explain middle western isolationism. More conservative than the rest of the nation, the West clung to nineteenth-century traditions after other regions had recognized the inevitability of a New World rôle for the twentieth-century United States.

[57] The debate is summarized in the *New Republic*, May 18, 1942. In the House the Middle West voted against Lend-Lease 94 to 41. The East favored the measure 71 to 40, the South 120 to 5, and the Far West 21 to 20. Middle western Senators voted 14 to 8 against the bill. In the East the vote was favorable by 11 to 6, in the South 29 to 1, and in the Far West 12 to 10. *Congressional Record*, 77th Cong., 1st Sess., pp. 2097, 2229.